TALIESIN REFLECTIONS

TALIESIN
REFLECTIONS

MY YEARS BEFORE, DURING, AND AFTER LIVING WITH

FRANK LLOYD WRIGHT

AND VARIOUS CONTACTS WITH OTHER PEOPLE AND PLACES

Earl Nisbet

MERIDIAN PRESS
Petaluma, California

Meridian Press
P.O. Box 387
Petaluma, CA 94953

Library of Congress Control Number: 2006922379
International Standard Book Number-10: 0-9778951-0-6
International Standard Book Number-13: 978-0-9778951-0-6

Dedicated to my Father and Mother

I cherish my mother, May Durian Nisbet, who taught me to love learning, and my father, Charles F. Nisbet, who interpreted that work is love made discernible.

Charles F. Nisbet

May Durian Nisbet

"There are some things which cannot be learned quickly, and time, which is all we have, must be paid heavily for their acquiring. They are the very simplest things and because it takes a man's life to know them the little new that each man gets from life is very costly and the only heritage he has to leave."

ERNEST HEMINGWAY, *The Green Hills of Africa*

 CONTENTS

Acknowledgments   xi
Foreword   xiii

INTRODUCTION   1

CHAPTER 1 :: CHILDHOOD   3

Beginnings
Onward
The Great Depression
Wheels

CHAPTER 2 :: WORLD WAR II   16

The War Years
The Boat Trip
Seven and a Half Minutes
    of Fame
Rocco Laginestra
On to the South Pacific
Camp Stoneman
Loran Estes
Adventures with Loren at
    Camp Swift
Rocky Marciano
Returning to Civilian Life

CHAPTER 3 :: BECOMING
AN ARCHITECT   31

Manuel Sandoval
The Lifeguard
Floyd page
Midglen
Frank Lloyd Wright
    (1867 to 1959)
The Taliesin Fellowship
On to Taliesin
Eugene Masselink

◼ A TALIESIN REFLECTION: 1

◼ A TALIESIN REFLECTION: 2

The Tea Circle
William Wesley Peters

◼ A TALIESIN REFLECTION: 3

The Taliesin Followship
    (the concept)

◼ A TALIESIN REFLECTION: 4

Spring and Summer 1951
Allen Lape Davison

◼ A TALIESIN REFLECTION: 5

John H. Howe
Kay Davison

CHAPTER 3   BECOMING
             AN ARCHITECT
             (continued)

             The Escapade of Barbara
               and Martha

             ■ A TALIESIN REFLECTION: 6

             ■ A TALIESIN REFLECTION: 7

             ■ A TALIESIN REFLECTION: 8

             ■ A TALIESIN REFLECTION: 9

             ■ A TALIESIN REFLECTION: 10

             John de Koven Hill

             Caravan West

             ■ A TALIESIN REFLECTION: 11

             ■ A TALIESIN REFLECTION: 12

             ■ A TALIESIN REFLECTION: 13

             ■ A TALIESIN REFLECTION: 14

             Life in Camp

             Mr. Wright Asks My Views

             ■ A TALIESIN REFLECTION: 15

             1951—Ongoing

             ■ A TALIESIN REFLECTION: 16

             ■ A TALIESIN REFLECTION: 17

             ■ A TALIESIN REFLECTION: 18

             ■ A TALIESIN REFLECTION: 19

             ■ A TALIESIN REFLECTION: 20

             ■ A TALIESIN REFLECTION: 21

             March 27, 1952

             ■ A TALIESIN REFLECTION: 22

             A Pirate Party

             Sequstering "My Room"

             The Price Tower (1952)

             ■ A TALIESIN REFLECTION: 23

             ■ A TALIESIN REFLECTION: 24

             ■ A TALIESIN REFLECTION: 25

             ■ A TALIESIN REFLECTION: 26

             Actor Charles Laughton

             Conversation with FLLW

             A Taliesin Tragedy

CHAPTER 4 :: ON MY OWN   91

             Christmas 1953

             Cabaña Tanglewood

             Hemicycle for Harry

             A Garden Lantern

             Blois House and
             Falconer House

             On Abstracting from Nature

             Drawings and Comments

             My Brother Harry

             Harry's Golf Balls

             Tahiti

             Moorea

             Willard Bascom

             Quinn's Bar

             Movie in Tahiti

             July 14: Bastille Day

             October 4, 1957

             The Next Week

             Progress?

             Matson Number Two

CHAPTER 5 :: SETTING UP
PRACTICE   140
The Crest: A House
in Hawaii
Tahitian Party
Johnny Hill in Hawaii
Longevar
Steve Oyakawa
Mother's Birthday
May Nisbet's Photo Gallery
Falconer's Phone Call
Bad Day at Black Rock
Projects
The Castle
Enter Clarence P. Chan
The Lion is King
Go-Aheads?
Travel to Spain
I Marry Mary Lou
Studio for Joe Gores
My Mother's Death (1968)

CHAPTER 6 :: SETTLING DOWN
IN CENTRAL
CALIFORNIA   179
New Horizons
Laginestra Letter
To Michelle
Wong Letters
Barbara and I Plan
Some Trips
Taliesin Fellows Northern
California

October 17, 1989
St. Martin
June 8, 1991
Second Seven and a Half
Minutes of Fame
The Incredible Roy Randolph
Seven and a Half Minutes
Forward
Variations on a Theme

CHAPTER 7 :: WORLD TRAVEL   205
To Travel or Not to Travel
My Trip to China
Forbidden City
The Terra Cotta Army
The Children's Palace
On to Spain
Costa Rica (2001)
My England and Holland
Vacation
Duke and Earl Visit the
Prince
Palms I Have Known
Closing Thoughts

 ACKNOWLEDGMENTS

Firstly: Thank you Father, Mother, and Frank Lloyd Wright

The Author gratefully acknowledges the efforts of the following:

Thank you, Kamal Amin:
I have observed with interest, at close range, as my friend Kamal developed his book project, and published his book, *Reflections from the Shining Brow,* about his experience at Taliesin. I was engaged in the excitement inherent in the process. As I developed this narrative, I felt firsthand, the same excitement.

Thank you, Stephen Pollard, Santa Cruz, California, for your editorial expertise in pulling wayward passages into line.

Thank you, Linda Marcetti: A special thanks to Linda, of Asterisk & Image, Aptos, California, for defining my color pencil layouts into sharp color graphics and organizing the contents into a formal book.

 # INTRODUCTION

Every happy family is alike, but every unhappy family is unhappy in its own way, so states Tolstoy in *Anna Karenina.*

I have not determined if there are more, happy than unhappy families, but I'm pleased to say I was a member of the former. Not until my teens did I realize that ours was a special family. Not that we were wealthy, au contraire, but we were rich with warm feelings toward one another. Simply stated, we looked after and loved each other, as I believe families should, but often do not.

As with most of us, I have had some good years and some dismal years. The good years have overshadowed the latter, and along the way, I have met some interesting people.

Living and studying architecture with the world's greatest architect, Frank Lloyd Wright, was the most memorable and the most effortless to relate, because it was such a wonderful experience. I only wish circumstances had allowed me to stay longer at Taliesin.

I do not write as a teacher of architecture, but rather as a chronicler of interesting events spent with the apprentices at Taliesin.

Naturally, there was life before and after Taliesin, and many of those I met became good friends. In part, this is a statement on their behalf, as some are no longer with us. I also wish to honor my parents, my wife, and my brother.

The incident that served as the impetus for this endeavor was the discovery of an old family photo album, and a group of architectural photos taken years ago.

To paraphrase Tolstoy on marriage, I was married twice, and if these unions were categorized based on happy or unhappy, I would say my first was a practice marriage. The second, to Barbara, was absolute heaven on earth.

My father and brother were matchless. I couldn't have asked for a better mother; I had the best. I couldn't have asked for a better wife; I had the best.

CHAPTER ONE : :

CHILDHOOD

In college, my life was forever changed when I read *An Autobiography*, the life story of the greatest of all architects, Frank Lloyd Wright. Now, many years later, my life's observations and reflections are coming together here.

BEGINNINGS

I was born in San Jose, California, on June 17, 1926, under the sign of Gemini, with the influence of the planet Mercury, a symbol of the god of commerce, travel and thievery. It is said that Mercury tends to make a person verbose, critical, high-strung, and even egotistical. We have a tendency to criticize, complain and be ungrateful. (My years in the army caused me to agree whole-heartedly with this evaluation). Good qualities include the tendencies to be adaptable, congenial, expressive and clever. Supposedly, we communicate in an idealistic manner and use our mental powers to achieve harmony and success in life.

I was born in my parents' bedroom, delivered by our family doctor, without complications, and assisted by my maternal grandmother.

ONWARD

My maternal grandparents were born in Holland and like so many, immigrated to the United States through Ellis Island. In 1880, they followed relatives who came before them and settled in Grand Rapids, Michigan. It was there my mother was born and spent the first six or seven years of her life. The family then moved to San Francisco, where her father passed away, and her mother raised eleven children on her own. Following her graduation from high school, my mother found a job in sales through newspaper ads.

My paternal grandfather was born in Scotland, where he lived all of his life. My grandmother, Jessie Knox, was born in England, and it was said that she could trace her lineage back to John Knox, founder of the Presbyterian Church.

My father was born in the northern-most part of England in Southshields, a city near

Author's maternal grandmother, Annie Durian, having immigrated from Holland, through Ellis Island in 1880 to become a U.S. citizen
: : 1942

Scotland. He spent his youth there, and lived a few years in Stratford-on-Avon, before moving to London to work for a cabinetmaker. After some time there on his own, he went to America and subsequently settled in San Francisco.

My mother worked at Nathan-Dohrmann, a prestigious San Francisco department store that sold art, china, silverware, gold items, cut glass, and other fine things. My father met her there and was taken by her sweet disposition, and soon they were dating. They courted for a year before one of the announcements published in the October 30, 1915 San Francisco Examiner was the marriage license acquired in the name of Charles Nisbet (age 25) and May Durian (age 20). Within a week, the two would be married in San Francisco where they both had been living.

After the wedding, the bride was presented with a Kodak box camera for taking photos during their honeymoon. They hiked along the Pacific Coast beaches to the village of Davenport, where my father had taken a job in a power plant.

Although they might have faced inclement weather in November, they were determined to experience this adventurous challenge carrying their tent and provisions for cooking on the beaches, on their backs. They would be explor-

LEFT
Mother's engagement
portrait (May Durian)
San Francisco, CA
: : 1915

RIGHT
Mother May Durian
prior to marriage to
Charles Nisbet
: : 1914

LEFT
May Durian after high
school graduation
: : 1912

RIGHT
Mother May Durian
and father Charles
Nisbet during courting,
San Francisco Park
: : 1915

ing sea life and the coastal birds for the 60-mile
hike to their new house, and the bride would
be able to record their experiences.

The hike was the beginning of my mother's
interest in photography. Admittedly her camera
was not the world's greatest, (which I still have

in my possession) but it was her introduction
to photography. A few years later she purchased a 35mm camera to begin more serious
photography.

She took photos of interesting village buildings, landscapes, and the nearby seashore, which

RIGHT
Father during his court-
ing days in San Francisco,
CA park
:: circa 1914

LEFT
Father seems quite
pleased with his catch
:: 1915

RIGHT
Father playing for
friends at a picnic

LEFT
Author's brother
"Harry" at age 4 years
:: 1921

RIGHT
Photo which won first
prize for author's mother
:: 1927

Author at age 3 years,
3 months. San Jose, CA
:: 1929

was within walking distance from her home.

Davenport did not offer classes in photography, so my mother purchased a book to learn how composition, shade, shadow, and lighting change photos. From that time forward she always had a camera nearby.

A few years later, they returned to San Francisco, where my grandmother still lived, and soon my brother, Harry, was born. My father's hobby was music, and he played the piano, organ, accordion, drums, harmonica, xylophone, and even water-filled glasses. After hearing a tune several times, he could play it straight through. He was also a gifted handyman as well as a cabinetmaker. Soon after my brother's birth, the family moved to San Jose, where my father started the first hardwood floor company.

They purchased a new two-bedroom house situated on a very large lot, and my father immediately began constructing an accessory building the size of a six-car garage. Only the

two front stalls were used for the family cars. In the remaining space, (large enough for four cars) he built wooden floors and storage racks for the oak, walnut, mahogany, and other hardwoods necessary for his new business.

Charles Nisbet's A-1
Hardwood Floor
Company, San Jose, CA
: : 1932

During this time, I came along. My mother was proud of her two sons, and she entered a baby picture of me in a contest to win clothing and canned baby food. The picture won first prize, and she kept a copy of it on our upright piano for many years. Years later, she told me that my photo had won first prize, but I didn't ask about my competition. For all I knew, it was a set of cross-eyed twins and a pit bull! Anyway, she was proud.

THE GREAT DEPRESSION

I was in my third year when the stock market crashed in October 1929. The prosperity of the 1920s had been unevenly distributed throughout the nation. Unskilled workers and farmers felt the brunt of the disaster, because production was greater than the ability to consume. Tariffs had cut into the foreign market for American goods. In early 1929 the expansion of credit, and installment buying, accelerated speculation in the stock market.

Eventually the depression spread throughout the world, bringing rise to new power struggles; and contributed to the rise of Adolf Hitler.

At the depth of the depression about one third of the labor force was unemployed and the gross national product declined about an even 50%.

I recall accompanying my mother to a government agency where they would hand out packages of cheese, bread, flower, and also fruit, when in season to those who would stand in line for several hours.

My parents had a large flourishing vegetable and fruit garden; so we were not in dire straight as were most in our area. In downtown San Jose people on the street corners were selling whatever they could. Apricots, apples, and pears would bring two to five cents each during the harvest season.

Some would also go door to door selling their wares, which was a difficult endeavor for two reasons. (1) The homeowner most likely could not afford the purchase, and (2) quite often they were not interested in what was being offered for sale.

Although I was quite young, I still remember the goat carts that would appear at our front door from time to time. These enterprising men would take photos of children in their carts and sell the photos to the parents for 25¢ each. Several came to our home during these hard times, and because my brother no longer cared to sit in goat cart for his photo to be taken, my mother was enticed to have my photo taken more than once.

WHEELS

Our country was still feeling the effects of the Great Depression when my brother and I were children, and even commonplace playthings were sometimes difficult to acquire. Most of my toys had been purchased for my older brother, so when he received something new, I would fall heir to another of his hand-me-downs.

When almost three years old, I received a small phaeton automobile equipped with a steering wheel for turning the front wheels. I would sit on the floor pushing it in one direction, then another, which kept me busy for some time. About a year later, my father took my brother's old tricycle from its perch on the garage wall and gave it to me. Dad had also made a small car for Harry: one that could be propelled by pushing pedals when seated, and turned with the small steering wheel he had installed. Another hand-me-down, but I was delighted with this one!

At about age five or six, I outgrew the tricycle and longed for a bike like my brother's. My father had purchased a used girl's bike that needed work. I cried when I saw it, as it lacked the horizontal bar designed for boy's bikes. It was also in need of paint, but Dad assured me he would paint it in my choice of color. Finally,

he decided to install a bar before painting the bike. I smiled. My father was quite clever, and no one noticed he had turned a "hers" into a "his" before painting the bike powder blue.

Other favorites were roller skates, used for skating on neighborhood sidewalks. Somehow, I had acquired an extra skate, which I took apart. I installed two of the wheels at the front of a 2" × 6" wooden board; the remaining two were placed at the rear. I then nailed a wooden box to this contraption and made handles for directional control. Soon, I was pushing my new vehicle around the neighborhood.

By age thirteen, some of my friends owned motor scooters, which were quite expensive, but my father, clever man that he was, built one

TOP
Author, age 3, taken by a Depression photographer
:: 1929

BOTTOM
Author, age 7, taken by a Depression photographer
:: 1933

for me. Using a 2" × 12" wooden board for the platform, he placed a wheel at each end and a gasoline washing-machine-engine mounted under the seat. The handlebars were equipped with a throttle for engine speed, and he devised a V-pulley arrangement with a lever that was pressed with your foot, when you wished to go forward.

At around fourteen, I had outgrown my motor-scooter-days. I yearned for a motorcycle; but my parents didn't approve of that mode of transportation. Riding in a friend's car one day, I spotted a motorcycle parked beside a farmer's barn, which was covered with rust and cob-webs, it was in very sad condition.

Since my folks would not approve, I asked my grandmother to loan me six dollars to pur-chase the cycle on a "hush-hush" basis. She was my favorite, and a great sport, so I was able to make the deal. The bike was a 1918 model, 4-cylinder Henderson. My friend, Buzz, and I brought it to his house so I could work on it in his parent's garage. It was necessary to take the

bike completely apart, and to clean and de-rust every square inch. The carburetor had frozen shut, and water had seeped into the oil from being exposed to the elements. Nevertheless, within a few months, I was able to start it. I had already repaired the magneto, and the Henderson didn't need a battery; so Buzz tied a rope to the rear bumper of his car and began towing me.

With two new tires on the bike, and the other end of the rope around my handlebars, we were off! I reached down to make adjust-ments and soon heard a "pop," another "pop," and then "pop-pop-pop," and the motorcycle was actually running! In fact, it was running too well; I had passed Buzz in his car, yet I couldn't release the rope from the handlebars. The engine was accelerating, but I was unable to slow it down, as, somehow, I no longer had control of the carburetor. Just as the rope grew taut, I was able to free it from the bike without falling, but the Henderson still wanted to run at maximum speed. At this point, I pulled the main wire from the magneto, and it finally stopped.

With a certain amount of diligence, the bike began to work properly. I repainted it and rode it a few years before selling it to the next victim.

A classic, bright-red Indian Chief was my next motorcycle. Thus began the habit of hill climbing with friends at Alum Rock Park in the

Future author on a motorcycle hill climb
:: 1941

eastern foothills of San Jose. Often, eight or ten of us would hill-climb at the park, but on one occasion only my friend, Bud Rouse, and I were there together. Bud's bike was a Harley, which, at the time, was the second-fastest motorcycle in northern California.

We had been climbing about an hour when my old Chief ran out of gasoline. There weren't any gas stations in the park, and the road out was uphill, so pushing it with Bud's size 12 boot would have been an act of futility. Also, attempting to buy a gallon of gas outside the park would have taken too long. So, we removed the gas caps from both motorcycles and lifted Bud's Harley high enough to pour some gas into my tank. A sloppy job, but it did work!

It wasn't long before Bud joined the famed American Volunteer Group. The AVG's fighter planes, emblazoned with shark's teeth captured the imagination of many. Bud became one of the hard-drinking, brawling-bunch of inexperienced airmen to volunteer for the legendary unit known as the Flying Tigers, and before Bud left for overseas, he sold me his Harley. Bud's father ran an automotive repair shop, and he was kind enough to hire me as a mechanic's helper. I continued working for Mr. Rouse until our family moved from San Jose to San Mateo during my high school years.

At age eighteen, I found the car I could afford: a Ford Model A roadster. The car was priced reasonably as it needed a lot of work, and it was powered by a V-8 engine! The seller delivered the roadster to our home, and after signing the documents, I took the car out for a trial run. About a block from home, I started to turn left when, to my surprise, the steering wheel came off in my hand! Meanwhile, the car continued on a straight course toward two gasoline pumps at the corner gas station. Each pump contained ten gallons of gasoline in overhead glass containers, and I began visualizing gas raining down on me with a flaming termination.

I started to panic, as I was still headed toward those pumps, while also trying desperately to get the steering wheel back on its shaft.

LEFT
Lt. Morefield and
R. Bud Rouse
:: 1942

BELOW
Author's first love on
four wheels, a 1930 Ford
"A-V8"
:: 1942

Soon the wheel was where it belonged,—but the threads had been stripped, leaving me with virtually no control as I continued to turn left. At the last second, I was able to veer away from the pumps, but I did run over some plants, while clipping a low fence at the corner of the station. Apparently no one saw this near-disaster or I certainly would have heard about it later, as we only lived a block away.

PHOTO: MAY NISBET

the Ford bumpers. The windshield was cut down six inches and a white padded solid top, made by "Carson" of Hollywood, was added, making it unique for its time.

After driving it for a few years, then selling it, I decided to rebuild the 1941 Ford convertible I had recently purchased. I installed a custom grille on the front end, removed extraneous chromium before applying new lacquer paint, and covered the dashboard with a soft padding. As I had recently returned from the service and would need additional funds for college, my budget for customizing the '41 Ford was limited. Still, it proved to be a fun car for traveling to nearby California beaches.

Most of the vehicles I have owned were either roadsters or convertibles. I suppose one could attribute that to my desire for fresh air.

Meanwhile, my father was quickly successful in his business, and because of the quality of his work, he laid the floors for several of San Jose's important citizens.

Two customers of my father's family became friends because of my dad's handicraft and his work ethics.

Jay Orley Hayes asked my father to install hardwood floors in his mansion, one of two brothers who owned an elegant fifty-sixty room Mediterranean style home in south San Jose.

This house, built in 1905, is now known as the Hayes Mansion, and is open to the public. Dad laid new oak flooring, and I assisted him with some of the nailing, and setting of the nails, then filling the nail holes. Dad then sanded the floors and applied the finish, while I did the final waxing.

The Hayes brothers were successful lawyers who became involved with the newspaper business by purchasing both the *San Jose Herald* and the *Mercury*. Eventually these evolved into one newspaper, the *San Jose Mercury News*.

Another local family who became friends was Alex J. Hart and family, a storeowner and one of the city's wealthiest businessmen. Hart's department store employed approximately 200

Slowly and carefully, I drove to Buzz's father's welding shop, where I learned about the stripped shaft. I asked Mr. Miller to weld the steering wheel to the shaft, as replacing the defective part would have been a major task.

My next auto was a 1936 Ford convertible coupe, which a friend and I worked on together. The '36 front end was removed and replaced with a '37 front end, which was fitted with a '40 Nash grille. New solid side panels were installed, and DeSoto bumpers substituted for people in our city of 60,000. The Hart family lived in a Victorian style mansion with two story columns, on *The Alameda*, a tree-lined street of prestigious homes in San Jose.

My father became acquainted with the Harts and was fond of their son, Brooke, a college student. In 1933, Brooke was kidnapped and held for $40,000 ransom. Before the exchange could be made, the kidnappers killed Hart and dumped his body into San Francisco bay.

Soon the two men responsible for Hart's abduction and murder were captured and held in the city jail. The news was broadcast by radio and very soon several thousand citizens of San Jose gathered around the jail.

Dad drove us to witness the turmoil on November 26, 1933. I was just seven then, and I clearly recall being hoisted on Dad's shoulders so I would have a better view.

The crowd quickly became a mob. Several men with a battering ram succeeded in forcing their way into the jail, and beat the jailers unconscious.

Thankfully I fell asleep at this point, and I didn't witness the two suspects being dragged across the street to St. James Park where they were hanged.

This was big news in San Jose and was recorded in newspapers throughout the U.S.

For some time my father kept the *San Jose Mercury* with photos of the murderers hanging from each of two trees. Later, the trees were also condemned for the crime, and were cut down.

The father of one of my pals offered me a part-time job at his soft drink bottling plant— with an increase in pay! I would be paid fifteen cents an hour plus all the soft drinks I could handle. I was in heaven. Dad let me change jobs, but it turned into something akin to working in a candy factory: one soon tires of the product.

My brother, Harry, had always been interested in having a strong, healthy body. Somehow, he became acquainted with the man who held the world's record for the one-arm barbell press. This person had a gym in his garage, and he invited my brother to train with him at night and after school. Soon, I decided I would ask to train there, and I was welcomed, but I worked with much lighter lifts since I was only about twelve at the time. Harry and I worked out there for several years, and I believe the training helped me later, when I became involved in high school sports. Although we moved from time to time, I always found a gym where I could exercise.

One of my earliest experience—one that has remained through the years—occurred when I was about four years old. My family and I had been lunching in my mother's rose garden, which contained over a hundred varieties of roses. A butterfly flew by and landed on a slice of bread. It perched there, flexing its wings, and when its wings were folded together, my father picked up the Monarch and held it in his mouth. When he let go, the butterfly continued to rest on his lower teeth, still flexing its wings. Several moments passed before it flew away. Dad said, "You see, certain things can't be intimidated." Since that time, I have learned that some animals, birds, and humans cannot be intimidated. With all living creatures, it is simply a matter of degrees as to whether or not they are timorous.

During my early years in grammar school, I became fascinated with comic strips, and would draw for hours, trying to replicate what appeared on the printed page. As I became proficient with bringing cartoons to life, I decided to become a cartoonist. After all, it seemed so easy and it held my attention, that is, until I took a drafting class in junior high school. Our teacher, Kurt Gross, was also a practicing architect, and occasionally he shared some of his beautiful work with our class. He made architecture seem so exciting my direction eventually changed from cartooning to architecture. We became good friends and remained so throughout his life

Although Harry was eight years my senior, we were best friends as well as brothers. As

Author's brother
Harry Nisbet's photo,
San Jose, CA
: : 1936

the eldest, he would always look after and protect me. However, he would also get me into trouble with the pranks he thought up. Once we took a truck-sized tire pump and reamed out the size of the outlet, so it would discharge a huge burst of water. Hiding in shrubbery, we filled the pump with water and waited for a passing car. My job was to aim the nozzle; Harry would then apply the most pressure possible, releasing a jet of water that would hit the windshield with a blast. I'm sure some drivers thought a summer squall had just blown through the neighborhood. This continued until I aimed at a neighbor's car, and he told our folks. That was the end of that idea.

We also fabricated model airplanes from balsa wood and paper, which flew by winding up the rubber bands that powered the propeller. We flew them at schoolyards, where there was enough space to adjust them to our satisfaction. When we grew bored with a particular plane, we flew it from the roof of our house at dusk. After winding the propeller, Harry would point the plane toward the direction we had chosen. I would then set fire to

the plane's tail, and my brother would send it off. Soon the plane would smoke, spiraling downward until it crashed in flames—much like the World War I movies we had seen at Saturday matinees. It was all great fun until someone reported the stunt to our parents. Another great pastime—gone up in smoke.

Our mechanical ability was tested when we acquired a single bed frame made of iron. First, we bolted two axles to the frame to support four wheels. Then a board was bolted to the frame to accommodate side-by-side seats. The front axle was pivoted in the center, to allow us to turn the wheels with an attached rope. This was makeshift, of course, and in no way legal since not only had we hooked up a small gas engine to our contraption, the "machine" also lacked brakes. If we chose to go forward, we used the lever we had installed to tighten the V-belt. And for reverse, we simply picked up our little runabout and turned it around. Fortunately, in those days, there was very little street traffic to consider as we drove around San Jose on a bed frame, or surely we would have been involved in some kind of accident.

Thinking back, I recall that our neighbors across the street had two sons close to Harry's age. Bob was a nice guy, but Ken was so crude you could cut his banter with a knife. It was hard to believe he belonged to the same family. Ken swore constantly about anything: the heat, the cold, flies, the color of his parents' car. Not only did he swear, which we did not like, but Ken always managed to pass gas whenever we stood around talking. He thought it was hilarious, and would laugh about it. One day I suggested to Harry that we make up a batch of candy with a special piece for Ken containing Ex-Lax, a chocolate laxative often used in those days. Harry though it was a great idea, so we loaded up Ken's piece with the purgative. My brother took the plate of candy across the street, making sure Ken took his special piece. We hung around for awhile, then went home for lunch. After lunch, we visited with the neighborhood boys for several hours, and then Ken started his old tricks. A few seconds later, his face held an expression we had never seen. He grabbed his pant leg and streaked for the house. Although our parents didn't find out about that trick, they probably wondered what happened to their supply of Ex-Lax.

When Harry and I were left to our own devices, we would occasionally roughhouse together. He was usually careful around me, due to the difference in our age and body weight. I admired Harry and wanted to be just like him, so if he wanted to wrestle, I would usually oblige. We shared a bedroom, and one night when it was almost time for bed, Harry pushed me onto the bed and we began trying to pin each other down. Soon, we were both standing on the bed, jumping around. For some reason, Harry lunged at me and I started to fall backward, arms flailing about. My head hit the hardwood floor first, and the rest of me followed. Some say that before they pass out they see black, well, I saw white.

Later, I learned that my fall had created such a noise that my mother heard it across the house. Harry panicked when she called out, as I lay there quite still, so he pushed me under the bed. Hearing our mother's footsteps, he pulled a heavy drawer from the dresser and placed it on the floor. When Mom asked about the source of the racket, Harry explained he'd pulled the drawer out too far and it had hit the floor. She then asked, "Where is Earl?" and he said I was in the adjoining bathroom. After she left, Harry quickly took a wet washcloth from the bathroom and placed it on my forehead in an attempt to wake me. That worked, but I still saw stars buzzing around for awhile. Also, an egg-sized lump remained on the back of my head for a couple of weeks. One thing had worked in our favor: During that time, I wasn't in need of a haircut or my mother surely would have spotted it.

CHAPTER TWO : :

WORLD WAR II

THE WAR YEARS

Shortly after Pearl Harbor, my father sold his hardwood floor business and took a job in a South San Francisco power plant where, he decided, he could do more for the war effort. Gas rationing was in full force, and to cut Dad's commute miles we moved north to San Mateo, which reduced his mileage by seventy percent. I completed high school at San Mateo High, where I first became aware of Merv Griffin when he complemented me on the redesign of my 1936 Ford convertible. Merv was a grade ahead of me, and he sang at many of our school dances. During summer vacations, Merv would go on tour with different bands; later, he became the lead singer for Freddie Martin's band.

While still in high school, I went to San Francisco to enlist in the Flying Tigers, as my friend Bud Rouse had already done. I passed the written test with flying colors, the physical like a tiger, but failed the eye test like a bat; so I was at the mercy of the draft.

I allowed myself to be drafted into the Army because I couldn't stand to be aboard any ship, no matter the size, and I did have a choice of services at that time. Hundreds of us gathered in San Francisco and took the train ride to Fort Ord, in Monterey, California, where we were there long enough for orientation, shots, and getting our clothing and duffel bag. In a few

days, we were shipped to various states. People from the East Coast would wind up being stationed in California, Oregon, or Washington. Californians would often find their training grounds in Maryland, or possibly North Carolina. I was shipped to Camp Fannin, Texas, which was a short distance from Austin. The next two years of my life were, without a doubt, the worst two years that I would have to endure.

After finishing basic training, I was assigned to go to the European Theater. No one ever explained to me why it was called a "theater." Was it because of the scenery or the buildings? Or because it had drama or a variety of costumes? Or was it because of the action? All I knew was, in that theater, people were trying to kill each other.

THE BOAT TRIP

I joined a multitude of GIs assembled at Fort Dix, New Jersey to receive our assignments that would take us to the front. It took several days for the top brass to get everyone headed in the right direction. The group I was assigned to waited a few days longer until the President Washington, a converted passenger liner, was loaded with supplies for our journey from New York City to Southampton. Finally, the day arrived and we marched aboard to claim our bunks on the newly retrofitted troop ship. All the below-deck areas were extremely crowded and humid. We felt that the last cool breath we took topside was the last breath of fresh air we would experience until the ship reached its destination.

Even with the overabundance of GIs aboard, the President Washington was a good ship, and our run across the Atlantic was smooth and uneventful. However, I am not a good sailor, and was often found hanging over the rail. A few days before sighting England, we experienced a real scare. A German U-boat was known to be in the same waters, but we were in dense fog, and fortunately neither ship saw the other.

During one of the days on our run, the paymaster asked that we line up to collect our monthly pay. As a private, I was paid twenty-one dollars a month—plus an extra four dollars per month for going into a war zone. I don't recall what I was paid aboard ship, but I proceeded to lose it all during a game of poker. That was one of my best lessons in life, and I haven't gambled since that time.

Arriving at Southampton, I was elated to finally step on firm ground. We marched in small groups from the ship to a train that took us through London, and on to Southend-on-Sea. Then, in the dead of night, we boarded a small ship for our voyage to Le Havre.

Fortunately, the war in Europe was winding down in early 1945, when I was assigned to General Patton's Third Army. After landing at Le Havre, we were ordered to line up in rows for inspection. A major walked down each row, his lieutenant beside him noting the names and serial numbers of those the major had selected for MP duty. It became obvious that he was basically choosing tall men who looked as though they could take care of themselves. Along with some others, I was chosen to stay in France for a few weeks of military police training, while many GIs from the ship were sent to Germany and Russia. I was thankful for that training period, as the war in Europe was finally coming to an end.

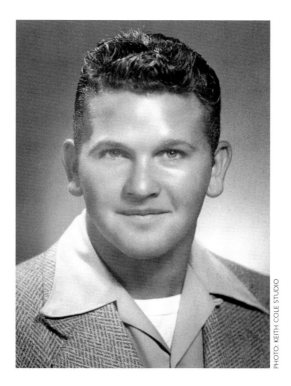

High school graduation photo for mother and father prior to entering the army
: : 1943

PHOTO: KEITH COLE STUDIO

After completing our MP training, we were each shipped to a different outfit to shore up the casualty spaces suffered by those commands. As an MP, I was sent directly to Patton's 14th Armored Division, who was guarding the infamous concentration camp, Dachau. Most of those prisoners had already been sent to hospitals when I arrived, but the stench from rotting corpses was still so bad, it was necessary to wear a cloth over one's face as a filter.

George Patton was not a stranger to the horrors of war, but even he vomited when some months earlier he had gone into the concentration camp at Buchenwald. At that time, (early 1945), hundreds of such camps were scattered throughout German-held land. Hitler's goal had been to "cleanse the race," and in so doing, six million Jews were exterminated, along with five million Communists, democrats, clergymen, intellectuals, Jehovah's Witnesses, gypsies, and homosexuals.

To illustrate how vicious the war had become, before our outfit arrived, U.S. forces swept into the village of Gardelegen to liberate prisoners still held there. However, the SS troopers had herded a thousand or more prisoners into a barn soaked with gasoline, then set it on fire. Immediately, it became a furnace with the screaming victims hurling themselves at barn doors, windows, and even cracks in the walls. Some had tried tunneling beneath the walls, but they became stuck and were burned to death. For those who might have escaped, SS troopers awaited them. In this particular case, only seven prisoners survived.

I wondered why such a place would need guards; who would care to steal anything? Still, we stayed until tractors arrived to landfill the open graves and take care of general cleanup.

A few months later I was assigned to the 45th Infantry Division. This particular MP unit had suffered the greatest casualty rate, percentage wise, of any outfit in Europe. The rationale was that MPs were ordered to stand at intersections while directing our tanks and troops toward the front. However, as the German artillery withdrew, those intersections were targeted and instructions given to knock out all mechanized units that followed, making it likely that the first bombardment would take out an MP and possibly the vehicle in question.

Next, our squad was ordered to keep the peace in Altotting, a small town in Bavaria. I was fortunate to have been trained as an MP, which meant I would ride in a Jeep or staff car rather than walk all over Europe—unlike most of our troops. We'd been notified by our officer-in-charge that a specially trained CIC sergeant, Chester B. England, had been assigned to our squad. When needed and under his direction, we would assist him, as Sargeant England was the agent provocateur investigating certain individuals in the area regarding their war criminal status. Later, we also learned that England was married to the entertainer, Judy Canova.

After taking over a small jail in the village, our function as MPs was to drive Sergeant England to the suspect's residence, arrest him, and then deliver him to the station for interrogation by England. If Sgt. England cleared the suspect, we would return him to his residence. Those with questionable stories were held for confinement until they could be transported to Munich for further interrogation.

With the war behind us, and the danger of snipers and skirmishes at an end, our squad of fourteen MPs had what the army called a "good deal." After taking over Altotting, we sought out and acquired an abandoned hotel for our stay. One of the men found an English-speaking Polish cook to live in and cook for us exclusively in exchange for his room and board. For weeks, our diet had consisted of something called "C" rations: a small box of packaged dry food with four cigarettes packed separately. I didn't smoke, so I traded with other GIs for candy, cheese, etc. The next grade up in the food chain was the "K" ration. I have no idea which Washington genius named our cuisine. "C" rations were always dry, while "K" rations consisted of canned food requiring a can opener, (or did the Washington genius think it was a "kan" opener?) "K" rations were somewhat better, but nothing like a cooked meal from the kitchen, which is where our Polish cook came in. For example: if you brought him flour, milk, eggs, cheese, mushrooms and butter, that evening we would have a feast! If one of our squad shot a deer or wild boar, the cook would outdo himself. During those times we would think of the men we'd met on shipboard who, no doubt, were eating their "C" rations somewhere in Germany or Russia.

Once, I asked a private in our squad to accompany me on fishing expedition. We loaded a metal laundry tub into our staff car and took off for the stream I had spotted a few days earlier. I asked my buddy to throw the concussion grenade I'd given him into the stream at the end of a pool about sixty feet long. On command, he threw in his grenade and a few seconds later, I threw mine into the opposite end of the pool. The fish that survived the first blast were not as lucky when my grenade went off. Beautiful speckled trout floated to the surface. We brought fifty-two of them back to our cook. In fact, we had so many fish, we asked the cook to invite some of his friends to dinner.

SEVEN AND A HALF MINUTES OF FAME

After several months of mundane routine, our captain decided we should have some time off for sightseeing. We were located not far from Berchtesgaden, and the captain wanted to visit Hitler's Eagle's Nest, built atop Kehlstein Mountain, some 6,000 feet above sea level. A stake-sided truck was ordered to transport troops from a medical unit, along with our MPs. We arrived in the early afternoon, and except for a few shelled-out buildings, the journey was great, the countryside and the snow-capped Alps absolutely magnificent.

Martin Bormann designed the Eagle's Nest, as a gift—on behalf of the Nazi Party—for Adolph Hitler's fiftieth birthday. Later scheduled for demolition, the Nest was spared through the efforts of former Governor Jacob. Once at the site, we scurried about to see how the Fuhrer had lived only months before our arrival. Both the views of and from the building were equally stunning. In short order, we began photographing each other with the Eagle's Nest as background. I was about to photograph two friends when I heard footsteps behind me. The person happened to be a *Life* magazine photographer, so I asked if he would like to photograph the three of us. "No," he replied, "just go ahead and take your picture." Later, I went inside to see Hitler's meeting room, and among the furniture was an oval-table about twenty-four feet long. While relaxing on a chair and my feet propped up on the table, I heard the click of a camera. I turned to see the *Life* photographer, who had just photographed several of us. That photo was used several weeks later on *Life's* cover, but as only my back was visible, I felt I'd only achieved seven and one-half minutes of fame. Three of us are pictured inside

the same issue, but again, I am only seen from the back.

ROCCO LAGINESTRA

While serving as an MP in Europe, I came upon several friends from San Mateo High awaiting reassignment to other outfits. They were only in the area a few days, but it gave me a chance to hear the news from home. Meanwhile, I had made new friends. One from my outfit turned out to be my best friend in all of Europe: Rocco Laginestra.

The first time we pulled guard duty together, we immediately bonded. Rocco was from Brooklyn, New York, and it seemed music was the nucleus of his young life. He told me about some of the many clubs, concerts, parties, and musical gatherings he had attended, and of the musicians he knew personally. He even carried his own music player through Europe so he wouldn't lose touch. Most of the music he played seemed like modern jazz. Rocco's music was new to me. In the past, I had always enjoyed classical music, or what in my neck of the woods was called "serious music."

Rocco told me about a friend from Brooklyn whose music I did learn to enjoy, that of Louis Prima. When Louie played and sang his songs, the world seemed to come alive; he wanted those around him to be as happy as he was. Later, Louie would marry his vocalist, Keely

Rocco Laginestra, my best friend in Europe during WWII

Smith, and produce many records. In later years, I saw them perform in San Francisco, Los Angeles, and Las Vegas.

Rocco was also a friend of prizefighter Rocky Graziano, who held the middleweight championship from 1947 to 1948. Graziano fought Tony Zale three times within a twenty-one-month period before finally winning the title; proving, I suppose, that three times can be a charm.

Hearing Rocco talk about his home state, I felt that while New York City was swarming with people, Brooklyn was more of a small town where many folks knew each other. During our tour of duty through European countries, Rocco and I had no idea as we kidded around that he would become president of RCA Records, and become not only a friend, but also an altruistic father figure to Elvis Presley, and be in contact with dozens and dozens of entertainers. I also had no idea that in a few years I would not only meet Frank Lloyd Wright, I would actually live with him for three years.

ON TO THE SOUTH PACIFIC

Many of our units were being broken up so veterans with the most combat time could return to the states. Those of us newer soldiers would form a new division and head for the South Pacific to finish the fight against the troublesome Japanese. I feared fighting on some island with the enemy slithering about, and felt I would only survive about a week due to my snoring. Before leaving the states, I'd learned from a Marine friend who had been there that during the night, Japanese soldiers would crawl to a trench where two American Marines slept. One Marine would be killed, by having his throat slit, and the next morning, the second Marine would go berserk after finding his slain buddy.

During my eighteen months in Europe, I had seen a cross-section of England from a train, the English Channel from a ship, and France,

Germany, Austria, and Bavaria from a truck. I would have preferred the truck, had I been driving, as most of the time we were jammed together on one of two long benches, duffel bags stashed at our feet. Lacking the space to move around, we placed our rifle between our legs—muzzle on the truck's bed and arms crossed over the rifle butt—while trying to catch some sleep. This actually worked, as by that time we were so tired we could sleep anywhere.

We had been transferred to a large staging area outside Le Havre. Thousands of soldiers awaited the ships to return them to the states for two weeks of R&R. My outfit of MPs would remain on guard duty while aboard ship as we had been assigned to guard military prisoners returning to the states for court-martial.

The following day we marched aboard, together with about thirty GI prisoners, into the bowels of the ship. Sailors called it the "hold" for good reason: it held your attention while making a mental survey of the forlorn area where you would spend the next five or six days. The hold would always be hot, humid, and would smell either of oil or vomit. The MPs on duty would live in those same conditions for the allotted time. Food was brought to the prisoners, but we MPs would at least have someone relieve us so we could go top-side for meals. Other than these short respites, we almost felt like prisoners ourselves, but for the fact that we would be emancipated at the end of the voyage.

I talked with several prisoners to learn why they had been arrested. Some had murdered their girlfriends; a few were in for rape, others for striking superior officers. I was amazed to find that one GI was being held for robbery. It seems he had robbed a French bicyclist while drunk, broke, and in need of money to buy more wine. Shortly, the police detained him, as the Frenchman had called ahead and given the ID number of the GI's tank to the authorities. The GI probably received five to ten years of hard labor for that stunt.

During our passage to New York, I noticed that one of the prisoners kept to himself, and that the others made no effort to engage him in conversation. Previously, while on duty in confined areas, I'd found it best not to attempt conversations with those who wished to be alone. There is usually an underlying reason for this type of attitude.

Somewhat later, I did get the story from a sergeant who had been in the same outfit as the silent PFC.

It seems the PFC had a French girlfriend whose husband had been killed by the Germans while serving with the French Resistance. The woman had a four-year-old son when she met the GI in a bar. She and the GI became close, as she was having difficulty supporting herself and her son. Whenever the GI could visit her apartment, he brought food he had obtained from an Army cook. After spending the night, he'd rush back to his unit in time for his duties, but the GI had decided to live in France. If he wasn't discharged from the Army while still in France, then, whenever the war ended he would rejoin his girlfriend, and they would marry in France.

They had already sought permission to marry from the highest-ranking officer in the GI's unit, but had been turned down due to regulations. The soldier chose not to be married by a French magistrate, which could lead to a reduction of his service benefits in the future.

Apparently, neither the French woman nor the PFC had family they could appeal to for financial help; so, they devised this plan:

Somehow, the GI persuaded his girlfriend to push her little boy under an American army truck, assuming he would be killed. The plan was to sue the U.S. Government for an amount that would keep them in cognac and comfort for the rest of their lives.

As with so many plans—implemented and perceived to be perfect—this one had a fatal flaw. Two witnesses had seen the woman deliberately push her son beneath the truck. While

Author being welcomed home from war by Statue of Liberty, New York, NY :: 1945

her lover was returning to the USA for military trial, she was held prisoner in a French jail.

As bad as conditions were on that small ship—with waves crashing over the bow during most of the trip—I was surprised I had not become seasick.

We finally steamed into New York harbor. All of us strained our eyes, trying to locate the Statue of Liberty through the dense fog. At last, the sun came out and there she was, shining like a beacon. We knew we were home.

We released the prisoners to the special MP unit awaiting them, and we then collected our gear and were taken to Fort Dix, New Jersey for deployment. After settling in the barracks where I would stay for several days, I called my parents to inform them I would soon be home. Rather than two weeks of R&R, we would receive a forty-five-day pass, as the war in the Pacific was looking much better for our troops.

(Frankly, the generals weren't too sure where to send us.)

I told my folks I would leave Fort Dix early the next morning for a camp near San Francisco, and would call them that night. Unfortunately, circumstances I would learn about later played havoc with our communication.

From Fort Dix, we boarded a C-47 transport for our flight to McClellan field near Davis, California. Upon landing, we were loaded into trucks for the short drive to Camp Stoneman. At that time, the largest telephone center in the world operated from Stoneman, which was capable of handling 2,000 operator-assisted long distance calls per day. Although we didn't have immediate access to the telephones, a telegraph office was also located on base. The most frequent outgoing message read: "Arrived safely, be home soon."

CAMP STONEMAN

In 1942, the War Department acquired nearly 3,000 acres for the Camp Stoneman site in Pittsburg, California, forty miles northeast of San Francisco. The camp was used both as a staging area and rifle range for troop training.

Named for George Stoneman, a Civil War cavalry commander and early governor of California, Camp Stoneman was active for only twelve years: May 28, 1942 to August 30, 1954. The camp served as an embarkation point for more than one million American soldiers destined for duty in the South Pacific Theater. The post's functions were to receive and rapidly process troops for overseas duty; i.e., complete and update records, arrange for last-minute training, provide medical and dental care, and to issue and service equipment.

Later, the camp was used as a depot for personnel replacement and reclassification and as San Francisco's Port of Embarkation for the distribution of troops.

During the camp's most active period, thousands of soldiers arrived by truck, but chiefly by train from the Santa Fe and Southern Pacific lines, which had spur tracks leading directly into camp. In order to ensure that troops scheduled for overseas duty were combat-ready, GI's were first inoculated for diseases specific to their South Pacific destinations. They then had physical examinations, as well as dental work if needed.

When our outfit arrived at Camp Stoneman, we were kept under wraps while receiving shots and medications for the South Pacific, our final destination. We were restricted, and could not use the telephones for two days. When finally I was allowed to call home, my mother answered, then burst into tears and could not talk. My father took over, and I then learned that a second transport had taken off from Fort Dix, shortly after ours left the ground. The second plane crashed, killing all aboard. Naturally, the tragedy was reported in the news, but since I hadn't been able to call home, my parents had assumed the worst.

When my mother was able to speak, I consoled her and explained the situation. I felt deep remorse for the GIs who had spent years fighting the Germans, only to die in a horrible accident on home ground. The following day, a fellow MP gave me a ride from camp to my home in San Mateo.

Being united with my family again was great. I sought out old friends to hear about buddies who had entered the service following my induction. And I learned that ten of the thirteen fellows I inquired about had enlisted in the Marines and were killed—either on Saipan or the Tinian Islands—in the South Pacific. That news provoked an eerie sensation. I reflected on those who were gone, the three still fighting overseas, and I thought about the South Pacific Theatre, where I would undoubtedly be sent within two months.

SPRING OF 1945

With so many men still serving in the armed forces, it was relatively easy for me to find work. After checking the local newspaper, I answered a building contractor's ad for a carpenter's helper. My goal was twofold: to help with finances at home, and to learn the rudiments of construction. I worked as a carpenter's helper for about a month, then, to comply with my orders, boarded a train in San Francisco for Camp Swift, Texas, near the city of Austin.

Camp Swift was planned in 1940, yet almost 3,000 buildings were constructed in the incredibly short space of 120 days. Initially designed to accommodate 44,000 troops, the camp reached a maximum of 90,000 GIs during peak periods. In addition, 3,865 German POWs were housed at the camp. Most were soldiers captured from General Rommel's elite Afrika Corp. Approximately eleven Germans still remain buried on Camp Stoneman's former grounds.

Following 1944, the Germans were left to work, unguarded, as escape attempts were rare. If such attempts were made, they sometimes ended with amusing results: One "escapee," when treed by a bull, shouted for help to those who were searching for him. Another, who had pocketed a hunk of bologna, was bitten in the buttocks by a tracking dog. Adding insult to injury, the guard dog was a German shepherd. Another attempt ended when one of the former elite was heard whimpering in the night, due to becoming trapped inside a drainage pipe.

After reporting to camp, I learned I'd be joining the MP unit of the Second Division, and was given new patches for my uniform. The new unit badge must be sewn onto the shoulder of the left sleeve, with the patch from my former outfit sewn onto the shoulder of the right sleeve. Settling in at my assigned bunk and footlocker space took much less time than sewing the patches on my dress uniform. Because of my limited talents at sewing, I would only sew on a patch when a clean shirt was needed.

LORAN ESTES

Another Californian, Loran Estes, had already been billeted in our MP barracks before my

My good friend Loran Estes from Long Beach, CA
:: 1943

Good Friend Loran Estes with his "Model B" Ford with a Winfield Flathead, Long Beach, CA
:: 1943

arrival, and from the beginning, I treasured his friendship. I found Loran a refreshingly moral, high-principled human being with nothing but altruistic thoughts for others. I relished our time together in the army and later in civilian life. I felt fortunate to have a friend of his caliber.

Loran and I shared a passion for automobiles and in rebuilding our cars. Both of us, he from Long Beach and I from San Mateo, worked hard to get the most power possible from the engines in our respective cars. We each had what Californians called A-V-8s; i.e., a Ford Model A coupe body with the standard 4-cylinder engine removed and replaced with a more powerful V-8 engine. With well-tuned, high-performance engines installed, these coupes would improve their performance by about forty percent.

Another bond was formed immediately: Loran and I were among the few soldiers in our squad from California. Some were from Oklahoma or Arkansas, but the majority came from Texas. Usually the Texans had much to say about any subject, and a great deal more when it came to their Great State of Texas. They claimed that since Texas was the largest state in the union; they had produced the biggest and best of everything. I soon became miffed over how wonderful it was to be a Texan, so I "rambled" (a Texas term) into a local book store to purchase the latest *World Almanac*, which I shared with Loran. Now, we would see who had the most power! We took turns studying everything that listed California as first, over other states, in any category whatsoever. After shooting down theories from anyone who bragged that Texas was the leader in such and such an industry, Loran or I would say "That might have been the case many years ago, but now California produces x times over what Texas can claim." We memorized fact after fact until the Texans were so apprehensive of our counter-attacks, their bragging finally stopped.

ADVENTURES WITH LORAN AT CAMP SWIFT

Note: Loran Estes has kindly supplied a great deal of the following information from his vast memory.

When Loran joined the 2nd Division at Camp Swift, 40 miles from Austin, Texas, he was chosen to be part of the Military Police company as a second echelon mechanic, which required him to spend most of his time in the motor pool. The closest town was Bastrop, just

4 miles away from the main gate, which maintained a population of 3,100, and boasted 27 liquor stores. Smithville, thirteen miles from camp, and proud to have a USO, was the GIs' "stomping grounds" whenever we could get away and provided we could commandeer a military vehicle.

The commanding general ordered a convoy be sent to Alexandria, Louisiana to pick up some PX furniture and return it to Camp Swift, a distance of 500 miles. The night before this trip, Loran and I went into Austin for some libation and a general tour of the city. We didn't return to camp until 2:00 a.m., and had to be on the road by 5:00 a.m. to escort this particular convoy. I had already been assigned for the trip, but Loran volunteered so we might find some fun along the way. The officers were grateful for Loran's skills, useful in the event of an accident or mechanical failure.

Our Captain ordered five MP Jeeps to run the convoy; i.e., direct civilian and military traffic.

The convoy, when rolling on the road was 13 miles long. Loran, in the lead Jeep, drove mainly on the wrong side of the road to arrive ahead of the convoy at Smithville, thirteen miles from camp, where he would direct civilian traffic.

The last vehicle in the convoy was a large wrecker, capable of hauling a 2-1/2 ton truck in case of accident or breakdown. Along the route, the driver became frustrated at continually speeding up and dropping back. Eventually, he had dropped back so far that when the convoy went through Houston, the MP directing traffic at a major intersection assumed the entire convoy had gone ahead. He then proceeded to the next town, leaving the intersection without military traffic control. When the wrecker arrived, with its driver assuming that an MP would be holding back traffic for him, the huge vehicle zoomed through the intersection and collided with a delivery truck from a pharmacy. The delivery truck rolled over; thousands of pills were scattered throughout the intersection along with shattered glass containers, and a good time was had by all.

The convoy proceeded on its way without incident and by the time it approached Lake Charles, Louisiana, it was getting dark and Loran was in the last Jeep at this time to pick up MPs who had been left at certain intersections. Meanwhile, the four advance Jeeps had stopped at a roadside diner to get a cup of coffee. As Loran caught up, with his MPs in tow, he saw the four Jeeps and pulled in next to them. He and the others went in for coffee also, and as soon as they were inside, one of the already seated MPs asked, "Where's Earl?"

Loran replied, "I don't know, the last time I saw him was at an intersection in Lake Charles. I didn't see anyone, and I'm the last Jeep to come through." In an instant, the lieutenant assigned Loran to go back and look for me, some 49 miles back from the diner.

On the way back to look for me Loran was quite tired, and was doing all he could to stay awake. By the time he arrived at Lake Charles, he looked for me at every intersection where an MP had been posted, but there was no Earl to be found; so he turned around to catch up with the convoy. Unbeknownst to all, I had been picked up by a truck and had already gone past the diner where the other Jeeps were parked; so I was not left at Lake Charles to die.

Finally, all of the convoy was intact and it pulled into the camp at Alexandria. All of us had taken extra blankets with us for sleeping purposes, because the highest temperature along the route was 34°.

The next day, while the rest of the crew was loading the PX furniture, our MPs decided to go into Alexandria to look around, and map out the trip back, which was really just a cover to get away from camp, because we would be going back the same way we came, the following day. We saw the sites we wanted until 10:00 or 10:30 in the evening; so our Jeep with four MPs decided to go back to camp for some shuteye. On the way back we saw a Ford truck with a stake body on it loaded with firewood, and it had somehow rolled backward into a ditch that was about six feet deep, but fortunately it had a gentle slope. A woman was standing beside the truck, and in a flash, we decided since we were soldiers, as well as scholars, and gentlemen, we would stop to help. We hooked our Jeep to the truck with our towrope and pulled the vehicle back onto the road again. We told the lady we would follow her home in case she had more trouble with the truck. She had told us the engine had quit unexpectedly, and that was the reason it had gotten away from her and rolled into the ditch.

When we arrived at her house, she invited us in for coffee, and we noticed she was a very attractive lady in her early forties. While having coffee and chatting, there was a knock at the door; it turned out to be her brother who had been looking for her, since she was overdue with the load of firewood. We noticed his head had quite a lot of blood on it, and he told us a horror story of how he had jacked his car up to change a flat tire, and in the process, the jack slipped out and hit him on the head, and by the time he arrived at his sister's house, he had a knot on his forehead the size of a golf ball.

During our tete-a-tete we found out the lady's husband was a colonel in the Army, and was still overseas. We gabbed until about three in the morning, and we were all getting very, very, tired; so we jumped into the Jeep to go back to camp in Alexandria to try to get some sleep. By the time we got there we had only enough time to eat and grab our bedding and throw it in the Jeep, because the convoy was already lining up for the return trip to Camp Swift. By now, three days had gone by and Loran and I, dumb nineteen-year-olds, had only slept about 3-1/2 hours each night.

Now the convoy was heading for Camp Swift, and we did just the reverse of what we had done coming to Alexandria, with the exception of the tow truck.

We had successfully gotten past Houston with no trouble, and at this time Loran and I were in the lead Jeep together, with Loran at the wheel heading for Columbus, while I was fast asleep in the passenger seat. Of course the farther Loran had driven from Alexandria, the more he was in need of sleep, and later he told me by this time he had driven off the road about six times with the bouncing of the Jeep awakening him each time; meanwhile, I'm still asleep.

Once in awhile I would wake up to ask Loran how he felt, and did he want me to drive? He would say he felt great. "God, no. I can still drive," I recall, was the answer to one of my questions, and I would slumber some more.

Apparently Loran was driving a bit slower than he thought he was driving because of his struggle to stay awake. He soon saw a gasoline station on the left side of the road lit with a hundred light bulbs strung on a wire.

I was still asleep when he pulled into the station and he rushed inside to gulp down a soft drink, believing it would keep him awake, and when he reached the door to leave, he saw the convoy going past the station, and of course, being the lead Jeep, we should have been several miles ahead by now. Loran didn't remember the past hour or so on the road, but he figured he must have done something right because the two of us were still alive.

Loran got back into the Jeep, and rushed past the convoy to finally arrive at Columbus, with me still asleep. The lieutenant asked Loran where the hell had we been, because he had arrived at Columbus an hour earlier. Loran gave him some mumbo-jumbo, and soon we were rushing about to get the convoy back to Camp Swift. Loran felt this particular trip was one of the highlights of our existence at this military base.

In early April 1946, we were to be moved from Camp Swift to Fort Lewis, Washington, the 2nd Division's new home until further orders.

Soon, we boarded a train for Washington via California. Loran and other Californians had been bragging about our fair state, but just as

we crossed the border into California, it began raining heavily, which drew a loud rejoinder from other MPs. The rain stopped as we started passing fields of lush crops, in beautiful symmetry with other farmlands. Although the non-Californians hated to admit it, they knew they were in paradise.

We disembarked at Pittsburg, California, then transferred by truck to Camp Stoneman. There, we would regroup and practice for the first Armed Forces Day parade in San Francisco, honoring the armed forces' involvement in World War II. Why, I mused, if we were to be honored, must we march?

The day of the parade, our MP regiment with color guard was the first unit directly behind the San Francisco Mounted Police. We marched on poorly maintained streets, due to the lack of labor during the war, and between streetcar tracks. And we were following horses that, on occasion, did what came naturally. In short, we were trying to avoid holes between the tracks, along with horse droppings.

We marched from San Francisco's Ferry Building to City Hall, which had a reviewing stand for the parade. The number of soldiers from the 2nd Division was estimated at over 10,000. While standing at attention in the reviewing stand, every so often a soldier would silently keel over into a "dead faint."

While stationed briefly at Camp Stoneman, I visited my parents in San Mateo, returning to camp with my custom 1936 Ford convertible. Loran and I would acquire evening passes, drive around the Bay Area to see what mischief we could get into, then stop and see my folks before heading back to camp.

One night Loran was driving my pride and joy back to camp while I happened to be asleep in the passenger seat, and a car was coming towards us the exact same moment I was dreaming we were going over a cliff on the right side of the road. In a flash, I had grabbed the steering wheel and was turning it to the left with all my strength so we wouldn't go over the cliff, at this same instant, Loran was turning

Second Infantry Military Police (RIGHT) marching in Armed Forces Day Parade on Market Street, San Francisco, CA :: 1945

the wheel to the right so we wouldn't cross over the center line and hit the oncoming vehicle. It was fortunate Loran also lifted weights and was able to finally overcome my slumberous effort. By the way, we didn't hit the car! I later left my convertible with my folks before we had to leave for Fort Lewis.

The war with Japan was nearing a conclusion, and with the atom bombs dropped on Hiroshima and Nagasaki, the Country's resistance waned. A great number of our service men and women would be separated.

After a week in the San Francisco area, we were put aboard a train heading for Fort Lewis, but it was well known, by then, that it would just be a holding area for soldiers to be discharged from the service, based on a point system. Troops with the most time in battle received the most points and were discharged first. Next came the soldiers with the most time in the service. After that, I thought, they probably selected you if you had the best crease in your trousers, or best shine on your boots. Whatever it was, I was one of the last to be relieved of military duty out of Fort Lewis.

During the weeks I was waiting to be discharged, the Army always wanted you to be doing something. We were soon to be civilians again, but the Army could not see us on our bunks, or in the PX drinking beer or even soft drinks. No, we imminent ex-soldiers were given a chance to report to the parade grounds for drill, to the supply sergeant for paint and brushes to paint the barracks, to the lieutenant at the gymnasium for lessons in basketball or boxing or weight training, or to the lieutenant at the baseball diamond for games. Since I had played some baseball in high school, I realized that half of the time you play this game, you would be sitting until it was your time at bat, so I chose the baseball diamond. And they say a diamond is a *girl's* best friend!

ROCKY MARCIANO

A game was set for the MPs of one unit to play some medics from another unit. I was chosen to play the position that I preferred to play, center field. Back in San Mateo I was pretty fast at fielding, and being in center field I could sometimes help my teammates in right field or left field. In choosing up sides, back home, after the pitcher was chosen, I usually came next or possibly third or fourth. It was another story here at Fort Lewis; no one had seen the others play before. Anyway, I was finally chosen and I looked at the medics selecting their players. One of them stood out with his constant gift of gab, a likeable fellow by the name of Rocky Marciano. He was their catcher and when our side was at bat, Rocky always had something to say to, or about, the batter.

Later, of course, everyone would know that during the next ten years he would become the only world's heavyweight boxing champion to retire undefeated, with a record of 49 wins, zero losses, and 43 knockouts. After Joe Louis retired as undefeated champion in 1949, money problems forced him back to prizefighting. He

finally retired again in 1951 after a KO by Rocky.

There would be more games, but this was the first that I saw Marciano as a catcher. He had a very good arm, and put several of our team out at second. When this first game was over, one of my teammates happened to be a friend of his and suggested the three of us go to the PX for a beer. One beer turned into another, which turned into another, and so forth.

During the next few weeks, Rocky did some boxing on the base, and I believe he even went to some nearby cities to fight as an amateur. I could see how he would win so many fights around the base, since he looked as if he might have done a lot of barroom brawling where he grew up.

I did well enough in my baseball playing for the first few games until the medics brought in a "ringer." He was a pitcher who had played professional ball for the New York Yankees. He was not yet a star, per se, but he had been signed, and then drafted into the service. After his windup and release, it seemed that it only took a second for the ball to pop into Marciano's glove. After watching him strike out our batters, I had great apprehension about going to the plate when my turn came to bat. I stood there, watching that graceful windup, and suddenly I heard a pop, and it was strike one. I was so transfixed by the experience of the fastest ball I had ever seen coming at me, I just couldn't move. Strike two, then I heard, "Strike three, you're out." Fortunately we only had a few more days of baseball before we got our walking papers. In the three or four games against that pitcher, I never got a hit. It was also fortunate, I thought, that *I was never hit.*

RETURNING TO CIVILIAN LIFE

The Army finally decided that Fort Lewis was now safe and didn't need my protection any longer, so they gave me an honorable discharge and handed me a train ticket to San Francisco.

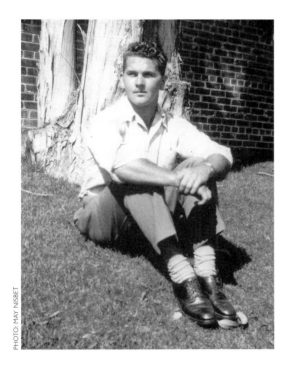

ABOVE
Photo of author by his mother prior to
becoming a soldier in WWII
:: 1944

RIGHT
Harry Nisbet ready for his college years
:: 1936

My honorable discharge stated: under Military History #30, Military Occupational Specialty and Number, Military Policeman 677. Under #31: Military Qualifications and Date, SS M1 rifle. Under #32: Battles and Campaigns, Central Europe. Under #33: Decorations and Citations, Meritorious Unit Award, European African Middle Eastern Service Medal, American Theatre Service Medal, Good Conduct Medal, Victory Medal, and Army of Occupation Medal Germany.

In order to help you find work after being separated from the Army, each soldier was given a paper titled "Separation Qualification Record," and mine went on to say: Summary of Military Occupations: Military Policeman: Served with the 14th Armored Division in the European Theater of Operations. Searched, and guarded German prisoners of war, working in connection with the Counter Intelligence Corps. Was required to accompany prisoners to various encampments throughout Europe. In addition to above duties, had responsibility of guarding Army installations and equipment and maintaining peace and order and the control of traffic.

Now I felt great; if there were any Germans needing to be searched, I might possibly get a job! I had called home and my brother had driven my mother and father to collect me.

They had also picked up my grandmother, who lived in San Francisco, and we all loved to dine at Fisherman's Wharf; so that is where we had a feast celebrating my homecoming. That meal with my family helped melt away the prior two years of the war's perplexity that beset me. I was home.

I found about, and immediately joined the 52/20-club. Congress had mandated a program whereby ex-GIs would receive twenty dollars a week for a total of fifty-two weeks to further or complete their education. I signed up at San Mateo Junior College, only because several of my buddies were already attending classes there. It was quite easy, and we found ourselves just partying most of the time. That finally became boring, so I registered at a private architectural and engineering college in San Francisco.

That worked out well for the next four years as I took the train to and from San Mateo four days a week and drove my car on Wednesdays in order to take my grandmother shopping. She was a wonderful lady, with old-world charm and a regal air about her, who would sit quietly making quilts, or pickle some vegetable, or can some fruit, or make the best coffee that I had ever tasted up to that point in my life; then to rest, she would sit at the table playing solitaire.

HOLLYWOOD FOR HARRY(?)

Around this time, those close to my mother began suggesting that Harry and I were good-looking enough to be in movies. After all, Mom had grown up with, and was still a friend of Henry Hathaway, the movie director.

Hathaway's directorial achievements included *Call Northside 777* (1948) with James Stewart and Lee J. Cobb; *The Desert Fox, The Story Of Rommel* (1951) with James Mason; *Five Card Stud* (1968) with Dean Martin and Robert Mitchum; and in 1969 John Wayne won his only "Oscar" for his work in *True Grit* with Glen Campbell. Our mother decided not to push the issue, since Harry wanted a career in law enforcement. After becoming a police officer for the City of San Jose, he was recommended for a position in the wealthy community of Atherton, California. As a high school junior, I felt a certain pride in my brother's job, and at times rode along in his patrol car. Harry had worked in Atherton for a year when he received a call to respond to a burglary in progress at a large, expensive home. Alone, he went quietly to the front door, which was slightly open. He took out his pistol and walked softly to the darkened opening. Not hearing anything, he pushed the door open and jumped inside the foyer. He looked to his left and saw someone pointing a gun at him, and his hair stood straight up. He nearly fainted as he realized that he was looking at himself in a full-length mirror. That was it for Harry, a few weeks later he resigned.

When our mother brought up the subject of Hollywood to me, I explained that my goal was to someday build beautiful buildings. I'd never felt my voice was strong enough for the stage or movies, nor did I find the idea appealing. Thankfully, she was not the typical "Hollywood mother" who pushes her child to become a star. She was sensitive, and she understood. The subject did not come up again.

CHAPTER THREE : :

BECOMING AN ARCHITECT

While attending college in San Francisco, I would occasionally have free time in the late afternoon. I would wander around the city, visiting various shops. One day I came upon Gump's, a fashionable seller of fine art, jewelry, china, and Japanese prints.

A sense of well being came over me while viewing the prints: simplistic drawings that told a story in but a few strokes. I had seen many museum-quality paintings, but this was my first experience with that particular art form. After learning the price of several prints, I soon realized it would take months for me to save and purchase one.

What to do? A few days later I checked out two books on Japanese prints from the city library as I felt I needed something soothing for my room. Among the many I liked, I chose four, and proceeded to paint copies of them. Not exactly Japanese, but they satisfied me displayed on the walls of my room.

I was assiduous in my studies, and focused on my dream to someday design and build beautiful buildings. My mother was quite aware of my goal, and on my nineteenth birthday presented me with a copy of Frank Lloyd Wright's *An Autobiography*. After reading the book, I loaned it to Chuck Bass, my best friend in college.

Chuck Bass and I were inseparable during our time in college, and we made it a point to stay in touch during the following years.

To supplement his income while attending college, Chuck drove a taxi; He also taught ballroom dancing at the Arthur Murray Dance Studio. He became an extraordinary dancer, and won a few ballroom dance contests with his partner in the bay area, but his favorite dance was the "Mombo." When Chuck heard of a nightclub with this particular Latin beat, he would call and invite me to accompany him. Chuck sought out the rhythm in the bay area and would also drive to Los Angeles, or San Diego. I wasn't a dancer yet Chuck tried to show me a few steps, but, for me, it was hopeless. I was content to sip a cocktail and watch his performance on the dance floor. He was usually the best dancer in the club moving to the rapid beat of the music. At all times Chuck's shoulders remained level, the criterion of an extraordinary Latin dancer.

After being together for a few years, (both in and out of the classroom), Chuck commented, "Earl, you understand me better than my parents or my brother." I was taken aback by his remark, as Chuck's brother was also an architectural student. After pondering his statement, I repeated what he had said, "Chuck, you also know me better than my parents or my brother."

We began seeking out various Wright-designed houses in California to visit and photograph. The owners were usually pleased

Author's drawing of
wood block print by
"Kuniyoshi" while in
college
:: 1947

to show us through their homes, especially
after learning that we were architectural
students devoted to Wright's work and his
philosophy.

At this period of our lives we were both
single, but Chuck had a romance in progress.
Soon after telling him I had been accepted at
Taliesin, Chuck and Sarina were married. Chuck
considered becoming an apprentice, but now
he would have to support he and his wife. The
young couple moved to Phoenix so he could
be close to Taliesin West, and Chuck immediately was employed with a local architect. It

wasn't long before he too fell in love with the
enchanting desert surroundings.

On several occasions I brought Chuck and
his wife to our camp and showed them the various buildings. Chuck was absolutely enthralled.

After a few years of desert life, Chuck and
his wife returned to the San Francisco Bay Area.
Upon my return to California during Christmas
time, in 1953, Chuck, Sarina, and I continued
attending art galleries, musical performances, and
on occasion, we visited FLW buildings.

In late 1954 Chuck and I drove to Los
Angeles to see a FLW exhibit called "60 years

of living architecture," a display of the master's drawings, photographs, and models. These were shown in a temporary building constructed expressly for the ceremony at the Barnsdall Hollyhock House site, which Wright designed in 1927. The Barnsdall house eventually became part of the Los Angeles Municipal Art Museum, and it is now open to the public.

MANUEL SANDOVAL

We soon discovered the V. C. Morris store in San Francisco, an exclusive gift wares shop being remodeled to Wright's design. We talked with the owners, Mr. and Mrs. Morris, who kindly permitted us to wander through the building among the pandemonium. One of the workmen

Author's drawing of wood
block print by "Buncho"
while in college
:: 1947

friends with Manuel. This evolved into discussions about architecture, design, and, of course, Mr. Wright. In time, Manuel invited us to his flat in the city for dinner. His wife, Ella, was gracious about having two students occasionally show up for dinner.

During these visits, Manuel shared some of his superb architectural drawings and designs. The furniture in their home was remarkable, as not only were the designs unique, with a somewhat Mayan motif; they were modern and attractive, while remaining pure Sandoval. The wood was unlike anything I'd ever seen with a superb finish in shades of rich, reddish-brown. When Manuel removed a cabinet door to show us its unfinished side, we gaped at the most inexpensive grade of Douglas fir plywood on the market. That certainly opened my eyes. Manuel had truly transformed a "sows ear" into a "silk purse." When asked how he had obtained that particular shade, he would not divulge the formula, saying this was something he would work on in the future.

Manuel had constructed fine cabinetry for Mr. Wright, both at Taliesin and for various clients throughout the country. Probably the most notable and challenging work was Wright's intricate, abstract-style office, done in several different woods for the Edgar J. Kaufmann Department Store in Pittsburgh, Pennsylvania.

Wright planned the office using a 4-foot square unit system proportional to the 8-foot ceiling height. Cabinets were kept to a height of 2 feet, corresponding to a half-unit, used vertically. Mr. Kaufmann's abstract style desk (designed by Wright) and the plywood relief mural above it became the focal points of the room.

The entire office was constructed of cypress veneer in carefully matched grains, plus a few other hardwoods added for accents. Loja Saarinen, wife of architect Eliel Saarinen, wove the fabric for the carpets and upholstery.

Eventually, the office was removed, intact, and is now part of a permanent exhibit at the Victoria and Albert Museum in London.

was cutting walnut boards for the beautifully curved shelving on the second floor. I had never seen such an attractive fitting of mitered cuts. When we stopped to compliment the workman on his craftsmanship, he introduced himself as Manuel Sandoval, one of Wright's first apprentices. Mr. Wright had requested, specifically, that Manuel carry out the intricate cabinetry for the Morris store. Chuck and I began stopping by after classes to see how the work was progressing, and soon we became

Author's painting for
his room, college days
:: 1947

Author's painting of Japanese wood block print by "Saraku" while in college
:: 1947

During those three summers working as a lifeguard, I saved six people from drowning and one fantastic-looking 20 year old blond girl from rape, (I changed my mind) so I was probably worth my salt—although as I write this, my doctor doesn't allow me any. While off duty one day, the lifeguard who replaced me lost a young man who had been swimming beyond the marked area. I was grateful this had not occurred on my watch.

While I was in college, my father retired from his position at the power plant in South San Francisco. My mother did not appreciate the heavy fog that occurred in San Mateo; so they moved to Menlo Park just a block away from the Stanford Golf-Course. That worked for me and I moved in with them, commuting to San Francisco by train to complete my education.

THE LIFEGUARD

While attending college in San Francisco, I worked two jobs during the summer. One as a carpenter's helper, the other as a lifeguard at Stanford University's Searsville Lake, a summer resort west of the campus. My boss, Chuck Coker, was a weightlifting competitor at Stanford while studying for a degree in physical education. When Chuck asked if I would like to work out with he and two of his buddies, I immediately accepted. His friends, both Stanford alumni, were Norman Norse, who held a California State Championship in the shot putt for Stanford, and Otis Chandler, whose family owned the *Los Angeles Times* newspaper. All three were stronger than me; which was okay—even they needed to rest on occasion.

Author as lifeguard at Stanford's Searsville Lake
:: 1947

FLOYD PAGE

I soon learned that a gymnasium had opened in Palo Alto, a short distance from Stanford. Floyd Page, owner and operator of the gym, had been working out since childhood, evidenced by his muscular development. He was a single man when I first met him, and soon we became good friends. Quite often, after closing the gym on Friday nights, we dined and toured the nightclubs together. Floyd was well known and respected around the area. He was also a great vocalist, and was usually asked to sing in the clubs we visited.

When needed, I would substitute for Floyd as an instructor. The gym was closed on Sunday, and during summer we would head for the Santa Cruz beaches to work on our tans, have a few beers, and flirt with the girls.

Floyd was well known and respected within the gymnasium circuit. Weightlifting and body-building stars often dropped by for a workout and a visit. These included: Clancy Ross; Dennis Nelson, (also in movies); Walt Baptist, (gym owner from San Francisco); Steve Reeves, (Mr. America in 1947, also a movie star); Jack La Lane, (TV personality with incredible stamina and strength); Vic Tannny (with his Hollywood gym for movie stars); and Mickey Hargitay, (Mr. Universe of 1955). Mickey played in movies and married actress Jayne Mansfield in 1958. Their daughter, Mariska Hargitay, currently plays a detective on the successful TV series, *Law and Order: Special Victims Unit*.

Floyd would sometimes be invited by other gym owners to visit, and occasionally he and I would work out with them. After completing a workout with Jack La Lanne, at his Oakland studio, we headed downstairs for lunch when an attractive, well-built girl began climbing the stairs. Jack said, "Guys, meet Beverly. For the past five months, we've been working on developing her breasts." He then said, "Bev, show these two your breasts." Without any hesitation, she pulled up her sweater, sans bra, to reveal what Jack had helped her accomplish. Jack was

"Professional Mr. America" Floyd Page and author after a workout with Steve Reeves and Clarence Ross in Ross's gym, Alameda, CA :: 1947

always dedicated to promoting better health.

On another occasion, Floyd called Clancy Ross, former Mr. America and gym owner from Alameda, to work out with him. Steve Reeves was also expected that day. Floyd couldn't seem to enlarge his calves, which Clancy knew. While Steve was still in his street clothes Clancy asked that he show his calves to us. Steve started to pull his trouser leg over his calf, tugging several times before the pants relinquished their hold. As expected, Steve's calves were huge. After completing our workouts at Clancy's gym, one of his members took our photo, which was later sent to Floyd's gym.

Floyd competed in several bodybuilding competitions, usually winning second or third place. Finally in 1948, he won the title of "Professional Mr. America" in San Francisco.

Some time after Loran and I were discharged from the Army, we arranged to see Floyd compete in the Mr. Universe contest, which was held in Los Angeles. Floyd was about

5' 10" tall and weighed just less than 200 pounds, and as Loran noted, "His body was hard as a sidewalk."

During the exhibition, a strength and endurance contest was held between three contestants, including Floyd, to show how many times each of them could bench press 325 pounds.

The first contestant, whose name I don't recall, was about 6' 2" tall and weighed about 220 pounds. He lay down on the bench and pressed the barbell 18 times. The second contestant was Alan Stephan, who pressed the same weight 21 times. The final contestant was Floyd Page, approximately 4" to 6" shorter than the previous two, and with a much slighter build. (Floyd had been training to, hopefully, bench press the most total weight in his weight class).

Floyd got into position and was handed the barbell, which he proceeded to press 26 times before the bar was taken from him. The consensus of most of the spectators was that Floyd would have accomplished 32 to 35 repetitions.

Listed in Ripley's "Believe It or Not" for having so little body fat in proportion to his muscular definition that it was impossible to pinch the skin on his upper arms, Floyd had again gained fame. Once, while in a swimming pool, I tried to teach Floyd the "dead man's float"—when facedown in the water, the swimmer pulls his knees to his chest with his arms. Floyd attempted to do just that, but when he brought his knees to his chest, he sank like a rock.

JOE GORES

One day, a strong, husky Stanford student came into Floyd's gym and began exercising. I learned that he lived in a boarding house fairly close to the gym, and that his name was Joe Gores. His major was English literature, and he wanted to write mysteries.

We began working out together, and soon we were hanging out after our exercise sessions. Before long, we went on a double date.

Author photographed mystery writer Joe Gores for dust jackets for his novels

Joe had been seeing a Stanford student named Marta. Although pleasant and brilliant, she was not the most attractive co-ed I had ever met. Joe had recently met Marta's girl friend, Mary Lou, who was shy but very nice looking. Joe's master plan involved having me entertain Marta while he worked his charm on Mary Lou. Although I didn't like Joe's idea of switching girl friends in midstream, I agreed to participate. The four of us went to an early dinner, took in a movie, then stopped at a coffeehouse.

Discomforting moments occur in our lives, and this was one of them. As the evening progressed, Joe and I had both turned our attention to Mary Lou. Marta caught on quickly, which was indicated by her change in facial expression. I tried chatting with her, but I had become so mesmerized by Mary Lou, I kept forgetting what I'd intended to say to Marta. The evening did *not* go as planned.

Later, we learned the girls would double date only if Mary Lou was my date, with Joe devoting his attention solely to Marta. We accepted their conditions and as Walter Cronkite said: "That's the way it was."

To supplement his lifestyle, Joe applied to David Kikkert Associates, a San Francisco firm that repossessed cars. (Sometime later, Joe would write about his experiences at DKA in a series covering street-level crime and detection). We decided to rent a house together—one close to both Stanford and the gym—although a considerable distance from Joe's nighttime "repo" work in San Francisco. I occasionally assisted Joe in the fine art of vehicle repossession. Once Joe had gained access to the vehicle in question, he would hot-wire the car and drive it to a spot designated by DKA, while I followed in his car. Joe's nocturnal adventures could be exciting, especially when attempting to repossess a car from a lonely, isolated area, and if the vehicle's owner took a "pot-shot" at him.

One night after hours spent repossessing autos, Joe was driving home alone via the Bayshore Highway when he decided to pull off the road for some much needed sleep. He parked his car about forty feet from the pavement, and within minutes fell asleep. He awoke in a hospital. It seems another motorist had fallen asleep and rear-ended Joe's car. Although Joe had sustained a neck injury, a few months later he managed to complete his studies at Stanford.

The long drives home, preceded by grueling hours spent repossessing cars, finally caught up with Joe. He rented an apartment in San Francisco to be closer to his "repo" work, which, in turn, fueled many of his mystery novels.

MIDGLEN

After completing four years of college, I moved back to my parent's home in Menlo Park. I continued working as a carpenter's helper—this time with a different contractor—and assisted him in the completion of a house. I'd heard that four of Mr. Wright's former apprentices were

building an unusual house in Woodside, about thirty-five miles south of San Francisco. With perseverance, I looked for and found the site. The house under construction was built of concrete-blocks and was similar to Wright's four houses in Southern California. I was very impressed with the design, and the former apprentices stopped working to chat and subsequently invited me to lunch. When they learned that I wished to become an apprentice at Taliesin, they began giving me advice, each in his own way. I told them about my previous work, and they invited me to assist in the completion of Midglen, the house under construction. This would mean a cut in pay, but I agreed to work with them until Midglen was completed.

While working on Midglen, I wrote to Mr. Wright to inquire about the possibility of becoming an apprentice at Taliesin.

In the interim, Midglen was completed and polished. Articles and accompanying photographs were featured in a local newspaper

Reply from Taliesin regarding my inquiry as to becoming an apprentice to Frank Lloyd Wright
:: 1950

Mr. Earl Nisbet
3029 Del Monte
San Mateo
California

Dear Mr. Nisbet: The Fellowship is over-crowded at this time - with about sixty in the group originally designed to be but thirty five. Mr. Wright has not been able to accept any applications.

If you happen to be in our vicinity you are welcome to stop by - we will be glad to show you around.

Sincerely yours
Eugene Masselink
Secretary to Frank Lloyd Wright

March 15th, 1950

FRANK LLOYD WRIGHT (1867 TO 1959)

FRANK LLOYD WRIGHT was undeniably the greatest architect of the twentieth century. He pioneered Prairie-style houses, and the Usonian idiom. Organic architecture followed, which he described as one that "Proceeds, persists, creates, according to the nature of man and his circumstances as they both change."

Following his birth on June 8, 1867 in Richland Center, Wisconsin, Anna Lloyd Jones Wright predestined her son's career by hanging pictures of beautifully designed buildings in his room. When Wright was two years old, Anna gave him a set of Froebel geometric wooden blocks to construct buildings of his own.

In 1869, Anna gave birth to a daughter, Jane, followed by daughter Maginel's birth in 1878.

Their father, William Cary Wright, was a music teacher and traveling Baptist minister who preached in Iowa, Rhode Island, and Massachusetts for the first ten years of Wright's life. In 1877, the family returned to Madison, Wisconsin, where Wright spent his school years. William abandoned his family in 1885, leaving Anna to raise their three children.

At the age of fifteen, Wright entered the University of Wisconsin as a special student hoping to study architecture. However, as that course was not available, he began by studying engineering. After two years at the university, he left for Chicago to find work in an architect's office.

Wright was twenty years old when the well-known architect J. Lyman Silsbee hired him. It was Silsbee who had designed All Souls' Unitarian Church, where Wright's uncle was minister.

Wright had seen buildings in Chicago that, he felt, made a statement. After learning they had been designed by Dankmar Adler and Louis Sullivan, he brought one of his drawings to their office, and he was hired as a draftsman and worked for their firm for several years. Wright and Sullivan became good friends, and in time, Sullivan financed the construction of Wright's house in Oak Park, Illinois.

After his marriage at age twenty-two to Catherine Lee Clark Tobin, Wright realized that his salary would not support a mortgage and a growing family of six children. He then began moonlighting—accepting clients without his employer's knowledge. Sullivan soon learned about this; they had a falling-out, and Wright was fired in 1893.

His first commissions during 1893 and 1894 were for residences in Chicago and the suburbs of Oak Park and River Forest. Some fifty-six were built, and most are still standing. A major design of that period was the W. H. Winslow house, designed for Wright's friend and publisher of House Beautiful. The design was an important example of Wright's "new style" characteristics, soon to become the basis of his constantly developing architectural language.

The Winslow house had individual merit of design, incorporating materials and form that set it apart from its neighbors, and which Wright would later develop these features into the Prairie Style. Some of the characteristics that remained throughout his life were: the stylobate-like foundation—one that anchors the structure to the ground—broad overhanging eaves; materials used in their natural form such as unpainted or non-plastered brick, and wood left in its natural state.

The Winslow house was unique for that period. It has since been designated by the American Institute of Architects as one of seventeen American buildings designed by Wright to be retained as an example of his architectural contribution to the American culture.

Wright also created the theory of organic architecture; i.e., buildings developed from their natural surroundings with orientation and requirements part of the actual design. The exteriors of his buildings favored natural colors with materials in their original state. His interiors emphasized a sense of spaciousness, planned with one room flowing into another. The living room could not be large enough nor the fireplace important enough to have an exalted feeling of enclosure.

He also invented or initiated various building techniques. Wright developed a system of pre-cast concrete blocks held together with mortar and pencil-sized steel bars. He was the first to use radiant heating in concrete floors, indirect lighting, air conditioning, and wall-hung toilets; he also coined the word "motel."

What Wright offered, due to his innate sensibility toward architecture, was a basic concept of design for American's needs and lifestyle during the coming age of technology.

Although conventional architects opposed his unorthodox methods, his principles are still evidenced (albeit to a lesser degree) in much of their work.

Frank Lloyd Wright's designs for businesses, churches, museums, banks, hotels, motels, resorts, a beer garden as well as a service station, proved to be both innovative and practical. During his 70 years in architecture he designed over 1,000 buildings of which 532 were built and over 400 are still standing. In short, he changed the way we think of interior space.

Because of Wright's fame, his personal life was subject to scrutiny by the press. Although he and his first wife, Catherine, had their share of domestic problems, she steadfastly refused to consent to a divorce.

Wright was involved in a scandal when he traveled to Berlin and lived with Margaret (Mamah) Cheney, the wife of a client. After two years in Europe, they returned to the U.S., and Wright then started construction on Taliesin (a Welsh word meaning "shining brow") on 200 acres of land his mother had inherited near Spring Green, Wisconsin.

A disaster occurred at Taliesin when a live-in chef went berserk, set fire to the house, and killed seven people, including Mamah and her two children. Wright received letters of condolence from all over the globe. One in particular intrigued him, and he arranged to meet the self-proclaimed sculptor, Miriam Noel. She was both interesting and sympathetic to Wright's situation. Before long, he asked Miriam to move into Taliesin. During this time, attorneys for both Wright and his wife were discussing a settlement, yet she would not grant him a divorce.

Wright accepted an offer to design the Imperial Hotel in Tokyo, which not only removed him from the U.S. for several years, it improved his financial situation. In 1922, Catherine finally agreed to the divorce Wright had requested in 1909.

PHOTO: BARBARA MORRISON

Miriam Noel and Wright were married in November 1923. However, Miriam had many problems, and one night she left Taliesin for good. Wright now faced another divorce. Miriam agreed to the terms in August 1927, and each went their separate ways.

During Miriam's absence, Wright had attended a ballet in Chicago where he met a young woman named Olga Milanoff Hinzenberg. Olgivanna, as she was known, had recently studied with George Gurdjieff, in Paris, at his Institute for the Harmonious Development of Man. She, also, had left her spouse and in 1925 Wright asked Olgivanna and her daughter, Svetlana, to join him at Taliesin. Olgivanna obtained a divorce, and in December 1925 their daughter, Iovanna, was born. Olgivanna and Wright were married on August 25, 1928.

THE TALIESIN FELLOWSHIP

The next few years were lean. Not much work came Wright's way, nor did funds from his writings and lectures add greatly to their income, Olgivanna then proposed that Wright open their home for students to "learn by doing," a practice similar to Gurdjieff's teachings.

Following Wright's talks at colleges and universities in 1932, thirty students registered for The Taliesin Fellowship, the Wright's first apprenticeship program with tuition fees of $1,000 each.

In addition to providing the necessary upkeep of the buildings, students would learn carpentry by completing the remodeling of parts of Taliesin that had been delayed for lack of funds. The Great Depression had arrived, and Wright's innovative new school would serve as a way to cope.

Taliesin would be a total learning environment. The school would develop apprentices in architecture, painting, weaving, construction, farming, gardening, cooking, also the study of music, art, and dance—all these while producing responsible, creative, and cultured human beings. As Mr. Wright often remarked, he wanted to develop the "complete man." (In today's vernacular, the word of choice would be "person.")

A few years earlier, as Wright worked with Dr. Alexander Chandler on the design for a luxury hotel in Arizona, (which did not come to fruition), he realized the comforts the desert offered in winter. Wishing to escape the harsh Wisconsin winters; Wright purchased several hundreds acres of rugged desert land from the government. The property was located in the foothills of the McDowell Mountains in Scottsdale, Arizona.

Wright chose a site and began drawings for Taliesin West, a "desert camp," where the Fellowship would construct buildings essential for withstanding the winter. This concept was unlike the usual relationship of apprentice to architect, whereby the young apprentice works in the architect's urban office.

Frank Lloyd Wright (1867–1959). The master strolling past one of his early works, the windmill "Romeo and Juliet" :: 1951 publicizing the grand opening, which was very successful. Wright's former apprentices had planned to build the house, sell it for a profit, then purchase another piece of land and repeat the process. Hundreds visited Midglen to view this unusual home of decorated, hand-made concrete block, but not one made an offer to purchase the house.

At last, a response to my letter requesting an interview with Mr. Wright! Gene Masselink, Mr. Wright's personal secretary, wrote that I could meet with Wright at Scottsdale, sometime within the next few weeks, to discuss my possible acceptance at Taliesin!

Thus far, I'd learned that forty-five to fifty-five apprentices lived with Mr. Wright at all times—at both Taliesin, near Spring Green, Wisconsin and Taliesin West, near Scottsdale, Arizona. With the exception of foreign students, young people were accepted for apprenticeship only after a personal interview with Wright. The waiting list usually numbered between four hundred to seven hundred.

During my work at Midglen, I'd met an ex-apprentice of Wright's, Alvin Badenhop. We became friends, and he suggested we drive to Scottsdale together. During that drive, Alvin gave me tips that would help with my interview.

When we arrived at Taliesin West, I entered Mr. Wright's office and introduced myself to Gene, who showed me to a waiting room, I sat there, knees shaking and thought, what on earth am I doing here? Would I be able to say the right things that would lead to my acceptance? I remembered the large waiting list, and my knees trembled even more.

Soon, the tap-tap-tap from Mr. Wright's cane grew louder with each approaching step. I had never, in my life, wanted anything more than to work for this great architect, and to learn about building and design. Very soon, I heard what would become the usual preface to his first words, "Hrrumph." The door opened, and there he was: an older man of medium height who exuded confidence and theatricality—both in

his manner and mode of dress. We shook hands, he offered a big smile accompanied by a twinkle in his eye, and I settled in comfortably for the interview.

Mr. Wright was more impressed with the work I'd done for my father in his hardwood floor business and my experience as a carpenter's helper, than with my formal education. He was known for saying: "He didn't want to unlearn anyone." I'd been instructed by the four ex-apprentices not to mention their names, as they had had a dispute with Mrs. Wright and had been asked to leave. Not until much later in our relationship would I learn the details.

After answering more questions, Mr. Wright thanked me for the interview, then invited me to look around the camp before I left.

While taking me around, Gene described how each building in the camp was used. One thing became clear: I saw enough to know that I wanted to participate in life at Taliesin, and I left there highly elated.

Upon returning to California, we learned that Bill Patrick, one of Midglen's four designers, had been commissioned by a couple to design a residence for them. He told us the bids had come in too high and asked if Al and I would help build the house. We discussed it, and the owner agreed with our conditions.

Construction began shortly after obtaining the subcontractors' bids through the owner, who would act as owner-contractor. The job proceeded well, yet I worried about being accepted at Taliesin before the house was completed. Would I be turned down if I arrived past the acceptance date?

At last, the owner-contractor accepted the job—with some minor changes. His father, who owned a business in Holland, offered to pay us double if we flew to the Netherlands and took our pay in Dutch guilders. Al and I were tempted, as our plane fare would also be covered. I desperately wanted to make that trip, as my maternal grandparents were from Holland. However, I had recently received a letter from Mr. Wright stating," Come along."

By late 1950, I'd purchased a new car, the 1951 MG-TD. Other than my travels with the army, I hadn't made many trips, so I decided to see the country while driving in March, to Spring Green, Wisconsin.

My footlocker packed with clothing, and my carpenter's toolbox filled with tools, were sent ahead by train to Spring Green. I found out later from Wes Peters, the Wright's son-in-law, that someone from Taliesin saw the items were in care of Taliesin, and brought them to Gene. I also realized people were expecting me to appear each day after my possessions arrived. Having said goodbye to Mary Lou, whom I had been dating regularly, and other friends and family, I set out for Wisconsin in my MG. Books and additional clothing filled the passenger space of my little car, and snow was everywhere when I reached my first stop: Reno, Nevada. Hotel rooms and meals were dirt cheap, with the hope that guests would stay longer to gamble. Stage shows with top entertainers were reasonably priced, so I stayed three nights. Recalling my earlier gambling experience on shipboard, I stayed away from the slots and gaming tables.

Having spent one night in Salt Lake City, (a Mormon city sans showgirl productions), I drove on to Cheyenne, Wyoming. By this time I had become fascinated by the scenery each state offered, each beautiful in its own way.

This native Californian had no idea how chilly one becomes when driving through the snow in a sports car fitted with canvas side curtains. At that point, I decided to proceed east through South Dakota and Minnesota, before arriving in Wisconsin. The MG, though fun to drive, was not the most practical of automobiles.

My last night on the road was spent in Rochester, Minnesota. After checking into a hotel and having dinner, I went to a nearby cocktail lounge for a drink. I began to wonder if the man sitting beside me was the popular singer of the day, Johnnie Ray—sans entourage,

but with his usual hearing aid. Later, after noticing Johnnie's name up in lights, I knew my hunch had been correct

ON TO TALIESIN

Anxious about arriving at Taliesin the next day, I requested an early call from the hotel desk clerk, and the closer I drove to Spring Green, the more impressed I became by Wisconsin's simple beauty. When finally I came to the Hillside Home School Mr. Wright had designed for his aunts in 1901, I knew I should continue on toward Taliesin. Proceeding up the driveway, I came upon polite-sign notifying visitors not to enter. Wait a minute, I thought, I'm not a visitor; I've been invited here by Mr. Wright himself! I continued driving to the parking area where, soon, Gene Masselink, Mr. Wright's secretary, appeared with a hearty greeting.

EUGENE MASSELINK

Destiny plays a great part in our lives. Many people are born, live, and die within a hundred miles of their birthplace. Whether or not Eugene Masselink's parents knew those facts, his family moved soon after Gene's birth on September 5, 1910, from Cape Town, South Africa, to Grand Rapids, Michigan. How very fortunate for the Wrights, and for those who experienced Gene's art.

While in his teens, Gene's artistic talent became even more recognized when his abstract paintings were exhibited in local art museums. During his student days at Ohio State University, Gene had attended a lecture given by Wright. Following his graduation in 1933, he was accepted as an apprentice at Taliesin, where he remained for the rest of his life.

When Wright decided that he needed a secretary, he put Gene in charge of attending to his correspondence, writing letters to applicants for admission to Taliesin, and making contact with clients and the press. Almost immediately he became totally knowledgeable regarding Wright's affairs. He would bill clients and also pay bills when there was money available to so do. He was entrusted with some of the most intimate of Wright's correspondence, locally and worldwide. He typed nearly all of the letters that Wright dictated.

He chauffeured the Wrights to formal affairs, met guests at train depots and airports, and arranged for their stay at Taliesin. In addition to overseeing parties and plays, Gene's exceptional high baritone voice added timbre and depth to many of Taliesin's performances. He executed, painted, and on many occasions oversaw the proper placement of the murals Wright designed for his clients.

Gene founded the Taliesin Press and created decorative elements for many Taliesin publications. He actually hand-printed most of Wright's "four square papers," (informational flyers folded into quarters) on the large platen press located near his private quarters. The latter part of Gene's life was spent at Taliesin and Taliesin West. In 1959, Gene served as a pallbearer for Mr. Wright's funeral.

In 1962, while working feverishly to finish painting the icons for Milwaukee's Greek Orthodox Church, soon to open, Gene died unexpectedly of a massive heart attack. Those who knew him were saddened by his early demise. We had lost a great friend and a unique artist, one who would have produced many more works of exceptional beauty.

A TALIESIN REFLECTION :: 1

Gene's cordial greeting seemed flat after explaining that he'd expected me two weeks earlier (following the arrival of my belongings by train), and rooms for apprentices had already been filled. My heart sank. Was I being turned away?

"Follow me," he said, "and we'll discuss this with Mrs. Wright." After being introduced to her, I waited nervously for Mrs. Wright's decision. She thought a moment, then asked if

Gene could arrange to clear out the guestroom, currently in use as a storeroom, for my use.

He agreed, and we were off.

On our return to his office, Gene explained that the "guest room" was in terrible condition. He'd seen my carpenter's toolbox and suggested I use plywood stored in the barn, plus any supplies needed to make the room livable. I now felt somewhat better. Still, I could not have known my good fortune at being assigned that particular room.

Gene called for someone to clear out whatever had been stored in "my room." After being shown the room, I noticed that my footlocker and toolbox had been placed beside a broom, a mop, and a dustpan. I would be scrubbing my own floor that night—before even contemplating sleep. As neither bed nor closet was evident, I slept on the floor in my sleeping bag. In due time, I realized that I'd be constructing both my bed and wardrobe closet with the plywood Gene had mentioned. A table and chair would follow whenever time allowed. The room's one window was about six feet high and eight inches wide. Not the place to be in case of fire, but it was *my* room!

Another revelation: the construction of bed and wardrobe closet would be done on my own time. Work assignments continued from early morning until past tea time, which was held daily at 4:00 p.m. Depending on one's assignments for the day, I soon learned to rest whenever possible. Personal endeavors could always be attempted the following day—or the next.

A TALIESIN REFLECTION :: 2

On my first morning at Taliesin, I was shown the canning kitchen and introduced to four pretty young women whom I would assist in canning vegetables. These were the wives of apprentices working elsewhere on the property.

Taliesin itself demanded much upkeep. The

garden required watering, spraying, weeding, and pruning. Because of the substantial size of each structure, the buildings were always in need of cleaning, dusting, and/or window washing. The Wrights often had weekend guests, which then meant clean guest rooms, living and dining rooms, also the garden room where guests gathered before dinner.

Several apprentices with prior farming experience usually maintained Midway, the family farm. In addition to the Wrights' personal horses, cows, pigs, sheep, chickens, rabbits, an Afghan hound or two also lived at the farm. Acreage was reserved for growing feed for the livestock, and barns were constructed to store the harvested grain. Fruits and vegetables were grown for the fellowship's use, and at times, apprentices would assist in their production. Midway's buildings also housed farm machinery and equipment for grading the roads.

Most of the apprentices gathered at the Hillside Home School, as many lived adjacent to the drafting room in two long rows of private rooms. Others lived nearby and convened at the school to teach, weave, paint, read, or study. Some worked in the kitchen preparing meals, others were responsible for cleaning the kitchen and dining rooms, decorating the public space, or removing the trash and garbage and taking it to the dump.

Later that first afternoon, I met Wes Peters, an affable man who had noticed my car with its cloth top. He suggested that I store my MG in a carport on Taliesen's upper level, for which I was very grateful.

The next morning, I learned it had snowed during the night, then rained, creating an icy walking surface. My shoes were not designed for these conditions, and I immediately began to lose traction. Very slowly, I walked to my car, started the engine and waited for it to get warm. Hillside, where daily fellowship meals were cooked and served, was too far to walk in these conditions. While waiting, I asked two other apprentices on their way to breakfast if they'd like a ride. Robin Molney and Shao Fung Sheng, were happy to be offered a lift, although this meant three people in a car with only two seats.

We crowded in and I started to make the first turn, which sloped downward, from the parking area onto the gravel road. Because of the slope I drove as slowly as possible, applying very slight pressure to the brakes, as I could feel ice beneath the tires. Those precautions didn't help—we went into a slide, sliding across the road as if in slow motion, until we hit an embankment, then rolled onto the car's left side. Shao Fung and Robin fell on me; meanwhile, I started laughing, but Shao Fung screamed and would not stop. I asked Robin to try opening the door from his side so they could get out. He was able to extricate himself and finally help Shao Fung from the car. She did not stop screaming until her two feet hit the ground. I finally climbed out and the three of us walked to breakfast.

Later, some of the fellows assisted in getting the car upright. My MG was still in perfect condition, with nary a scratch.

I place my driving skills in snow country on the same level as those required for horseback riding. That, however, is another story.

THE TEA CIRCLE

Frank Lloyd Wright chose the name "Taliesin" for the residence he designed and built for himself at Spring Green. Welsh for "shining brow," the title was appropriate, as the house clings to the brow of a hill situated above the left bank of the Wisconsin River. Minimal excavation of earth at the site provided space not only for guestrooms, but also for a furnace room beneath the main house.

In 1914, a fire consumed the living quarters of this great structure, originally constructed from native limestone, cypress, and an integral colored plaster surface, which was subsequently redesigned and rebuilt. A similar fire occurred in 1925. Taliesin was again rebuilt into the form now standing today.

Author photographed
at Taliesin "Tea Circle,"
Spring Green, WI
: : 1951

The Tea Circle actually began as a semicircular stone bench. A series of retaining walls connected the upper portion of the hill garden to the entry court one story below.

Two existing giant white oaks were incorporated into Wright's design. Not only did the trees anchor the circle and the building to the ground, they provided shade one hundred feet in diameter for those taking tea during the heat of the day.

Aside from the fellowship's formal weekend gatherings, the Wrights rewarded their apprentices' hard work by closing the day's chores with a high tea at the semi-circular stone bench at 4:00 p.m. A large Oriental bronze bell had been hung from one of the oaks, and when struck, it notified all to drop their work and appear at the Tea Circle, dressed as they were. The tea cook awaited them!

A teacart or table was placed in the center of the circle; here the apprentice would select a snack to eat with his tea. He would then sit on the stone bench and usually converse with others regarding their work. Should an apprentice be extremely hungry, he might be tempted to have seconds, however all eyes would fall on him and he had better be just "pouring tea."

Our duties were assigned by Mrs. Wright and posted weekly on a bulletin board. Chores were delegated to the apprentices on a rotation basis. Usually, the tea cooks would prepare snacks appropriate to the tea. These edible delights varied, as did the tea itself, whether it was served iced or hot. Absolutely all treats were to be baked by the tea cook. Never could the tea cook circumvent baking by purchasing desserts in town.

The task of tea cook lay within the fellowship's culinary realm. After proving one's worth as a tea cook (by having tea and snacks prepared, on time, daily) Mrs. Wright might consider you for the position of breakfast cook for the entire fellowship.

Mrs. Wright also determined how long one would have to endure arising early and following her recipes for the fellowship breakfasts. If one was steadfast in their weekly stint, and didn't ruffle any feathers, in time they'd be promoted to the job of regular cook for lunch and dinner. That experience would enable a person to qualify as cook for a large restaurant, if they so chose.

WILLIAM WESLEY PETERS

William Wesley Peters was born on June 12, 1912, in Terre Haute, Indiana to Clara and Frederick Peters. After attending Evansville College from 1927 to 1930, Peters enrolled at Massachusetts Institute of Technology to study marine and structural engineering. Ships were but one of his many interests. Peters built intricate models of famous sailing ships and various automobiles, also the highly decorated Faberge-style eggs, which, on their own, were worthy of display in any museum.

It was at MIT where Wes heard a talk by Frank Lloyd Wright explaining how the newly formed Taliesin Fellowship would function, and he was eager to join.

In 1932, William "Wes" Peters was the first to join Wright's Fellowship, which allowed him to become both an apprentice and charter member, and to learn and assist the great architect.

During the next few years, Wes, together with Eugene Masselink and John H. Howe, became Mr. Wright's three most valued apprentices. Each, in his own way, became devoted to working with and assisting the master.

For decades, Wes performed many engineering calculations for Wright's greatest works. These included: Fallingwater, the Guggenheim Museum, the Johnson Wax Buildings, the Greek Orthodox Church in Wauwatosa, Wisconsin, the First Unitarian Meeting House in Madison,

Wisconsin, and dozens of other major buildings and residences.

Some time before Wes became the Wrights' son-in-law by marrying Svetlana, Mrs. Wright's daughter by a previous marriage, he performed jobs in the drafting room, on the farm, or with general construction and repair work. Wright was aware of Wes' positive energy, his natural take-charge manner, and his ability to follow tasks through to completion. Wes' self confidence marked him as a future leader of Taliesin apprentices.

Wes needed that confidence when he fell in love with Wright's adopted daughter, Svetlana, who was only fifteen at the time. The Wrights felt that Svet was too young to consider marriage so they tried, in vain, to break up the relationship. Nothing would deter the young pair's plans to leave so they could eventually live together. Wes left for Evansville, and Svet moved in with a musical family named Cree. Svet and the Cree's daughter, Margaret Jean, studied music together, and in time, Svet became an accomplished pianist and violinist.

Before long, the Wrights realized that Wes and Svet were truly in love, and they were asked to return to Taliesin. Months later, the young couple's first son, Brandoch, was born. In due time, Svet gave birth to Daniel.

In 1946, during Svet's third pregnancy, and while driving with her boys in a Jeep, she lost control. The vehicle crashed and toppled into a riverbed, killing all but Brandoch, who was thrown clear. This tragic loss affected everyone at Taliesin; Svet had been revered and loved by all.

A TALIESIN REFLECTION :: 3

The morning after my encounter with the icy driveway, Wes gave me a task for the following month. First, he showed me around the diesel power plant that provided electricity for all of Taliesin. He then explained how to start and maintain the power, and how to power-down each evening. I would now arise at 4:30 a.m.

daily to insure that electricity would be available by 5:00 a.m. (This early start was mostly for the cook's benefit in starting breakfast on time). At 10:00 p.m. each night, I would flick the switch off and on several times, informing all that power would soon be terminated.

Here I was, a night person—if my mother could see me now! As a youngster, I'd been so hard to awaken she would have to shake me several times. If that didn't work, she would place a wet washcloth, dripping with cold water, on my face. That usually did the trick.

Wes had heard about my car tipping over and asked to see my MG-TD. As a fellow car buff, his was not an unusual request. After describing my dilemma of the previous day, I explained what I knew about the MG's features. We agreed that the earlier TC version, with larger wire wheels, was more attractive than the stamped-out wheels on my current model.

At that time, Wes owned a Jaguar XK-120, which was parked nearby. He was anxious for me to see it, and when he removed the car's protective covering, I was stunned by the beauty of the Jag's design. As he was about to drive to Madison on business, he invited me to "jump in."

Proceeding cautiously over the same driveway that had given me problems the day before, Wes continued at a slow speed until we arrived at the paved highway. When the engine had warmed sufficiently, he pressed the accelerator to the floor and soon we were flying down the road at 105 miles per hour. Wes was an excellent driver, and he would slow down to posted speeds when nearing towns or schools, then return to 105 miles an hour. Although he liked to speed, I always felt comfortable as Wes's passenger.

On our way to Madison, he mentioned having spoken to Bill and Barbara Morrison, who I had also talked with about repairing cars and tuning engines. He then inquired about the fine points of maintaining my Ford A V-8, and my 1936 convertible. By the time we reached Madison, he had decided to put me in charge

of maintaining the Wrights' automobiles. That was fine with me, as it was something I liked to do.

Wes parked his car, stating he would return in about thirty minutes. After he left, I wandered into a drug store to buy another wind-up alarm clock. I planned to set the alarms for a ten-minute difference each morning, as I dreaded the thought of the Wrights waking up without electricity.

When Wes returned, he surprised me by saying that we'd be having lunch at one of his favorite restaurants. He ordered steaks for us both with a huge portion of French fries on the side. I watched, in amazement, while he poured a half bottle of ketchup over his food. Along with his meal, he also drank two bottles of Coke. I chose not to use ketchup on my food, as I'd worked in canneries during summer vacations at home, and had witnessed what sometimes winds up in the ketchup.

What amazed me more than anything was he never complained of heartburn, this particular day, or the several times that we did the same thing during the next three years. I came to believe his favorite meal consisted of ketchup and something else.

THE TALIESIN FELLOWSHIP (THE CONCEPT)

During the early 1930s, the Wrights were certainly aware of how the Great Depression was affecting their personal and business lives. The influx of new clients seeking Wright's architectural skills had dwindled, while the overhead needed to keep Taliesin functioning drained their resources.

After discussing their situation, they decided to open Taliesin to young people throughout the world who wished to become architects. Living with the Wrights in beautiful, natural surroundings, they would become apprentices and learn from the master architect himself.

New apprentices would pay an annual fee for room and board. In addition, they would participate in the growing and canning of the many varieties of fruits and vegetables grown at Taliesin, and in the care and feeding of farm animals, so that all could sustain and live in this unusual community. Also, they would study nature and learn art, painting, pottery, music, drama, and weaving. And they would learn building and remodeling—whatever was necessary for shelter.

Each apprentice would assist in the kitchen; later they might become a cook, a breakfast, or tea cook. They would clean the kitchen and public spaces by removing and burying trash. They would learn to work with their hands by felling oak trees on the property and then by sawing the trees into planks to be used later for construction. They would quarry stone and make cement; they would dig river sand for making concrete and mortar, then combine it into an organic work of art. Future apprentices at Taliesin were all eager to learn and participate in these tasks. Most of those who came to Taliesin and participated in this way of life left with a better sense of understanding and an intrinsic love of nature.

Mr. Wright's *An Autobiography* and his talks at colleges and universities inspired many to seek him out. Affectionate fledglings came from China, Japan, India, England, France, Ireland, Greece, and Italy, as well as many of our states.

Mrs. Wright usually made out the weekly work schedule for the apprentices who were junior to the seven highly experienced senior apprentice. These "seniors" were under the direct supervision of Mr. Wright.

For some reason, Mrs. Wright felt I would never become a cook, no matter the level. She did think I was a natural at cleaning pots and pans to the degree that I was on kitchen duty almost every third week. With about thirty junior apprentices doing common chores, it seemed I should be assigned kitchen duty only once every three months, but it never worked out that way.

Occasionally, I would be assigned to pick up garbage and trash at Hillside, Midway, and Taliesin. I'd then dig a large pit, far from the

buildings, and bury the refuse. Because I was one of the newer apprentices, I was amenable to whatever she asked. There were stories that: if one questioned anything that Mrs. Wright asked to be done, she would have you for breakfast. In the event of back talk or disrespect, the person at fault would be asked to leave the fellowship. So, I dug pits and washed pots.

Between chores and in the early evenings, I found time to plaster some of the worst holes and cracks in my room and to apply a finish coat of paint to the walls. I also completed the bed frame and built a wardrobe closet in one corner. Recalling what Manuel Sandoval had shown me about finishing Douglas fir plywood, I started my experiment. Using a few colors over a base coat of stained dull varnish on the Douglas fir, I wiped thinned oil colors with rags to obtain a translucent effect. It turned out looking like a special wood, since I had also wiped in a hint of gold color for highlights. Whenever I had visitors, they usually commented favorably on the cabinetry. I, too, was pleased with the results.

As the weeks passed, I realized how fortunate I'd been that another apprentice had taken the last available room at Hillside before my arrival. Most new fellows start by living with a large group of apprentices near the drafting room or the kitchen. Only when a room became available, and an apprentice had been there long enough to prove himself to the Wrights, would he be selected to occupy a private room at Taliesin.

The abandoned guestroom was pleasant, located directly below Mr. Wright's grand piano, and several times a week following dinner, I heard him playing—mostly Beethoven—or improvisations based on those works. The music could be clearly heard, as an overhead heating register in my ceiling was connected to the floor register located near Mr. Wright's piano.

The heat register also served as an inconvenience. Sometimes, as I read, discussions emanating from the Wright's living room would creep into the pages of my book. Soon, I would be concentrating on their chatter rather than my book. The topic was usually irrelevant, and I could continue reading. I only noticed heated discussions between the Wrights occurred only twice. When this happened, I simply took my book into Mr. Wright's nearby office and read for a few hours.

During my first year at Taliesin, I became so proficient at carpentry that my assignments were for finish work only; i.e. work of a quality clients or overnight guests might observe. This put me a step up from a novice; soon, even Mrs. Wright became aware of my work.

⬛ A TALIESIN REFLECTION : : 4

While enjoying my first permanent assignment as mechanic and maintenance person for the Wrights' vehicles, I decided to torment another apprentice for his aloof and unapproachable attitude toward me.

Any attempts at becoming acquainted with Bruce Brooks Pfeiffer were brushed off. Constantly in a rush, though never seeming to have work of any kind, Bruce walked briskly by whenever I saw him. He was talented in the field of music, and played classical piano pieces for our formal dinners on Sunday evenings. He also appeared to be very close to Mrs. Wright. Still, I still felt slighted by Bruce's standoffish ways.

I'd finished washing Mr. Wright's car, the Riley, when I noticed Bruce backing his MG-TC into one of the carport stalls. Knowing he would soon be driving to Hillside for breakfast, I decided to deal with Bruce's boorish attitude. I grabbed a hydraulic jack and started jacking up the rear of his car. With Bruce's MG situated barely above the carport's gravel floor, I then blocked up both sides of the rear axle—just enough so my stunt would not be obvious.

I was checking the oil and other fluid levels on the Wright's vehicles when Bruce walked briskly to his car and started the engine. He waited for it to warm up, then shifted into low

gear. Nothing happened. (Naturally, his car would not move with both wheels off the ground.) He shifted into second gear, then reverse; still, the car would not budge. Noticing his agitation, I walked over to inquire and was told that regardless of which gear he shifted into, his MG would not stir.

Not only was Bruce uninitiated about the workings of an automobile, his driving skills, as I'd already noticed, were sadly lacking. I had observed his driving qualities a few times and I thought he might kill himself, sooner or later, behind the wheel. I immediately started giving him some mumbo-jumbo about the way MGs were built, and that it was important to be careful that the "thermotrockle" in the drive shaft did not slip out of position. He absorbed all this, knowing that I also owned an MG. I then explained that his car was a few years older than mine, and that the factory had corrected the problem on the newer models. I then stated I would look at his car after servicing Mrs. Wright's, so he wouldn't expect the offer of a ride to Hillside.

He thanked me for whatever I could accomplish and began walking to Hillside. At that moment, I thought I should have waited until there was snow on the ground for him to plod through.

With Bruce well on his way, I retrieved the jack and let his car down to the ground again. I was still in the area when he was dropped off at his car. He inquired what I'd done, and I answered that I'd realigned the "thermotrockle," and he should try it again.

Bruce started the engine, and it moved forward when he placed it in gear. Then he put it into reverse, and voila, it also went backward! He was amazed that I knew so much about cars and thanked me profusely. (I later heard that he'd told all his friends about my mechanical skills).

From that point on, Bruce actually spoke to me whenever we met; in fact, we became good friends. Yet I was still concerned about his lack of driving skills, and asked him to follow me to an open field where I could give him some pointers. With Bruce as my passenger, I demonstrated how to maneuver out of a slide or skid, and how to drive fast without having the car tip over. Then, with Bruce at the wheel of his car, I guided him through the same maneuvers. An hour or so later, he seemed much more comfortable behind the wheel.

SPRING AND SUMMER 1951

At Midway, with some of the crops already harvested, the soil was prepared in rotation for the planting of the next vegetable crop. The chicken coops were cleaned and ready for the first laying, and the barns in shape for the dairy cows. Meanwhile, a local farmer who had decided to sell his land offered his pigs to Mr. Wright for a good price. Following a quick discussion, a deal was made.

The pigs would also require housing, so Mr. Wright designed units for each of his new arrivals. A few apprentices constructed the units, setting them up at the edge of a curved road leading into Midway. This changed the area into what resembled a section of an urban subdivision, so Mr. Wright ordered a street sign labeled: "Pork Avenue."

The apprentices had given appropriate names to some of the "girls" (dairy cows) at Midway. For example, one with large, soulful eyes was named "Jeanette," for Jeanette McDonald. Another quite shapely cow was known as "Mae West," while a certain bovine was dubbed "Marlene" due to her long eyelashes. I named one because of her beautiful pair of; well, she was called, "Lena Horny."

Near the end of May, the Wrights and their daughter, Iovanna, left by steamship for Italy to attend the upcoming exhibit: "Sixty Years of Living Architecture." The collection, which would tour several countries, included Wright's models, photographs and drawings. The first stop, scheduled for Florence, was to be held at the Strozzi Palace.

While in Florence, Mr. Wright was awarded the de Medici Medal, a recognition of honor from the city whose citizens had also been supporters of Brunelleschi and Michelangelo.

Returning home on the ship, Wright redesigned the Guggenheim Museum with renewed energy. He proposed a new set of working drawings be completed, delegating the task to Jack Howe, who asked Curtis Besinger to assist him.

Many parts of the building were changed, necessitating new structural calculations and a new set of working drawings, which would be revised many times over the following months. Ultimately, the Guggenheim was the most difficult building Mr. Wright had ever conceived, considering the changes and the building permit required by the New York City Building Department.

ALLEN LAPE DAVISON

Davy, as he was known at Taliesin, was a fun person to be around. It could be said that most who met Davy liked him immediately. He could tell a joke or be serious or silent—to the degree that one might think they were in church.

When I first met Davy, he was already married to Kay Schneider, an apprentice from Germany who had arrived at Taliesin by way of Switzerland. Kay served as Mrs. Wright's private secretary. The Davisons had a baby girl, Celeste, and a son, Tal, who was nine years old.

Davy did wonderful delineations for some of Mr. Wright's buildings; he especially liked to produce night renderings. Few architects care to prepare night renderings for their clients, but his were spectacular.

Davy's delineations included the Madison Civic Center, Guggenheim Museum, Arizona State Capitol; the twin cantilevered bridges in Pittsburgh, Pennsylvania, and the Pittsburgh Civic Center, also various residences. He was quite knowledgeable about construction methods, and he supervised several of Mr. Wright's houses. These included the Dr. A. H. Bulbulian and Thomas E. Keys residences in Rochester, Minnesota, and the William L. Thaxton residence in Bunker Hill, Texas.

A TALIESIN REFLECTION : : 5

While starting a new set of drawings, Davy Davison, who had already completed several presentation drawings for Wright's clients, began working on a night view of the Guggenheim's exterior. He had also been completing the working drawings for two other clients and, at that point, needed help. Davy asked Wes if I could assist them, so I was assigned to work with Curtis. After being shown where the building's specifications were to be hand-

lettered on the drawings, I began my work. I finished on time—just as Davy completed a magnificent rendering of the Guggenheim, which was later made into a poster.

Although the Unitarian Church in Madison was dedicated in February 1951, it had not been completed. The members continued to hold meetings in the building—unfinished due to lack of funds. This upset Mr. Wright, who decided that the Taliesin Fellowship should complete the necessary work.

Initially, Wes and Curtis were appointed to help complete the project. One day, while using Wright's tractor on the driveway approaching the entrance foyer, Wes was caught between the tractor and the low roof. He sustained bro-

Abstraction sketched in Frank Lloyd Wright's office, August 21, 1951

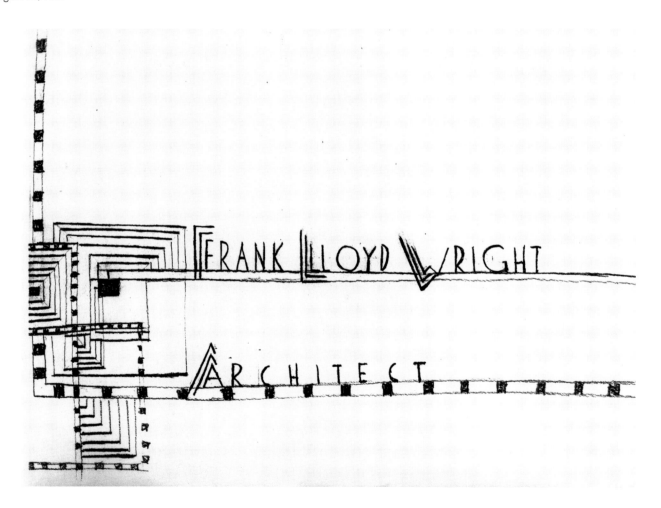

ken and cracked ribs, which prevented him from continuing any kind of physical work on the project.

Wright began sending other apprentices to see what they could accomplish; soon, most of the Fellowship was helping the Unitarians.

Because of the lack of funds, Curtis designed new seating for the church. His design was based on a single sheet of plywood—cut and assembled so that the only "waste" was in the sawdust on the floor.

With the project close to completion (and to Mr. Wright's satisfaction), the second dedication, including an address by Wright, was scheduled for August 21, 1951.

Dressed in their finest, all at Taliesin left for Madison to attend the new, formal opening of the Unitarian Meeting House. All, that is, but me.

Gene had asked that I remain in Mr. Wright's office to answer the phone. Gene seldom left his office, but recently he'd been at the church, applying gold leaf to Wright's words, which were carved into the fascia boards, and he needed more time to complete the project.

The night of August 21 has become memorable to me: after sitting around for some time, the telephone rang. Within seconds, I was talking to Quentin Blair, of Cody, Wyoming, who wished to speak to Mr. Wright about designing a house for his family. Although Blair was somewhat apprehensive about talking to Wright, I assured him that Mr. Wright was easy to converse with, and would return his call in a timely manner. We hung up, and I wrote Gene a note to present to Mr. Wright the next morning.

In those days, only a few night calls came into Taliesin. To relieve my boredom, I began drawing an abstraction that included Mr. Wright's name in the design. I drew it freehand, as neither a T-square nor triangles were handy, so I plodded on and completed my work just prior to Gene's return that evening. While explaining Blair's call to Gene, I observed him taking an interest in my drawing. He must have

appreciated my work, as from that moment through the remainder of my time with the fellowship Gene called me "Brother."

I was thrilled that such a great talent as Gene would say something nice about what I had done. I knew it would not stand up to anything of his, but it was a nice complement.

JOHN H. HOWE

At Taliesin, John H. Howe was always known as "Jack." Born May 17, 1913 in Evanston, Illinois, Jack graduated from Evanston High School and joined the Taliesin Fellowship in 1932 as a charter member. He became Mr. Wright's chief draftsman, and no doubt produced more of Mr. Wright's drawings than any other apprentice from 1932 until the master's death in 1959.

Jack was a true workaholic. One would see him long after dinnertime, bent over his drawing board, where he remained until midnight. After a few hours of sleep and some breakfast, he would start the process again.

Jack assisted Wright until the advent of World War II, when he claimed conscientious objector status. He was imprisoned at Sandstone, Minnesota, where he remained until 1946. He then rejoined Wright at Taliesin, continuing as one of the Taliesin Associated Architects until 1964, when he left to accept a position with Aaron Green in San Francisco. (For many years, Aaron Green was Wright's West Coast Representative for the Frank Lloyd Wright Foundation).

Several years later, Jack opened an architectural practice in Minneapolis, which prospered until his retirement in 1992. The West Coast still beckoned, however, so Jack and his wife, Lu, moved to Novato, California, where he died on September 21, 1997.

Before my time at Taliesin, I had sought out every possible publication that featured Wright's buildings. Actually, I was more interested in the drawings than the photos, and I could detect differences in some of the drawings. One could determine if Howe or another

PHOTO: ROBERT GOEPEL

John "Jack" Howe, chief draftsman to Frank Lloyd Wright since 1932; credited with the majority of client renderings and exhibit drawings until the master's death in 1959

and colored pencils on tracing paper, then mounted on a board. It depicted a graceful sky-scraper with lavish amounts of patina copper applied vertically. Horizontal fins shaded the glass in various portions of the building. Once more, subtle colors executed by an artist's deft hand made an exceptional building come alive.

KAY DAVISON

Although born in Hamburg, Germany, Cornelia "Kay" Schneider Davison arrived at the fellowship by way of Switzerland. Her entrance in 1935 soon blossomed into useful work and activities for the Wrights. Kay became a costume designer for Taliesin festivals emphasizing music and dance. She was also a painter of note. In later years, Kay gave lectures on painting for the Frank Lloyd Wright School of Architecture.

Mrs. Wright was aware of Kay's skills, and soon Kay became her personal secretary. Within a short time, Kay became almost as close to Mrs. Wright as her own daughter, Svetlana.

Olgivanna Wright was able to evaluate a person's character within minutes of her first conversation with them. Always in control, she would immediately decide if an individual would be accepted as her friend, and if so, whether that friendship would develop into a casual or close relationship.

In selecting Kay as her secretary, Mrs. Wright's motives soon became clear. Kay reported all sorts of community gossip, idle rumors, or scandal to her and, in turn, Kay became something of a power in her own right. Some of the apprentices began to fear Kay only on a lesser scale than they feared Mrs. Wright.

As with many organizations, cliques developed over the years. Some in the fellowship were loyal to Wright's architecture and his life style; others were involved with Mrs. Wright and her work, an offshoot of her studies with Gurdjieff. While Wright continued designing buildings for clients, Olgivanna was involved in

member of the fellowship had executed the rendering. I appreciated Jack's color-pencil drawings more than any I had seen—with the exception of Mr. Wright's. To see Jack's color perspectives of Wright's buildings come alive— from rough sketch to pencil layout to the final realization—was a true revelation.

I was privileged to be in the drafting room when two of my favorite drawings by Howe were rendered:

The first was used for one of Wright's little-known projects, the Masieri Memorial in Venice (1953). The Wrights had first visited the memorial site because of the personal friendship between Wright and Mr. Masieri.

Jack depicted the building as seen through the archway of an existing structure, and as it was located in Venice, the structure was reflected in the canal. He used soft colors for his choice of colored pencils, resulting in an ethereal feeling. In fact, the rendering was done with brown ink, pencil, and colored pencils on tracing paper, and later mounted on a board. When completed, it was signed "FLW/Jan 20/'53."

My second favorite drawing was of the H. C. Price Company Tower in Bartlesville, Oklahoma (1952). This drawing was done with brown ink learning everything possible about those in the fellowship; thus, she was able to exert control over them.

Kay was adept at gathering information and sharing it with Mrs. Wright, this soon became common knowledge. So, if one wished Mrs. Wright to be informed about something, it would first be relayed to Kay, and posthaste, Olgivanna would receive the news.

Mrs. Wright was the person in charge of creating the weekly work schedule for the entire fellowship. That is, with the exception of the senior apprentices who worked directly with Mr. Wright in the drafting-room.

One day, Mrs. Wright gave Kay a demeaning task: Olgivanna handed Kay a laundry bag containing her underwear and asked her to hand-wash the delicate unmentionables. Upset at being asked to perform such a menial chore; Kay gave the task to Barbara Morrison, who had been at Taliesin for several months. Barbara stood her ground by saying that if Kay wanted Mrs. Wright's laundry done, she would have to do it herself. Later that evening, Kay could be seen at the laundry room sink, hand-washing Olgivanna's under garments.

THE ESCAPADE OF BARBARA AND MARTHA

I spoke with both of these beautiful girls, Barbara Morrison and Martha Paul who were involved in the following confrontation, but neither of them could recall who made the overture to the other. This is quite understandable as it happened at Taliesin back in the summer of 1951, but it bears retelling.

It seems there was a very large cow's head in the walk-in cooler adjacent to the fellowship kitchen, and Barbara thought, or Martha thought it would look awesome in apprentice Steve Oyakawa's bed.

In the afternoon, when no one was about, the two girls placed the heavy bovine component on a large circular tray, and proceeded towards Steve's bedroom.

As they were in the process of transporting it, they had a problem of it sliding around on the tray, and a few times it nearly slipped off and onto the floor. As they were in this secluded circumstance they met up with a group of visitors who were being shown through the building, and a few of them gasped at what they saw, but Barbara and Martha carried on.

When they made it to Steve's bed, they rolled up a comforter and arranged it under the bedding to look as if a person was occupying the bed. Then they placed the cow's head on the pillow and stuck a thermometer in its mouth, as if it might be ill. Next they were thoughtful enough to place a bouquet of flowers on the bedside table. Soon everything was to their liking and they made their way back to the kitchen to wash the platter and put it back.

It was a good feeling, as they succeeded in their devious plot, but as everyone knows about 'the best laid plans of mice and men,' it just so happens with 'the best laid plans of mice and *women*,' also.

Someone had noticed what was going on and Steve was told what the girls had been up to. It just so happened Steve was the breakfast cook this particular week, and when Steve cooked eggs sunny-side up for both Barbara and Martha, he included a cow's eye on each of their plates. Needless to say, neither of the girls ate their breakfast that morning. One might say the punishment was "an eye for an eye."

The cow's head did not go to waste for apprentice Bodil Hammergard, from Denmark, the regular cook that week, made soup with it.

A TALIESIN REFLECTION : : 6

The summer of 1951, Mr. Wright decided the fellowship should have a picnic—most of us had worked long hours harvesting the sorghum crop, thrashing it by hand. Sorghum is similar to sugar cane, although the stalks are cooked down into molasses rather than being refined into sugar. It is said that, "If you have never thrashed sorghum, you haven't lived."

When sorghum has grown to its fullest and the leaves start to dry, one walks through the field with two sticks and begin to flail away, knocking all the leaves to the ground until the field resembles a sea of poles. During this operation, one sweats profusely; the short fibers from the tall plants rain down as if blown from a fiberglass insulating machine. Gloves, hat, and a long-sleeved shirt are worn, also a bandanna around one's neck. Regardless of how well one is covered, about an hour later you'll start itching in places you thought were properly covered. At this point, you shower as often as possible, but after two or three showers a day, the itching continues. The crop must be harvested in only a few days, as trucks will arrive to pick up the sorghum at a pre-set time and day. Therefore, we worked ten-hour days for three or four days in order to harvest the crop on time.

During his youth, Wright had done sorghum thrashing for his uncle, and he knew we would appreciate a picnic upon completing our task.

Food was prepared and packed on the stake-sided truck, along with whatever was needed. We were lining up for our outing at one of Wright's favorite picnic spots, Brenmar Hill, a few miles from Taliesin.

Gene Masselink had the Wrights settled in the family's Riley, designated as the lead car. The stake-sided truck containing food and several apprentices was next, and I quickly followed in my MG-TD, since I didn't want to be last and collect a great deal of dust and dirt from the four other cars making up the convoy.

Gene started off and the rest of us fell into position, single file, along the two-lane highway. Bill and Barbara Morrison had squeezed into my passenger seat. Several apprentices, including Sheng Pao, were standing at the back of the truck. Without warning, Sheng Pao's hat flew off and blew across the road into the oncoming lane. I had been looking in my rearview mirror often enough to know that no one was trying to pass us. I then pulled out a bit to make certain no one was approaching us. All was clear;

so I swerved out and was able to reach down and grab Sheng Pao's hat without having to slow down. Everyone on the truck started shouting and applauding, while Bill and Barbara expressed praise for my accomplishment. I was just happy I hadn't missed the damn hat.

Awhile later, some of the fellows told the Wrights what they had witnessed. Mr. Wright called me over and said: "Well, Earl, I heard you did some pretty fancy driving."

"It was nothing, Mr. Wright," I replied, "it was just my California hat trick."

A TALIESIN REFLECTION : : 7

Much of my first year at Taliesin was spent performing chores in the fellowship kitchen. During the week we were assigned, there was much to be accomplished, as approximately fifty-five apprentices were fed three times a day. Those assigned for kitchen duty quickly learned that on each of their shifts, they would be paired with a different apprentice. Not having worked closely with someone beforehand could turn the job of completing tasks on time a real workout.

I was fortunate to be assigned to fellowship kitchen duty several times with Morton Delson. We worked and thought together almost as one, which made our job so much easier. After completing a task, we would jump to the next chore in order of importance. As a novice, preparing food three times a day for such a large group and completing it on time was quite demanding, but I always found it easier when working with Morton.

Quite often, the Wrights would invite clients or important friends to spend the weekend at Taliesin, but no special meals were planned for that week. Near the end of our week's work, Morton and I felt we could use a vacation from chores. Morton didn't have a car, and my MG was itching to hit the road and see more of the countryside near Spring Green, where we were located. Since he had preceded me at Taliesin, I suggested that Morton request time off for us both from Mrs. Wright. He did, and we acquired our vacation time painlessly; so the next morning, directly after breakfast, we left for new horizons. As neither of us had much extra cash, we planned to seek out YMCAs along the road where we could bed down, followed by a nice shower in the morning.

Our purpose was to visit some of the buildings Mr. Wright had designed over the years. From Spring Green we drove to Madison to view the Unitarian Meeting House— still under construction, but almost completed. Our next stop was the Pew house, also in Madison. The Pews were both at home and showed us through all the rooms in their home. We then set our course for Milwaukee to view "Wingspread," the Johnson house. Unable to speak to anyone there (we could view the house only from the locked gate), we proceeded on to the Johnson Wax Building. A male employee who expressed interest in Frank Lloyd Wright's work escorted us through the building, and when he learned we were still at Taliesin, he showed us several private offices and meeting rooms not open to the general public. After a delightful three hours, we headed for Chicago and the Oak Park area, where Wright had completed so many fine buildings. We spent two nights at the local YMCA; which allowed us to view the Robie house, Mr. Wright's personal studio, the Unitarian Church, and several houses designed early in Wright's career. Although disappointed at not being able to examine each building's interior, we felt their exteriors were magnificent.

We then drove to Benton Harbor, Michigan, to view the Howard Anthony house-completed about a year earlier. This was one of my favorite Wright-designed homes. Howard Anthony was truly a great friend to the Wrights. Many times, he would send supplies to Taliesin to enable Wright to continue remodeling whatever he wished to accomplish. In fact, Anthony had donated the stack of plywood, some of which I used to renovate my room at Taliesin. As usual, we arrived unannounced, and were surprised

to find Mr. Anthony at home in mid-afternoon, as we had expected him to be at his Heathkit electronics factory. Upon learning we were from Taliesin, he was gracious and quite friendly to us both. He showed us through his simple, yet magnificent home, and later barbecued steaks for the three of us. Mr. Anthony also invited us to stay with him for two nights, which gave us the opportunity to drive to other nearby houses before returning to Benton Harbor.

We were fortunate to view the interior of the Dr. Palmer house in Ann Arbor, but other homes in Michigan we wished to see could only be viewed from the outside. These included the Maxwell Smith house, the Affleck house in Bloomfield Hills, the McCartney house, the Eric V. Brown house, and the Levin and Winn houses in Kalamazoo. They, of course, were all different and most refreshing to see in their beautiful countryside locales.

Since both Morton and I were almost out of money, we decided to head back to Taliesin. Arriving late in the evening, we each went to our rooms. The next morning we asked Wes Peters what our jobs would be for the day. He stated that we were "called on the carpet," meaning we must see the Wrights about a particular problem, and I should appear first. Knowing that when someone was "called on the carpet," they would be scrutinized by the Wrights—and if the matter were serious, you would be asked to leave the fellowship. I wasn't sure what to expect, but I took off immediately. At that time, I was at Hillside, and upon arriving at Taliesin, I asked Kay Davison where the Wrights could be found. Saying she would call them, she asked me to wait in the loggia. When they appeared, they sat beside each other in high-backed chairs. I wasn't offered a chair, which I viewed as a bad sign. Mrs. Wright began by stating that we had returned two days late; they had a responsibility to our parents in knowing where members of the fellowship were at all times, and why hadn't we called to advise them we were all right? She hinted at my influence over Morton, "a nice person," and that I would lead him astray simply to "have a good time."

About then Mr. Wright jumped in and asked what we had been doing while we were gone. Apparently, we were due back two days earlier, which Morton had not relayed to me. I explained that we'd set off to view as many of Mr. Wright's houses possible in the time allotted, and nothing more. I mentioned Mr. Anthony's hospitality and the good wishes he'd sent. Mr. Wright cleared his throat, indicating his desire to speak, then proceeded with, "Mother, it seems they were just a bit overly enthusiastic in furthering their education, and they won't be doing it again." Mrs. Wright gave me another two-cents worth, then excused me, saying it wouldn't be necessary to send in Morton. I was quite relieved after learning what had upset the Wrights.

Morton and I did take one more "vacation" the following year, but we made certain to return on time.

Before my arrival, Morton had been at Taliesin for about a year. Both Ogliavanna and Mr. Wright were fond of him. He later supervised some of Wright's buildings under construction near New York City and Morton's office in Manhattan. Those he supervised were: the Hoffman house in Rye, N.Y., the Kalil house in New Hampshire, the Cass house on Staten Island, also a prefab in Blauvelt, New York, and, I believe, two others. In addition, Morton served as Wright's East Coast representative; he worked on the Guggenheim Museum, its annex, built sometime later.

With the passing of time, I am happy to say that Morton and I became very close friends.

◼ A TALIESIN REFLECTION : : 8

During fall of 1951, the Wrights gave a lecture in Detroit and while there, met a young Greek violinist, John Amarantides, originally from Athens. John was interested in both Gurdjieff's teachings and the dance movements that Mrs. Wright had organized at Taliesin. Because of his exceptional talent, John was invited to play for the fellowship at Taliesin, and one Sunday evening, with Curtis accompanying him on the piano, John completely captivated his audience. After observing the fellowship in their practice, he joined us later that fall.

For some time, John continued to be associated with the fellowship's music. Following Wright's death, John designed a U.S.A. two-cent stamp with the master's portrait in blue.

The push was still on for completion of the new working drawings for the Guggenheim—with Jack looking for every possible candidate to assist him.

When Jack noticed I was free one afternoon, he asked Wes if I could help him. Jack put me to work on the layout of a parking lot for the Guggenheim. After giving me basic instructions, I was left to my own devices. In order to achieve the correct dimensions for the actual parking area, I did an overleaf from another drawing.

Placing the entry and exit off-street (per Jack's instructions), I then drew the general layout of the parking areas, plantings and planter boxes, also the lighting required for vehicles—both above the parked cars and at ground level. The automobile's designs were my choice, so I delineated some as if already parked, with others appearing as if they had just arrived and were searching for a parking place. The cars I designed for the sheet were without the curved lines usually found on most architectural drawings. Instead, these were drawn as an abstract, yet simple form. My designs were similar to those for stealth aircraft that would appear twenty years later, yet with the shape and proportion of an automobile.

A few days later, with all drawings completed, Mr. Wright approved and signed each sheet, and prints were made of the revisions. Later as I reviewed the drawings Jack appeared, saying: "You won't find your parking lot sheet in there, Earl. Your automobiles were too good; in fact, they were a visual distraction, so I had some-one else make another layout."

So, there you have it. On my first day in the drafting room to actually assist the Master, my drawing was "distracting." I was bewildered and perplexed at the same time.

▣ A TALIESIN REFLECTION :: 9

In the summer of 1951, Mr. Wright and Wes discussed replacing the loggia's glass doors, which had been installed in 1925. Wes asked my help with taking measurements. An order would be placed with a shop in Madison; the doors would be manufactured to a slightly oversized dimension, then planed to a close fit to reduce air infiltration.

Once the order was placed, the oversized doors made from 1-3/4" thick red tidewater cypress were delivered the following week.

Wes asked apprentice John Paul and I to remove the old doors and hang the new ones. While doing this, we left the hinges on the sup-porting members and adapted the door stiles to receive the other half of each hinge.

The procedure was much more difficult than we had imagined. Each door measured approxi-mately 2 feet wide by 9 to 10 feet high, which made them cumbersome to handle. Also, they needed to be set in pairs and to meet correctly —with an overlap at the center of the meeting stiles. Because the job required that each door be hand planed, sanded, then finished with a wood preservative before hanging, it took almost a week for us to fit the ten doors into their final, permanent position.

Wright built the original Taliesin I in 1911, but very soon a fire damaged most of the living quarters, requiring Taliesin II to be re-built in 1914. All went well until a second fire destroyed much of the residence. The final rebuilding of Taliesin III was completed in 1925; therefore these were the doors John and I replaced in 1951. While alone in that particular area one day, I wondered about the new doors' longevity. I felt we had done a much better job

of protecting the wood from the elements. Leaded paint had been applied to both the top and bottom of each door—as protection from moisture—which, no doubt, had caused the previous problems. On the last day of working on the paired doors, I was alone in the loggia. While gazing at the hills across the valley, the overall effect reminded me of a Japanese screen—absolutely stunning. I hadn't heard Mr. Wright's footsteps until he was at my side. I was certain he'd been observing our work in progress, as his bedroom was nearby.

After greeting me, he proceeded through one of the paired doors to the terrace beyond; then he looked at the total effect from the out-side. When he came back, he asked me to tell John we had done a nice job.

I thanked him and said I would relay the message to John on his return. Mr. Wright then said, "Earl, what do you think of the log-gia?" I replied that it was a great complement to the beautiful living room; I then stated that when approaching the loggia through the masonry piers with its low ceiling and then returning to the high-ceilinged loggia was a magnificent feeling. I understood why he'd used some of the art pieces broken during previous fires. (He had directed masons to imbed them in the room's new stonework). However, I added, having the masonry grout painted with gold leaf didn't seem organic to me. Mr. Wright listened, paused, then said, "We won't be doing that any more." Turning, he walked from the room.

Through the years John, his wife, Martha, and I have kept in touch. One of John's letters men-tioned our work.

"Fact is," he wrote, "I brought up the subject of hanging the paired doors in the loggia, which served the new terrace at the time. You and I installed them (four or five pairs) and it was no small deal. You'll recall they were probably 9 or 10 feet high and individually no more than 2 feet wide, making for unusual proportions and bulky to deal with. It was during this time you guided me in the correct use of the plane."

A TALIESIN REFLECTION : : 10

This is my understanding of how the bird walk
came to be. In the spring of 1951, while both
were in the living room, Mrs. Wright mentioned
to her husband that the balcony in the loggia
should be closer to the trees, to the southeast.
Wright went to the window and gave it some
thought.

The next morning he gave Wes a sketch of
the design, which later would be turned into a
scale drawing. Wes then drove to the area to
verify building a stone column to support two
steel beams. This, in turn, would be the main
support for the elongated walkway dubbed the
"*bird walk,*" by Mr. Wright.

Wes calculated the moments for the beams
and ordered two steel beams. He then asked
me to accompany him to the site so we could
determine the distance from the house to the
base of the stone column. After we staked it
out, several apprentices began excavating, by
hand, for the concrete footing that would be
poured for the column. The following day,

we apprentices started hauling stone from
the quarry to stockpile for George Hass, the
German stonemason. George would then
select the stones needed for a column built
in keeping with the existing walls.

Using a mortar mixer, we added cement to
the sand obtained from the Wisconsin River, and
in this way kept up with George laying stone,
and talking to himself, and laying stone, etc.

We built a wood scaffold around the column as it rose in height, and we made it adequately wide since George, not only being an
older man, was also adequately wide, and we
didn't want him falling.

The stone column was topped off with
two steel plates with anchors imbedded into
the mortar so that the steel beams could be
securely welded.

Wes climbed a ladder to determine where
the ends of the beams would be located,
directly into the existing wall of the living room.
He then brought Wright's tractor to the site,
and had three very large and heavy wood
beams delivered to the site. These would be
used as a gin pole, with block and tackle, which
served as a job-built derrick.

As Wes operated the tractor, several
apprentices helped with the staying of the
base of the gin pole and with tying off the
steel beams. With the combination of a powerful tractor and many strong men, the beams
were finally in position. Using an arc welder,
Wes welded the beams to the steel plates
already imbedded in the stone column.

I was never able to view the connection
Wes made to the house, as he was usually on
the only ladder at the job. Additional ladders
and apprentices were later called in to complete the construction, as it would soon be
time to leave for the desert.

Among those who worked on the *bird walk*
were Wes, in charge of construction; Steve
Oyakawa from Hawaii, Duke Johnson from
Piedmont, California; Morton Delson, from
N.Y.; Nils Schweizer, from Orlando, Florida;
Dennis Stevens, from Palatine, Il.; Jackson Wong,

Steve Oyakawa (BACK-
GROUND) and author
beginning construction
on Taliesin's "Birdwalk"
: : 1951

PHOTO: BARBARA MORRISON

from Portland, Oregon, David Dodge from England, Joe Fabris from Canada, and myself.

Steve and I did much of the framing, since we came back to the job after teatime for a few hours, and we were usually the first to start in the mornings. Day by day, Mr. Wright could be seen in the living room viewing our progress. When we finally got a plywood floor down, he came from the living room to appreciate seeing Taliesin from another viewpoint. Although pleased, he was impatient to get the job finished.

Jackson and Steve, (plus another person whose name I've forgotten), did most of the plastering. The plywood flooring was hot-mopped and ready for the flagstone saved from the quarry. This turned out to be a complete fiasco, as it was getting so late in the year the mortar and mud took too long to dry. "Mud" consisted of a highly-watered mortar poured around the flat walkway stones already set into the mortar, as a finish, to level the floor as much as possible.

Wright wanted the project finished, so we carried out his wishes. However, the caravan was also being prepared for the trip to Arizona, and we knew the mortar and mud would not completely dry before the temperature would drop to freezing. Steve and Duke rigged up a canvas covering for the walkway, then placed a portable heater-blower at the living room doorway, to assist in drying the floor before it froze. This was an "okay" plan, but time didn't allow them to also cover the bottom of the walkway. Too much moisture remained in the floor, leaving the stones to freeze and crack out of position.

Next spring, it was necessary to remove the flagstone, mud, and mortar and begin anew. It was Dejavu all over again.

JOHN DE KOVEN HILL

Born in Cleveland, Ohio, John de Koven Hill first came to Taliesin in 1937 at the age of seventeen and soon became another "right hand"

for Wright. Gifted with a natural ability to coordinate colors and textures, John was at ease both at building projects or work in the drafting room. During his later years at Taliesin, John did the interior designs for some of Wright's buildings, and also supervised their construction.

He loved all growing things, and he planted several beds of flowers around Taliesin East. His was an innate gift of making any building look better for the flora he introduced to the site.

He also worked on various models designed by Wright for his clients.

Johnny, as he was known in the fellowship, also had musical talent. He sang in the chorus and accompanied others at the piano. He seemed to have no end of talent, as well as being a handsome and genuinely likable man.

During Johnny's years at Taliesin, he became so proficient at construction work that Mr. Wright asked him to supervise the construction of some of his better-known residences. Among those were the Lowell Walter house in Quasqueton, Iowa; the Douglas Grant residence in Cedar Rapids, Iowa; the Carroll Alsop residence, in Oskaloosa, Iowa, and the Jack Lambert residence in Oskaloosa, Iowa. He also supervised the mounting of exhibitions in the USA and abroad, in addition to supervising the construction of some sixty-eight Wright buildings. In time, Johnny became one of Wright's most trusted associates.

Over the years, Wright's work was published in *House Beautiful* magazine, and their editor, Elizabeth Gordon, and Wright became good friends. When she asked for his recommendation for a talented individual to assist in the magazine's architectural department, Wright immediately suggested John Hill. Wright also mentioned that John would provide much by enlightening the public to the advantages of building truly organic structures.

John was perfect for the job, as he had been trained in architecture and design and knew how buildings should be constructed. His taste in clothes was impeccable, and he dressed well for any occasion.

During the three years prior to John's leaving in 1953 for *House Beautiful* in New York City, John and I had become good friends. We said our good-byes, but Taliesin was a bit lonelier without John's presence.

Elizabeth Gordon soon discovered John de Koven Hill's worth as Editorial Director of the magazine. Johnny published articles and photo layouts of Wright's work, and suggested many innovations for the magazine. He also brought other architect's work to the publication to inform their readers of quality architecture and interior design.

He stayed with *House Beautiful* for ten years before returning to Taliesin, but not before the Hearst Corporation recognized him as having influenced the culture of the United States.

CARAVAN WEST

Ten days before leaving for Arizona, it began to snow. Gene and the Wrights assigned drivers for the family vehicles needed at the desert camp. Gene would drive the Wrights in the caravan's lead car; Duke and Jackson would drive the dump truck containing tools and equipment needed for our upcoming work.

The stake-sided truck was loaded with canned goods preserved by the fellowship, along with ham, eggs, and whatever might survive the trip of seven to ten days. Some of us included our footlockers, suitcases, or boxes of supplied. Finally the truck was loaded and covered with a canvas. I believe Ralph Smith, from Burlington, Washington, was the driver and Robin Molney, from New York City, was his assistant. Private cars followed within viewing distance until our arrival at the first scheduled stop. The fellowship would stay overnight in a hotel or motel, depending on availability. This would be repeated the following day, although the Wrights would planed to include worthwhile attractions and historic sites along the way.

I asked Wes to seek permission from the Wrights so I could drive alone to Arizona, allowing me to view some of Wright's houses along the way. That was agreed, provided that I arrive in camp at the scheduled time of the caravan. I thanked him and mapped my course.

Most of the fellowship left together with the Wrights except for those assigned to close the house and studio. Several stayed at Midway through the winter to care for the animals, and attempt to keep them warm.

My first stop was at Charles City, Iowa, where I located the Alvin Miller house. It was both delightful and serene. I appreciated the use of stone and cypress boards, to say nothing of the fantastic view of the Red Cedar River.

My next stop was at Quasqueton, Iowa, to visit the Lowell Walter house and their river pavilion on the Wapsipinicon River. An unusual feature of this house was its reinforced concrete roof with a curved fascia. The walls were of red brick with interior walls constructed of walnut boards.

No one was at home at the Miller house, but this time I was fortunate to find Mrs. Walter at the mail box as I pulled up. After explaining that I was with the fellowship, she invited me in for coffee and to see the house.

She mentioned that she and her husband were very pleased with the house and that John De Koven Hill had supervised the construction. After touring the interior, she gave me a key to the pavilion and its boathouse below, to view on my own, as she was preparing for a meeting.

My next stop was at the Douglas Grant house in Cedar Rapids, Iowa. Again, I was fortunate, and found Mrs. Grant working in the garden. I explained my mission, and she invited me inside.

Before we reached the front door; she told me this chilling tale. As the bulldozer operator was preparing the site, he suddenly shouted, "My God, I'm dead." That he was, because the blade of his tractor had cut into a (previously unknown) underground power line. Hearing this, I felt the hairs on the back of my neck rise up.

A unique approach to the living room had been used in the Grant's three-story house. From the entry, one descended three levels beside a masonry wall that the Grants had quarried and laid themselves into an interesting horizontal pattern. Thousands of small pieces of limestone could be seen with their edges showing, with most of them 3/4" to 1" in thickness.

After the tour, I thanked Mrs. Grant and again checking my map, I headed southwest for my next objective.

The drive in my MG was uneventful—with one exception. This occurred in a small town during early evening. An officer of the law pulled me over, claiming that I had been speeding, although I hadn't seen any signs posted. He stated I'd gone through a "speed zone" at forty-six miles an hour, whereas the posted speed limit was thirty-five-m.p.h. I explained that I was from California, and in California, a speed zone permits you to speed. After glancing at my California driver's license, he allowed me to proceed.

Before leaving Taliesin, some of the apprentices who had been with the Master for several years suggested that we, the newer apprentices, purchase some rum in Mexico to prepare for the colder nights on the desert. That soon became one of my goals for the trip. Upon arriving at El Paso, Texas, I parked my car and took a bus into Ciudad Juarez, to find a *tienda de licor*. For about two dollars each, I purchased two one-gallon bottles of white rum, wrapped in wicker to avoid breakage.

Returning to my car, I drove to Tucson, Arizona, where I spent the night, and the next morning, I headed for Scottsdale. During those times, I enjoyed Scottsdale, where many stores had hitching posts and rails for their customers to tie up their saddle horses.

After viewing the area, I decided to drive out to camp. At that time, in order to get to Taliesin West, one would drive over graveled roads that went through washes (dips in the surrounding land that carried water during

Caravan ready to leave Wisconsin for Arizona :: 1951

rains). The amount of water coming down a wash depended on how much water fell up stream. If one wasn't careful, a car or truck stuck in the bottom of a wash could be swept away for a great distance; therefore, folks were advised to wait until the fast-running water completely subsided.

Arriving at camp, I parked my MG in the apprentice's parking area before entering the office. I then introduced myself to an apprentice, as Gene and the family had not yet arrived.

A TALIESIN REFLECTION :: 11

I decided against living in a tent manufactured for the fellowship, as I had brought my sleeping bag and a very large canvas cover. In time, I planned to build my own tent as others had done. In fact, some were still standing, awaiting occupancy for another season.

I slept on the canvas, pulling it completely over me in the evenings to ward off moisture; otherwise it might have frozen in my hair.

Many used redwood boards in various lengths and condition were available for my project. Old canvas was also in plentiful supply, because the drafting room roof had been re-canvassed the previous year. The desert's harsh weather demands that fabrics such as canvas be replaced every few years.

I decided to build a small fireplace in my tent, and naturally, an abundance of stone and sand could be found in the camp. Here again, at Taliesin West, we were responsible for certain chores; therefore, tent building would be done on my own time, which worked for me. The shape of my new abode was designed around the dimensions of the used boards available at the time.

The tent's roof was low at the fireplace end, making it easier and quicker to build a short fireplace. The canvas roof pitched upward from the fireplace to its termination, at the "view" end, allowing me standing height within the tent. I fabricated a drop flap, closing off the tall end of the tent, (located at the opposite end from the fireplace) in case of heavy rains or extremely cold weather. With the flap tied securely above, I could watch the sunsets from my bed or while sitting on my footlocker.

To create a friendly area for other apprentices to visit, I built a patio of flat stones, leveled

My desert tent, Taliesin West, Scottsdale, AZ :: 1951

in sand, with grout poured around them for neatness and stability. I added a few canvas chairs for guests, and I made a plant box filled with native cacti. For the ultimate in outdoor living, I devised a hanging garden from a plow disk. From my point of view, "my space" had turned out quite well. Still, it needed a final touch.

From the day of my first interview with Mr. Wright at Taliesin West, I had been moved by the huge Indian rock displayed at the front of his office. The rock's natural colors were beautiful, and the designs carved by the Indians were intrinsic to the desert.

I felt I must have such a rock for my new patio. I wandered off, behind camp, along the base of the McDowell Range, and before long I found one that looked as though people had camped around it in bygone days. This rock was a lovely, endemic specimen with native drawings etched upon its face. I had tried moving it before, aided by a six-foot metal bar, but it would not budge. I looked around and found another, but this was twice the size of the first rock. Now I was really dejected, but I had a plan.

A much smaller rock—plain, but colorful—was only a few yards from my tent. Using a wheelbarrow from the tool-shed, I moved it to my patio. Over the following weeks I carved "Indian" designs on the rock with a hammer and chisel until I was satisfied with its appearance. Other members of the fellowship also enjoyed the rock's placement and its effect. I saw it as a friend in the desert for the three years we were together.

Many years later, my good friend Jackson Wong, who had remained at Taliesen West long after I'd left, told me a humorous tale. It seemed a new apprentice from Italy, (one with a title, money and/or influence) had my petroglyph "Indian" rock removed, and it is now on display at a museum in Italy.

One evening, Mr. Wright wandered out in the desert and saw me applying canvas to my roof frame. When he asked where I'd found the canvas, I explained it had been removed from the drafting room. He answered that it looked quite new. I then stated I had painted the canvas with white lead paint so it wouldn't leak, as I knew he would not want to absorb the price of new canvas for this experimentation. Satisfied with my reply, he smiled and wandered off.

I wondered if he had ever considered painting the old, used canvas, rather than replacing it with new!

◼ A TALIESIN REFLECTION :: 12

Early in 1951 when I arrived at Taliesin in Spring Green, some of the first apprentices I became acquainted with were Bill and Barbara Morrison, also from Northern California. We were all interested in cars, and had much to discuss. Bill soon learned that previously I had overhauled automobile engines, transmissions and rear ends. In conversations with Wes, he also learned I had been put in charge of maintaining the Wright's vehicles.

I had a "field day" checking fluids, topping them off when necessary, and running the engines of Wright's cars, so they were always ready to go. At times, I drove the cars into Madison for special service, which was always a nice change. In the fall, all vehicles were ready for the caravan trip to the desert, and off we went.

Wright's 1940 Lincoln Continental, his pride and joy, made the journey west to camp unscathed. His was No. 5 (off the assembly line), commissioned by Edsel Ford and designed by E. T. Gregorie. The Continental was the first vehicle honored for design excellence by the Museum of Modern Art. Wright publicly declared the 1940 Lincoln as the most beautiful car in the world.

One day his daughter was driving the Continental and had an accident, which required repairing the vehicle. Wright proceeded to redesign the auto by filling in the rear window and adding half-moon windows

to the sides of the passenger area. In addition, the metal roof over the driver's compartment was cut out and replaced with a removable fabric top.

We'd been at Taliesin West only a few weeks when, after gassing Wright's redesigned Cherokee-red Lincoln, I decided to wax the car, as the finish seemed so dull. At the time, I didn't know that Wright wished his Cherokee-red cars to maintain their satin finish, especially in the desert.

After polishing his car, I felt it looked splendid. Later, I was told that when Wright saw his Lincoln, he went into a fit of rage. When Wes found me, and learned I'd done the wax job on my own, he then explained to Wright that it was an accident, as I'd not been aware that Wright did not want his cars waxed. I was glad not to have been near Mr. Wright that day, although he did give me strange glances for some time afterward.

◼ A TALIESIN REFLECTION :: 13

Late in 1951, while at Taliesin West, I was assigned to help re-stain part of the shop and pottery area, along with Steve Oyakawa, Barbara Morrison, Martha Paul, and another male apprentice. We had picked up our brushes, rags, and Mr. Wright's favorite Cherokee-red stain to start painting.

Although I'd been at Taliesin for nearly a year, hardly anyone knew about my prior life in California. I say this because I was in an area of the shop alone, painting away, but I could hear others in our group discussing mysticism and the occult. This continued until one of the apprentices asked about my views on the subject. Since "weird stuff" was often the norm from California, they wanted to know if I had witnessed anything unusual or mystifying.

I mentioned working with a tarot devotee who had taught me how to read palms. Their attention soon focused on me. They stopped working and drew closer. Steve, closest to me, answered "Yes!" when I asked if he wished to have his palm read and quickly held out his hand.

Holding his fingers gently, I revealed the brush previously hidden behind my back, and painted his hand red—(read!). Gazing, astonished at his hand, his face held a look I can see to this day. I was off and running, into the desert, while trying to avoid cactus as I glanced over my shoulder. It was a good thing I had a head start and was able to stay ahead until the situation cooled down!

A TALIESIN REFLECTION : :14

By 1951, when the fellowship had expanded to about fifty-five apprentices, Mr. Wright decided we needed another bathroom at the desert camp. He designed a combination men's bath and locker room, to be constructed near the shop area. When the drawings were completed, several of us were assigned for the construction.

Hand-digging the trenches for the stone masonry walls was difficult, as many hard layers of clay and rock had to be penetrated. The desert provided an abundance of rubble stone and face stone. We also brought back sand and gravel from nearby washes, which we used for the concrete mixed at the site. Wes ordered the form boards, which were delivered to the job from a Phoenix lumberyard.

The forms were constructed over the trenches we'd dug. We then began laying face stone, which would later be exposed when the forms were removed. Rough rubble rock and stone were used to support the face stone within the forms while they were filled with concrete. This practice continued for several days, and soon the walls reached a height of eight to ten feet.

During this time, I was quite short on funds. I hated to ask my parents for extra money, so I learned to do without until my next twenty dollars arrived. The desert played havoc with our clothing in general, and I needed a new pair of boots, as mine were quite worn. The sole of

Author at work on a poured masonry wall for the new men's bath and locker room, Taliesin West : : 1951

my left boot flapped about, compelling me to walk with an exaggerated high step. Daily, I'd been tying string around my boot to hold it in place.

While building the men's room masonry walls, we frequently exchanged jobs. One day, I was near the top of the form work, placing concrete behind face stones and into the rubble, while stomping the concrete to bind the walls to the stone. We were about to stop for lunch when I climbed down and noticed that the entire bottom of my left boot was missing. I had literally "poured my sole" into that wall.

LIFE IN CAMP

Spending the winter in Arizona, rather than enduring the ice and snow of Wisconsin was a treat, although my chores had not changed that much. Mrs. Wright still insisted I perform the most menial of tasks. These were divided, weekly, between working in the fellowship kitchen, picking up garbage and refuse, and burying the trash.

Layers of rock, sand, and gravel had to be penetrated when digging these holes, and the refuse had to be buried quite deep, or a fox or coyote would dig it up, leaving a huge mess that would attract flies.

One day while sitting on a rock to rest, following much digging, I heard an unidentifiable noise. It sounded like many small wheels in need of oiling, and it grew increasingly loud. Although I looked in both directions, nothing surfaced.

Within a few moments, I saw the source of this sound. Approximately one hundred and fifty quail, of all sizes, had formed a straight line and were marching across the desert eating anything they could find, dead or alive. Soon the desert floor was cleansed of all animal life, as the quail were only about two feet apart.

My presence did not disturb them at all. When they finally saw me, they moved slightly to one side until they passed by, then they closed ranks and once again were in a straight line. They were fascinating to watch. The quail "parents" were accompanied by their young, and a few came up to my boots and stared at me before they, too, left. They were not in the least intimidated by me, nor the size of my boots.

Although life among the desert's birds and animals was enjoyable, the situation within the camp could be perplexing. Some of the apprentices grew anxious whenever they were directly involved with Mrs. Wright. Stories were told wherein she would ask an apprentice to "pack up and leave" on a moment's notice. She was a strong-willed woman who insisted that things be done her way, or else. The "or else" probably caused the fellowship to diminish in size by about twenty apprentices over the years.

I learned about Mrs. Wright's personality quirks both from former apprentices and those still remaining with the fellowship. These were revealed while sitting around a campfire with friends, discussing world events, while drinking a-hot butter rum or two. One of the wives mentioned that she had deterred her husband from going directly to Mr. Wright with whatever he objected to about Mrs. Wright's domineering ways. She finally convinced him not to do so, as it would have led to them both being asked to leave.

Occasionally a newly arrived apprentice would learn that he or she would not be assigned to the drafting room right away—a position desired by all apprentices—but instead would be selected for menial chores. Their dissatisfaction which would eventually become known to Mrs. Wright, and the new apprentice would be served his/her "walking papers." In one case, a young man arrived before lunchtime took lunch with the fellowship and after learning what would be required of him, left before dinner.

I felt that because Taliesin was Mrs. Wright's home, she could decree how the place should function. Acutely aware that I was doled out more than my share of fellowship kitchen work and garbage detail, I had decided to simply tackle my assignments as they fell into place, as this was the trade-off for being with and learning from Mr. Wright. I felt that Mrs. Wright was, in fact, testing us, mindful of the time she had studied with Gurdjieff in Paris. She carried herself with a regal air which, in my view, added to her charm and mysticism. During our time in the desert, she gave talks after dinner on Tuesday evenings, and many apprentices went into town, rather than listen to her opinions, but I found them interesting and informative and attended all that I could.

MR. WRIGHT ASKS MY VIEWS

We had arrived from Wisconsin a few weeks earlier, when Mr. Wright emerged from the little kitchen as I walked by. He stopped me, wishing to chat before proceeding to the drafting room.

"Earl," he said, "what do you think of the buildings we have here?"

I had always been enormously impressed not only with the quantity of Wright's work, but also with the masterful quality of his designs. In my view, each of his designs, whether a residence, skyscraper, church, or a mere contrivance such as a wastepaper basket, was a masterpiece in its own right. Considering the vast number of his designs for clients, I was also impressed that he had produced so much as an artist, and that he would take the time to speak to apprentices, or guests, on a one-to-one basis. Now he wished to know my feelings about the structures at Taliesin West!

I mentioned my first drive from California to Taliesin West for the formal interview with him, and how impressed I was when approaching the camp silhouetted against the McDowell Mountain Range. The buildings were a perfect blend of texture and color, causing them to appear married to the ground. Many of the outer building's surfaces were battered or sloped in such a way they mirrored the backdrop of the sloping hills.

As I approached each individual building, I began to realize the greatness of the aggregate, with respect to their varied usage. I went on to say I was delighted to walk among the gardens and enclosures, which seemed to be actually growing from the desert.

A TALIESIN REFLECTION : : 15

The fellowship settled into making necessary repairs and remodeling buildings according to Wright's requests. As for me, I remained in the fellowship kitchen more often than I had expected. While working as kitchen helper one afternoon, I was the last person to take a break. I was finishing up when Mrs. Wright walked up to me, and abruptly said, "You're not afraid of me, are you Earl?" Without hesitating, I answered, "Why no, Mrs. Wright, should I be?"

Her face took on a bewildered expression, and without responding she turned and walked away. During my years at the fellowship, that was the only time I found Mrs. Wright to be speechless.

Whether her opinion of me changed following that encounter, or if she thought I had "met the test," things switched about. Several weeks later when my name appeared on the work list, I'd been assigned to the *family* kitchen rather than the *fellowship* kitchen—a privilege by having lighter duties and in working closer to the Wrights during their private gatherings. This was a welcome change.

My first morning in the family kitchen I met with Kay Davison, Mrs. Wright's secretary, with whom I would work that week. We met an hour before the Wrights would awaken, and Kay instructed me in my duties. First, I would build a large fire in Mr. Wright's bedroom, making sure the room was comfortably warm when he dressed. I would then return to the small family kitchen to assist Kay with the Wright's breakfast.

Once inside Mr. Wright's bedroom, I was not prepared for what I saw. A table lamp some distance from his bed gave a small amount of illumination, and I saw Mr. Wright lying on his back. As I came closer, I noticed that his blankets were pulled down and his upper body was uncovered, although he was wearing *long johns*. His mouth was slightly open, but he did not move. I could not detect the rise and fall of his chest. I froze. I thought he had passed away in his sleep. Frightened, I moved closer until I heard the faint sound of his breathing and was quite relieved. After building a huge fire, I left the room.

Following Kay's instructions, I set the table in the dining alcove. When the family's breakfast was under control, she asked me to return to Mr. Wright's room and awaken him. She would do the same for Mrs. Wright. She asked that I not wake him harshly, but while tending the fire speak to him gently until he awoke. I did just that and soon he asked who was in the room.

I said, "Earl, Mr. Wright." "Oh, yes," he answered, and off I went, relieved that he was OK and that he would be getting up.

Kay asked that I make toast for the family while she finished poaching the eggs, which were being cooked in a special pan, in cups, and were slippery if placed directly on a plate. I thought they should be placed on toast as my mother had done, but Kay said Mrs. Wright wanted them on the side with potatoes and parsley.

When the Wrights were ready to be served, Kay handed me the breakfast plates. I had taken about three steps into the alcove when I tripped on one of the floor stones and fell toward the table. I caught myself on the table's edge, holding two plates of poached eggs. Mrs. Wright's plate struck first. I watched it land without breaking. Mr. Wright's plate hit hardest, and I watched helplessly as two poached eggs left the plate and slid across the table toward him. As he stopped them with his hand, I thought I was finished as an apprentice.

Silently, Mrs. Wright glared at me. Mr. Wright asked if I was OK, and I replied that I was. I was about to return his plate to the kitchen when Mr. Wright picked up the errant eggs and placed them on his plate. Mrs. Wright asked that I return them to the kitchen, but he said, "Mother, these will do just fine," and I was excused.

After that episode, I was sure I would be reassigned as a fellowship kitchen helper the next day, but I was kept in the family kitchen for the rest of my time at Taliesin.

1951—ONGOING

During the winter, while checking the oil level in Mr. Wright's Lincoln, I saw one of the longest limousines I had ever witnessed pulling into the parking area. Very quickly, the chauffeur opened the door for Wright's new client, Nina Anderton, and her brother from Beverly Hills. They proceeded to Wright's office, where Gene escorted them inside for a discussion of their requirements.

During a short period of time, Wright worked out two plans so they could obtain several small rental shops on the Anderton parcel, located in the fashionable downtown section of Beverly Hills. The plans were similar as each contained a complex of small shops around a central court, in a split-level arrangement, with half-levels on alternate sides of the court. The various floor levels connected to a gently sloping ramp spiraling upward and terminating at the copper lighting spire on the upper floor.

The first design indicated a massive stucco wall facing the street. However, it did not allow the amount of glass frontage desired by the Andertons. Wright reworked the design to allow an all-glass facade, which was finally approved. Curtis Besinger (a talented musician who gave me piano lessons which, unfortunately, didn't take), completed the final working drawings.

That winter, Wright also designed two Usonian Automatic houses. These structures were constructed of pre-cast concrete blocks of various shapes and sizes and were held together with steel rods and liquid grout.

One was built in Paradise Valley, Arizona, for the father of an apprentice, Arthur Pieper, recently married to Bodil Hammergard of Denmark, also an apprentice.

Normally, Usonian Automatic homes were constructed with a double concrete-block masonry wall containing insulation between the supporting walls. However, for the Pieper residence, son Arthur fashioned the molds for the 3" thick blocks. He also poured the concrete, knit the blocks together with reinforcing steel rods and grouting, and raised the walls, assisted by non-professionals. This is what Wright considered the "automatic" aspect of construction: when one constructs (assisted by family or friends), as much as possible in their day-to-day work.

The second Usonian Automatic was designed and built for Benjamin Adelman in Phoenix, Arizona. This design was somewhat different than what might be expected in a concrete-block house. The structure consisted of a two-story living room and kitchen lighted from glass openings in the block pattern. It also had a roof fascia of concrete block I had developed when assigned to the drafting room during that period.

Gene Masselink contributed a beautiful wall mural for the living room, fashioned from gilt and silvered pieces of mirror.

The previous year, Wright had designed an all-masonry, curved, inline plan for son, David, and his wife. This was an above ground dwelling reached by a spiral ramp.

David, who was involved in the design, manufacture, and promotion of concrete block, had asked that his father design the house with standard block shapes, so that later he could use photos for the promotion of his block. Wright did just that, with the exception of a special frieze block used at the edge of the concrete floor slabs.

David's project, located in a beautiful orange grove in Phoenix, was nearing completion when he and his wife were invited to Taliesin for dinner. I happened to be working in the family kitchen when David discussed the problem of having very little control over parking cars for future guests at their home. Parking areas were not delineated on the grounds; therefore, guests and trades people would be parking on what was designated as future planting areas. When David presented a drawing of the problem area to his father, Wright drew a straight line from the center of a supporting pier to the street. This would become a low, all masonry wall I would be assigned to build the following week, assisted by another apprentice.

While constructing the wall, Mrs. David Wright always appeared with a delightful lunch for her husband, the other apprentice and myself. This, I felt, was truly euphoria!

When David first purchased the orange grove, he gave his permission for the apprentices to pick oranges for the fellowship. Several times during my stay at Taliesen, I was assigned

that job. It was always a joy to take in the grove's heady aroma and to view David's magnificent home.

A TALIESIN REFLECTION : : 16

Perhaps because of Wright's advanced age, or that the drafting room was always open to drafts, but he finally agreed to have that room glazed. Gene arranged for a company in Phoenix to install glass in all the open bays throughout the room.

Early one Saturday morning, trucks arrived with two crews ready for the installation. They were very efficient, and the installation was completed by four o'clock that same afternoon.

By coincidence, Duke Johnson had gone into Scottsdale for the day, and he returned to camp about five o'clock in the afternoon.

Meanwhile, Mrs. Wright asked me to locate her husband, as she wished to discuss something with him before dinner in the Cabaret Theater.

I found Wright in the drafting room, deeply involved in conversation with Jack Howe about the working drawings he'd been completing for one of Wright's most recent houses. I waited patiently for the opportunity to give Wright the message. After a few minutes, we all head a loud crash: Duke had entered the drafting room and, unaware of the recent installation, walked through one of the new plate glass windows. Startled by the sound of breaking glass, but worried that Duke might have been injured, we rushed to him. Duke was clearly shaken by the experience but, fortunately, he had not been cut.

A TALIESIN REFLECTION : : 17

While working at one of my numerous stints as family kitchen helper, Mrs. Wright gave me some instructions to relay to Gene for that night's movie and dinner.

I knew Wright had gone to Phoenix that morning for a hair cut from his barber at the

Adams Hotel. I noticed him coming toward me, and passing the drafting room, rather than stepping inside to see how the projects were progressing. When he was about 20 feet away, I noticed that his usual porkpie hat was not so usual. The brim was down to eye level, and his bushy sideburns were not in evidence. All of Wright's photos had clearly revealed his abundant growth of hair, especially at the sides of his head.

When he'd advanced close enough for me to say, "Good morning, Mr. Wright," instead of his usual greeting, his response was simply "Humph." Not only was he agitated, but he chose not to be seen or to make conversation while heading to his private quarters.

I gave Gene Mrs. Wright's request for changes to the evening's festivities, then returned to the family kitchen to help prepare the Wright's lunch. Opening the door, I heard Mr. Wright ranting to Olgivanna about the "stupid barber who had scalped him." He said that his regular barber had had an emergency at home, so he sat in with a new barber.

Did that barber not understand Wright's instructions for his haircut, or was he trying to give him his money's worth by the excessive removal of his hair? Regardless, when I saw Mr. Wright without his porkpie hat, he looked like a wet chicken, having feathers, but looking nearly bald.

He was still agitated when I served his lunch. "Pissed" would better describe his mood, but Mr. Wright would not openly speak that way. For the next several weeks, Mr. Wright would not be seen without some type of headgear.

A TALIESIN REFLECTION :: 18

Several years before I joined the fellowship, Wright had tried to get the public-power company to bring electricity to camp by installing underground lines. Although he would absorb the cost, they had refused. Now there was a possibility of supplying power from another direction, with the last mile or so installed underground. Wright approved their proposal and, finally, we had electric power! This was a blessing for those whose chores included starting up the old diesel generating plant. The plant not only produced exhaust fumes, but the noise could be heard throughout the usually placid desert. I hadn't yet been assigned this particular chore in Arizona, but I certainly recalled losing the extra hour of sleep required to get the power plant up and running in Wisconsin.

In 1951, Taliesin West experienced one of the most severe winters they could ever recall, and certainly, Wright felt it too. He decided to build a fireplace in what was previously called the "garden room," and to enclose the balcony at the end of the room to achieve more seating area. The changes would create a living room atmosphere for the growing fellowship and for the Wrights' occasional guests.

As usual, Wes' job was to insure that these changes were completed on time and in accordance with Wright's wishes.

Several of us constructed the forms for the fireplaces' poured masonry walls. Others knocked out the wall that had separated the garden room and balcony. Some brought in sand, rubble rock, and face stones for the portion of the fireplace that would be visible.

One day while we were hard at work, I overheard Wright tell Wes that we should have special stones for the face of the fireplace hood. Later, when Wright had returned to the drafting room, I told Wes that I had seen some unusual, rounded rock beyond the village of Cave Creek, (a supposed hideout for an Indian chief in the past). Wes grew excited, as he had also seen these rocks. He asked that I take Robin Molney along to find something unique.

While Robin located some six-foot pry-bars and two shovels, I hooked up the Jeep to a flatbed trailer, and we met in the parking area.

Shortly we were on the road, discussing our home states and how we became interested in Wright and his fellowship. I mentioned the V. C. Morris store in San Francisco, and how I had become friends with Manuel Sandoval and his wife. Robin also knew about Manuel's workmanship and was impressed that we were friends.

He mentioned being from Brooklyn, New York and that his former girlfriend was Rita Moreno, who wanted to be in movies and had already been on Broadway with Eli Wallach. He didn't explain why they parted, but later Rita became a famous actress, best known for her performance as Anita in *West Side Story* (1962), for which she won an Oscar.

Rita was the only female performer to win four of the most prestigious show business awards: the Oscar, Emmy, Grammy and Tony award.

Later, Robin became well known in skiing circles. After leaving Taliesin, he moved to Aspen, Colorado to set up his architectural practice; later yet, he became mayor of Aspen.

As we approached the area where I had seen the unusual rocks, I asked Robin to check his side of the gravel road, and I would check the driver's side. We found many rocks, but I had forgotten how large they were. Any that we found would have required a crane to get it off the ground.

It was a desolate area with absolutely no one around, so I wandered off the road to find a boulder we could handle. Finally, I spied one backed up to a small bluff. Robin immediately said it was much too large for us to handle, but I felt if we dug some sand from the tire tracks, which would lower the trailer bed, perhaps we could muscle it onto the trailer. As we'd brought shovels, we removed enough material for the trailer bed to just touch the underside of the rock. We spent almost an hour to get it loose and moved over the axle of the trailer, then blocking the rock to prevent it from rolling off.

When Wes saw what we'd brought back, he could hardly believe his eyes. He immediately told Mr. Wright, who also wondered how we had managed to get the rock on the trailer. I replied that it happened to be in the right location to move it.

Wes had a group of fellows roll the rock into what would become the living room. He began taking measurements, as some of the form would require a circle cut into it so the rounded rock could project into the room. He was quite excited to get it right.

When I returned from parking the Jeep and storing the trailer, Wes asked that I look for another large complementary stone for the hood. I set out walking behind the Wrights' quarters to the base of the McDowell Mountain Range. There were many prospects, but I wanted another special stone. I started climbing the gentle slope while looking all about, but none seemed right until, suddenly, one beckoned to me. This rock was about seven feet long and one foot wide, but only about two inches thick.

After resting a few minutes, I hefted the rock to see if I could carry it back by myself. First, I stood it upright, then heaved it to my shoulder and while it was heavy, I thought I could manage the job. I started down the slope and all was fine until I stumbled over a rock and pitched forward. I intended to ease the rock to the ground gently as possible, to prevent it from breaking. However, my boot picked up a cholla ball on the end of my toe, and I inadvertently kicked the ball into the back of my left calf. I screamed so loud, I thought that they might have heard me in Chicago. Well, the stone landed hard on the ground; two feet had broken from one end, but that was not my immediate concern, I had one of those damned balls in my leg with about fifteen barbed stickers penetrating my skin.

I looked for a place to sit without further cactus invasions, and to remove the cholla ball. Using two small, flat stones as levers to pry the ball from my flesh, it seemed to take forever, but after fifteen or twenty minutes it popped off; leaving several barbs in my calf.

Disheartened over losing two feet from the overall length of the stone, I decided to leave the smaller piece behind.

While carrying the main portion back, I

couldn't help thinking of how the Indians had supposedly tortured some of the white settlers they had captured. They would strip them of all clothing, then throw them into bushes of cholla. I wondered how long they would survive after suffering that torture.

I told Wes what had occurred, and that the stone would have been more impressive in its full length, but it was still used to offset the rounded stone.

If you see the fireplace in the Scottsdale living room, please let me know if you like the effect.

A TALIESIN REFLECTION : : 19

The fellowship had just settled in for the winter of 1952 when I decided to grow my first mustache. I had been mostly doing outside work since we made the trip down from Spring Green, and as I was shaving one morning, I decided to see what I would look like with a mustache; so I resisted shaving above my upper lip.

After that first day I would watch in the mirror to see how it was coming along. Well, not much was happening day by day, but I just knew that I would have a proper mustache soon.

A couple of weeks went by and the hairs started to grow out, but to me, my mustachio did not look very full. Perhaps I shouldn't look at it too closely each day, but it was hard not to, it was mine. I noticed, if I moved my head from side to side I could see some progress. One trouble was that the hairs that were growing out to form my new and very first mustache were about the same color as my skin. I thought when they were all the right length the mustache would become a definite enhancement to my face.

Soon I felt my mustache was at the proper length, trimmed well and quite neat, but somehow I was not getting any comments from any of the apprentices, male or female. I tried using a pencil to darken it a bit, but that didn't take too well, and I didn't want to buy a makeup

type of coloring, so I just left it alone. This went on for about a month, and absolutely no one ever commented on it, good or bad; so I decided to shave it off.

The next morning I cut just half of it off, showered and went to breakfast, then on to work. I thought someone would then remark about what I had done, but no!

This went on for about a week until early one morning I was seated for breakfast across from apprentice Joe Fabris. The sun was just coming up and it shone directly into my face. With that happening, Joe looked sort of bug-eyed and pointed at my face and stuttered, "You-you-you only have half a mustache!" so I told him what I had been doing, and that he was the first one to notice.

I shaved the other half off before going to work.

A TALIESIN REFLECTION : : 20

Having recently completed construction on the fireplace, and also enclosing the living room at Taliesin West, Wright then decided to redo the entrance to the room from the west, making it more presentable.

He did something I never thought I would see. Wright instructed four of us to paint the natural-colored concrete floor in a red tone. I had seen red-colored concrete floors in several of his houses, but those had been done using colored stain as an ingredient within the concrete. This new situation was quite different, as the concrete, in its natural state, had been in place for years.

As we proceeded to paint the concrete floor, I noticed some fellows dipping their brush up to the hilt with paint, allowing the brush to drip as they began painting. Since the concrete had originally been scored on four-foot centers, much of the paint ran into the scored marks, which was not removed. It was not for me to comment upon, as each of the three apprentices had been in the fellowship longer than I had.

I continued painting the floor in my section by dipping the brush into the paint a short distance and wiping the excess paint back into the can. I then started on the cracks, dragging the brush lightly until the surplus paint had been eliminated, then painting the flat surface in two perpendicular directions. By lightly dragging the brush in one final direction, an even finish was obtained.

Ready to proceed to another area, I noticed Mr. Wright was watching us paint. I had no idea how long he'd been there, but upon making eye contact, he beckoned me forward. "Yes, Mr. Wright?" I said.

"Where did you learn to paint?" he asked.

I explained my father's hardwood floor business, and that he was also a painter, and he had taught me to paint.

"You're doing nice work," Wright commented, he then turned and left the room.

I was delighted by his remark.

A TALIESIN REFLECTION :: 21

When Charles and Minerva Montooth decided to marry, they discussed it with Mr. Wright, who suggested that they exchange vows in the Cabaret Theater. This took place a few weeks before their actual wedding on February 23, 1952.

I was working in the family kitchen that week. When the big day arrived, I was scheduled to serve the family and the wedding party in the theater. Mrs. Wright had dental problems that Saturday and could not attend. Kay Davison also would not attend, as she would be caring for Mrs. Wright.

Hilla von Rebay, artist and curator of the Guggenheim Foundation, as well as a friend of the Wrights, had been discussing the Guggenheim Museum with Mr. Wright, and she also would attend the wedding. The bride's sister, Sarah, later joined the fellowship, also came out for the ceremony. Some of the principals who joined Mr. Wright at the family table were Iovanna Lloyd Wright, Wes Peters, Roland

and Hilla von Rebay, and the father of Minerva and Sarah. The theater looked great and was decorated with many tall flowers. Following the wedding, the choir sang beautifully; in fact, Gene Masselink's voice was in exceptional form that evening. Soon, it was time for snacks and I began serving the champagne brought by the bride's father for the reception. Since champagne was my favorite libation, I placed a towel over my left arm, letting it project beyond the hand that held my glass. As the evening progressed, I would pour several glasses for guests, followed by one for myself. This continued until Wes and Roland voiced concerns about not having enough bubbly, which they began mixing with ginger ale. After dinner, and making sure the tables were cleared before the movie, I slipped away with the remains of one bottle of champagne.

I hadn't planned to see the movie, so when my work in the kitchen was completed, I completed the bottle of champagne and jumped into my MG and headed for a party in Scottsdale.

I barely remember getting there, but I do recall they were not serving champagne. Someone placed a glass in my hand, and I was off and running. I don't remember what I was drinking for the next couple of hours, but eventually the party wound down, and I headed back to camp. In those days, Shea Boulevard, the main road to Taliesin, was not paved. Starting up the road, I realized I was speeding when someone would try to flag me down. Were they policemen or saguaro? I continued at a fast pace, bouncing on the bumpy road until the suicide doors on the MG opened and neither of them would remain closed. At times, I wandered off the road from time to time and it seemed as if large mosquitoes were biting my arms and legs. After reaching camp, I went to my tent and set the alarm—in a couple of hours, I would be needed in the kitchen. It seemed the mosquitoes were still bothering me when I awakened, and I realized what had been "stinging" me. Apparently while driving with the doors open, I'd hit cactus on both sides of the car, and both of the doors had scooped up cholla balls. They covered the car's interior and had been sticking me with their needles! The cholla's needles are armed with small barbs, and quite a few remained in my skin, which meant I'd need to pull them out with a pair of pliers.

I felt I had been cheated because this was definitely not a fun morning, and I didn't recall the night before!

Following my kitchen duty, I inspected my car. Several cholla balls remained on the seats, and some were stuck to the interior leather doors. There were so many, I needed two pairs of pliers to remove them. For several weeks, I could feel barbs that had broken off in various parts of my body, until the last of them festered and finally came out. It would have been nice to have a "designated driver" with me in those days.

A few days later, a surprise awaited me when Gene tracked me down. "Brother," he said, "your mother is waiting to see you in Mr. Wright's office."

In our correspondence, my mother had mentioned taking a trip through Mexico with her sister, Margie, who would travel at the drop of a hat. Mom hadn't given a clue as to when they might stop at Taliesin West, but here they were.

I was showing them the buildings and explaining their functions, when Mr. Wright walked up. After introducing the ladies to Wright, he suggested that we three join he and Mrs. Wright later for dinner, which we did.

Pleasant conversation preceded our dinner. Due to my aunt's passion for travel, here I was seated at the Wright's dining table, served by others while hearing the Wrights' opinions on various subjects. I was in seventh heaven. The Wrights were always genteel, even with those they had just met.

I was also delighted that my mother had finally seen examples of the architecture I had believed in for so long, and I knew she would further enjoy the sites in Mexico.

MARCH 27, 1952

Wright's exhibit "Sixty Years of Living Architecture" had already been shown in Florence and Zurich, and was soon to open in Paris before traveling to Munich and Rotterdam. Gene had made travel arrangements so the Wrights, together with their daughter Iovanna, would be in Paris for that opening. They planned to be gone for several weeks, during which time Gene would have surgery on the hip he had injured a few years earlier.

Bill and Barbara Morrison invited a few apprentices to climb Mt. McDowell, directly behind the camp, for a campfire, sleep-out, and to view the sunrise the next morning.

I agreed to go, along with Jackson Wong, from Portland, Oregon, Russi Patel from India, Steve Oyakawa and Ron Salisbury, from Vancouver, Canada, and Mr. and Mrs. Aubrey Banks from Chicago. I gathered my sleeping bag and other supplies, plus a heavy piece of canvas as a groundcover to, hopefully, protect me from any overlooked pieces of barbed cactus.

We set out for our climb after dinner, when there was still enough light. Our chosen campsite was at the top of a high hill, not an actual mountain requiring climbing gear. The ascent was pleasant and uneventful with lots of chatter and several rest stops so we could view the scenery at different levels.

We arrived just before sunset, so we hurried to spread out our sleeping bags and place some large stones into a fire pit. The fire would be built with pieces of dead cactus, which were always in abundance.

The sunset was beautiful, and as the sky darkened, we saw Phoenix, some twenty miles away, and we could also see lights from other townships, as separate entities. Naturally, we could see Scottsdale, closest to our camp. Tempe and Mesa were also close to Phoenix, but in 1952, they were still isolated by a strip of darkness. At this point Barbara said, "It looks something like ships on a vast ocean." Her statement was a good metaphor, as by then the sky was completely dark.

Russi told philosophical tales from his native India that kept one thinking for weeks. He also was quite a philosopher, and we would listen intently whenever he began to speak.

The fire began to wane, as did our conversation; soon all were asleep.

At first light the next morning, someone called out for us to get up to see the magnificent sunrise. A beautiful white-orange color appeared behind a mountain range, then a horizontal band of gray mist formed before the mountain, which seemed about thirty miles long. As the sky turned pale blue, the band of mist remained while we descended into camp. This was one of those special scenes, one that lingers in memory for years.

On our return to camp, someone called out that Gene wanted to see me in Mr. Wright's office. I dropped my sleeping bag at my tent, then proceed to the office. As I entered he said, "Hi, Brother, did you have a nice time on the mountain top?" I stated that it was fabulous, and I would like to repeat the hike sometime, but never would I see a sunrise to match the one we'd seen that morning.

Gene finally explained why he'd asked to see me. He was sorry, but he had received a telegram from my brother stating that my father had died from a heart attack. His statement shook me, as it was so unexpected. I asked Gene to explain my trip home to the Wrights, but that following the funeral, I would return to Taliesin.

I packed only what I would need for the drive to Menlo Park, where my parents had lived for the past several years. As I drove the Arizona roads leading to a major highway, I kept thinking of my father, who I had last seen a year before. There was so much I'd wanted to share with him: the Wrights, Taliesin, how fortunate that I'd become an apprentice to Wright, and especially Mr. Wright's question about where I'd learned to paint. Now it was too late.

I wondered if my brother had been able to contact our mom, traveling somewhere in Mexico with our aunt. I was certain the trip had been our aunt's idea, and from past experience I knew they would travel on a whim, without an itinerary.

While speeding down Highway 10 in Arizona, I heard the inserts in the engine rods loosen, and immediately shut off the engine. I'd been driving at eighty miles per hour for some time and was fortunate to coast to a small "Mom and Pop" gas station. After explaining my situation to the proprietors, I rented a garage for the MG and proceeded to hitchhike to Los Angeles. From L.A., I caught a bus to Palo Alto, where my brother picked me up.

Harry had called some hotels in Mexico, but was unable to locate our mother. I stayed with Harry and his family for several days while he tried, in vain, to contact her. There was no other recourse but to have the funeral while both our mother and aunt were still somewhere south of the border.

Several days later Mom arrived, shocked to learn she would not be able to tell her husband about the trip she'd been on, and that he was forever gone. We gathered around Mom for several days to console her, but nothing takes the place of a lost one.

I explained to Mom that I would have to purchase parts for my car, which had broken down in Arizona, and I would have to repair the engine, and then I would drive it home and sell it. This was accomplished, and with the funds received from selling the MG, I bought an older Chevrolet convertible and gave Mom the balance. A week later, I packed the convertible to rejoin the fellowship in Wisconsin.

During the drive, I was torn between loyalty for my mother and my love for architecture and working with Mr. Wright. Although she had stated that I was still young and needed to find my way in life, it was not easy to leave that lovely, gentle, woman.

This time, I'd decided to take a more northerly direction east to view other states. At Lassen Volcanic National Park, there was still a foot or two of snow on the ground, and it was there that the engine in my old Chevy decided to break a rod. Enough already, I thought, as I shut off the engine. After pulling over to the roadside and taking out my tools, I removed the head from this six-cylinder masterpiece. I then jacked up the front end, dropped the pan, and removed the broken connecting rod and its inserts. Leaving my car at the roadside, I hitchhiked to Susanville and took a hotel room for the night.

The next morning, after buying the necessary parts, I hopped on a bus. The bus driver was kind enough to stop near my ailing Chevy, and within a few minutes, I began the repairs.

Soon I was on the road again, heading northeast for Wisconsin. I enjoyed seeing different vistas on this trip, especially driving through Yellowstone National Park for the first time.

I pressed on through Montana and North Dakota before arriving in Minneapolis, where I located Wright's recently completed Henry J. Neils residence. This was a large house, constructed of scrap marble that had been meticulously grouted, cypress boards and a cedar shingle roof. The Neils's allowed me to take several exterior photos. Later they invited me to stay for dinner; following conversation about Wright and Taliesin, they suggested that I spend the night, as a storm was threatening. I politely declined, as I wanted to push on to Spring Green. After driving about fifteen miles, a rainstorm and a tremendous gust of wind hit my car and the convertible top tore away from the frame. Canvas flapped behind me, as rain pelted down with more water than I could drink in a lifetime.

Immediately, I returned to the Neils's house, where they provided me with a garage for my car and a room for the night.

By morning, the storm had passed, and after breakfasting with the Neils'es, I drove quickly as possible toward Taliesin. When the convertible top ripped from the frame, it created thousands of small pieces of canvas and threads in the car's interior. Upon arriving at Taliesin, I cleaned the car thoroughly, but for months after that, threads would continue to appear. To save money, I sent away to Sears for a convertible top kit, which I installed.

While in California I'd read a news report of a fire at Taliesin, Wisconsin. This was a brief piece without details. Not until I had returned did I learn the complete story.

Having returned from a successful trip to Paris, where the showing of Wright's work were well received, and as Mr. Wright was driven around Taliesin, he had observed high weeds around the buildings at Hillside. He directed apprentices to clear those weeds closest to the buildings and to burn the balance. The wind had been blowing away from the buildings as Wright attempted to start a fire, but he ran out of matches and sent Davy for more.

The fire smoldered until the wind changed directions; then suddenly erupted, and began burning near the building. Before it could be put out, the fire spread into the building, to the upper floor of the classroom area, the dining room, and then to the theater. It consumed the entire roof and walls of the upper level, with the stone walls left scorched, but intact.

Repairing the fire damage became the foremost priority in the days ahead. Several of us were doing the construction, as Wright wanted his plans realized before the summer's end. Removing the charred oak timbers took several days. Then followed a thorough cleaning before the start of new work.

The new work was designed to be more fireproof. Heavy Douglas fir timbers replaced the oak timbers that had burned away. Fortunately, the sandstone walls needed cleaning only and could still be used. The dining room and its roof were completed quickly, and the new dining area seemed nicer than before.

The theater roof was another matter, as it had not been redesigned to Wright's satisfaction. He preferred keeping the theater small, on a more intimate scale, while Mrs. Wright and their daughter, Iovanna, wanted a larger stage for practicing dance movements. Wright's solution was to slightly expand the size of the stage, but to also lower it so the stage would seem to appear larger. Wright designed a curtain made from monk's cloth and appliqued, multicolored felt in an abstract pattern.

🚩 A TALIESIN REFLECTION :: 22

One summer in Wisconsin I was directed to grade all the gravel roads at Taliesin, Midway and Hillside. None of these roads were paved, therefore, they had to be smoothed and reshaped after the winter's slush, snow and ice.

In earlier days, when he was more active, Wright had actually done the grading himself. He relinquished this task reluctantly, as he absolutely loved grading. Previously he'd used an antique mechanism with four wheels, a steel platform to stand on, and two large controlling wheels to change the tilt of a large blade, somewhat centered between the other four wheels. Additional controls were used to raise and lower the main blade. This contraption didn't have an engine; it had to be pulled by a tractor, and not only had it not been sold for scrap, this was the apparatus I was assigned to use.

While grading, one had to allow for rainwater to drain away from soil, which might cause the water to pool. Also, when approaching cattle guards, the grading should create a smooth transition to the iron grates in the road. It was a demanding job, but it was fun.

One day while grading the road over the hillock between Hillside and Midway (and pulled by another apprentice on the tractor) Mr. Wright appeared, dressed in his suit and porkpie hat. He'd been strolling from Hillside to the job site to view our work in progress. All was fine until he showed up. He began to "direct" the blade's operation by raising one hand while waving his cane with the other.

Naturally, the blade could not move as fast as Wright's cane. Frantically, I would spin the large controlling wheels, but the gear ratio could not keep up with the desired reaction time. Meanwhile Wright kept directing with his cane, somewhat like an orchestra conductor, as the blade tried to match his instructions.

The tractor was so noisy I couldn't hear his instructions clearly, nor were his hand and cane gestures understandable. Finally after about ten minutes of whirling his cane, Wright was exasperated enough to walk back to Hillside. With him gone, we did a nice job of reshaping the roads.

A PIRATE PARTY

Mrs. Wright's past association with George Gurdjieff, and her involvement with movement and dance, caused her to become immersed in plays and costume parties for the fellowship. For example, a notice on the bulletin board would appear alerting us to an Arabian Night's party on the following Saturday evening, or some other designated party, causing the entire fellowship to search the stage wardrobe or storage rooms for appropriate costumes. Completing an ensemble wasn't easy, as the number of available outfits did not match the roster of apprentices. Most times, we'd have to borrow accessories from each other to complete our costume.

Often, Mrs. Wright would give us only several days' notice for, say, five skits to play on the following Saturday night. This required willing fellowship members to take charge and select five groups of fellows, each group writing an appropriate skit, then directing a brief satire on a topic of the day. Some of these were quite humorous, and enjoyed immensely by Mr. Wright.

Wes and Mrs. Wright collaborated on one of the best parties given and attended by the fellowship. As a lover of all things nautical, Wes had found a large wooden boat on a lake in Madison that was for sale, and Mr. Wright agreed to purchase. Wes was to convert the boat into a three-mast schooner to be used for a party later that summer. The boat was moved to the upper pond at Taliesin where it could be worked on from time to time.

Pirate Party, Spring Green, WI (unknown, Barbara Morrison, Heloise Swaback, Mr. Wright, Mrs. Wright, Wes Peters, Iovanna Wright, Kay Davison, unknown) :: 1951

Meanwhile, repairs to the fire damage at Hillside were proceeding under Wright's close supervision. He insisted that anyone—not absolutely needed elsewhere—should work on reconstructing the dining room and theater. His goal was to have all work completed before leaving for Scottsdale that winter.

Because of Wes's love for ships and boats, he would try stealing fellows from other jobs to work on his boat conversion. Of course, if Wright learned about it Wes would answer to him. However, Mrs. Wright encouraged Wes as she was enthusiastic about the forthcoming Pirate Party.

Following several weeks of work, the schooner was ready for the Pirate Party. This had been planned to include those of the Wrights' guests still onsite. Attending were Gene's parents, Dr. and Mrs. Masselink, Mrs. Barney (Mr. Wright's sister) and others, including some of Wright's grandchildren.

The party began at one edge of the pond. Soon the galleon, with three sails unfolded, came into view and all stopped whatever they'd been doing to enjoy this colorful sight. It was impressive to have a boat of this caliber on "our property" for a private party.

The boat had been loaded with exotic loot in boxes and barrels, guarded by several bearded pirates. Several dancing girls (undoubtedly stolen along the way from an Egyptian chieftain's harem) were also on board. These included Barbara Morrison, Shirley Oliver, Maxine Pfefferkorn, Heloise Schweizer, and Iovanna Lloyd Wright.

By far, this was the most successful party given during my years at Taliesin. The Wrights and their guests sat on blankets and cushions while the fellowship danced about and served food and drink for all. There was something to watch until dusk, when Wes began shooting fireworks over the pond from the galleon. Meanwhile, apprentices lit a hundred candles attached to paper plates and floated over the basin, adding to the pyrotechnic display.

SEQUESTERING "MY ROOM"

While rebuilding the theater, Wes informed me that Mrs. Wright had asked that I move from Taliesin and take a room, in need of repairs, at Hillside.

While inspecting the guestrooms at Taliesin (prior to having clients arrive shortly for the weekend) Mrs. Wright noticed the distinct change in my room since it had been assigned me. Immediately, she'd decided it was now suitable for guests. This meant I would be moving from the room I had reconstructed more than two years ago.

I was not elated at the prospect of working on yet another room in poor condition, especially after working a full day on the theater. However, I was also a guest. So I moved.

THE PRICE TOWER (1952)

One of my favorite Wright-designed buildings emerged in 1952. Based on Wright's design of 1929, (known then as St. Mark's Tower for New York City), that project was never built. His new Price Tower would be a more distinct design.

The Price Tower was Wright's pioneering experiment in the multi-use skyscraper. A tall, richly decorated structure, the Tower was originally designed as combination business offices, shops, and apartments. This he called "The tree that escaped from the forest."

This began when Harold Price Sr., an Oklahoma oilman, contemplated expanding his flourishing pipeline construction firm in Bartlesville. His sons, Harold Price Jr. and Joe Price, felt that having a famous architect design his new structure would not cost much more than if an "average" architect served as designer. They convinced their father to invite Wright to design a three-story structure, complete with parking lot for ten or twelve vehicles.

Mr. Price wanted his new building to become not only an asset to the community, but also an efficient entity for his firm.

The sons called Taliesin and received an appointment for the three of them to discuss the possibilities of having Wright design the building. Initially, Price Sr. did not believe that Wright would be interested in designing such a small building.

In June, the Price family flew in their company plane to discuss their proposition with Mr.

Kenn Lockhart began constructing the Price Tower model, but because of a time factor for a showing, he solicited assistance from Curtis Besinger and Kamal Amin to complete the project :: 1952

Wright. While listening, Wright grew impressed with how Price Sr. had built his company from a small welding shop to a huge contracting firm that installed pipelines in several states. Price Sr. explained his requirements as Wright continued to listen. Soon, Wright offered his wisdom by stating that three floors were most inefficient, although he did accept their commission.

Wright had decided that Price was a venturesome man who would understand the value in building a tower of twenty-two stories that he delineated, based on St. Mark's Tower. He suggested that Price lease whatever space was not required, leaving the tower as a multi-use structure. Initially shocked at the building's height, Price finally agreed to a nineteen-story tower.

The building was constructed of steel reinforced concrete. The floors were cantilevered from the main central vertical mass, forming a taproot foundation system. This freed the exterior walls from being load-bearing, thus making each wall, in essence, a hanging screen.

The hanging screens consisted of gold-tinted glass, copper louvers, and copper faced parapet walls. This was planned on a unit system consisting of 60-degree parallelograms. The size (on ground) was laid out at 2' × 6" across and 1' × 10-5/8" on the side. The nineteen floors, plus spire, towered 221 feet above ground.

Wright felt a need for a building to house both workspace and an area for dwelling. In brief, one would live in an apartment and walk across the hall to their workplace, thereby reducing dependency on automobiles. Most of the upper floors contained three offices and one dwelling unit. Three elevators and a stairway provided access to the ground floor.

Over the years, the Price Company continued to grow until it occupied six floors of office space. The seventeenth floor housed a small office and living room used by the firm. The eighteenth floor contained a small conference room, plus the upper level of the seventeenth floor's apartment space, also used by the firm. Price's private office on the nineteenth floor included a roof garden. Wright also designed a built-in desk and glass mural for Price's office space, plus a mural for the seventeenth floor.

In 1980, the Price Company was reorganized and relocated to Dallas, Texas. Phillips Petroleum Company purchased the tower and utilized it until 1987, when the oil-market crisis occurred, causing the building to be vacant for the next three years. In the early 1990s, Phillips put the building up for sale. However, cultural groups convinced them to execute a four-million-dollar renovation, transferring ownership to the recently formed Price Tower Arts Center.

The building was then converted into an inn, where one may now stay in a Wright building, complete with all the amenities of a state-of-the-art luxury hotel.

In a 1991 Architectural Record Survey (not limited to Wright's work), readers were asked to select the most significant buildings in the world from the previous 100 years. Twelve of Wright's buildings were selected, including the Price Tower. One of seventeen structures designed by Wright, The Price Tower earned special recognition from the American Institute of Architects as representative of his contribution to American culture.

Wright also designed two houses for the Price family. One is located in Bartlesville, Oklahoma (1953), the other in Phoenix, Arizona (1954).

In July 1952, the Raul Bailleres family wished to build a Wright-designed home on a site overlooking the ocean in Acapulco, Mexico. This was in an area of large, smooth boulders that Wright incorporated into his design for the large, circular house. The roof was designed as a low, thin-shelled concrete dome with a large circular opening at the center of the span. The living room was open, yet partially shielded, with a more prominent boulder used as a feature. Part of the interior would be heated by a large fireplace and cooled on hot days by the evaporation of water sprayed over the roof.

On the ocean side of the house, the patios

were quite generous. They consisted of a series of stepped patios terminating at the swimming pool area, where overflowing water would splash over the boulders below.

Unfortunately, this magnificent plan was never built, although the Bailleres'es were a wealthy family who already owned a palacido in Cuernavaca.

About the time the Bailleres'es plans were finished, the City of New York requested clarification on some of the working drawings for the Guggenheim. Wright reviewed their request, and in due time furnished solutions to their queries. He then turned over the matter to Jack Howe for the completion of the revisions.

A TALIESIN REFLECTION : : 23

In summer, 1952, Mrs. Wright had intercepted a phone call from the Richard Smiths, for whom Wright had designed a house in Jefferson, Wisconsin in 1950. Although still quite new, the Smith's house had experienced roof leaks. The owners had asked both the general contractor and the roofing contractor to repair the leaks, but their efforts had failed. The Smiths wished to speak directly to Mr. Wright about the problem. However, Gene Masselink, who had taken the call, first informed Mrs. Wright, and as she didn't want her husband to hear about it, she informed the Smiths that someone from the fellowship would repair the roof.

Mrs. Wright then contacted Davy Davison, who chose Steve Oyakawa and me to drive to Jefferson and, hopefully, repair the roof.

One Saturday, we left before dawn in Davy's convertible for the drive to Jefferson. Arriving at the house, we asked for a ladder to climb to the roof. Sometimes leaks "travel;" i.e., they start higher up on the roof then appear at a lower spot, out of alignment, which makes finding them difficult. We soon found: (1) small holes at the junction where the masonry projects up, beyond the roof, and (2) the stepped flashing at the roof-to-wall condition was not done

properly, causing small openings that would allow infiltration of water.

We then drove to town, purchased some small flashing sheets and a can of waterproof mastic, and made the repairs. As the job was completed at dusk, the Smiths invited us to stay for dinner.

On our drive back to Taliesin, we were tired and getting sleepy. Davy told us his trick for staying awake while driving. He would wet his upper eyelids with his finger, open the driver's side window and hang his head out the window. Somehow, I have never gotten that sleepy.

Mrs. Wright was informed about our repairs to the Smith's roof. Thankfully, this was once Mr. Wright didn't have to learn about yet another roof problem!

A TALIESIN REFLECTION : : 24

I'd learned that an apprentice had driven the dump truck into the desert to gather stones for the new men's locker room, with disastrous results. Somehow, he hadn't shifted gears properly, resulting in a transmission repair at a garage in Scottsdale.

Wes asked that I ride to the garage with him, so I could drive the truck back to camp. On the drive to Scottsdale, we chatted about cars, drivers, and the merit of one truck over another, etc.

We arrived there at noon, so Wes decided we should have lunch before stopping at the garage. He ordered his usual rare steak, potatoes and Coca-Cola with catsup by the bottle. I ordered the same, but that my steak be well done, with *no* catsup!

After lunch, he dropped me off at the garage, and went about doing business for Mr. Wright.

The shop foreman explained I'd have to wait, as the truck was not quite ready, so I bought a local paper at the news rack nearby. I'd read a few articles when I learned that the truck was ready to roll.

In the early 1950s, the roads from the outskirts of Scottsdale to Taliesin were all gravel roads, with many ruts and holes to contend with. By the same token there was hardly any traffic, nor any trees, along Scottsdale Road. For miles, all one could see was desert when going to and from camp.

The dump truck was an older model, to be driven slowly and with care to insure it from returning to the shop for repairs, so I did just that.

Turning onto Shae Boulevard, the road was clear without even one Indian on horseback; so I picked up the newspaper and began to read. The road was also straight as the proverbial arrow; so I'd read a few lines, glance at the road, then return to the paper.

This continued until approaching camp, where curves showed up in the road, so I drove even slower. I parked the truck and walked into the desert to my tent. I was still full from the steak I'd eaten earlier, so I skipped dinner that evening.

The next morning, while walking by Wright's office Gene came out and said, "Hey, brother, why didn't you stop to help Bruce (Brooks Pfeiffer)? Didn't you see he and his MG, broken down on Shae?"

Puzzled, I tried to digest Gene's words before replying, "No, I didn't see him; I happened to be reading the paper at the time!"

A TALIESIN REFLECTION : : 25

Following Wright's Sunday morning talk at Taliesin West in November 1952, he asked the fellowship to consider living in the desert, per se. He then asked that we design a canvas tent he would eventually order from a tent maker. New apprentices would use these, also anyone who wished to change their current habitat to a newly designed tent.

I considered this for about a week. On December 9, 1952, while alone in the drafting room I completed my design for a tent structure that *would not leak*, (as had happened to

other apprentices living out in the desert).

When poles support a shaped canvas tent, the possibility immediately exists that the tent will leak wherever the supports touch the canvas—and that happens to be everywhere! New canvas sheds water nicely, but as it gets older, canvas becomes subject to water infiltration.

My solution: use permanent slabs of concrete floors poured in various locations around the camp. Permanent, painted metal frames would support the apprentices' tents by hanging them with canvas clips that snap over the metal frames. Without the supporting poles (causing leakage), the *hanging tent* could be unsnapped from the metal frames and stored indoors whenever the fellowship left for Wisconsin.

The design was almost completed when Mr. Wright walked in. Noticing I was alone, he asked what I was drawing. I explained this was my tent design and started to rise, but he motioned that I remain seated. I moved over to make room for him. He surprised me by placing his arm around my shoulder as he looked at my design. Elated at this display of comradeship, I proceeded to explain my work.

Previously, I'd felt that Wright wasn't getting much response from students about submitting their tent designs. Hardly any discussion had occurred within the fellowship.

After explaining my design, Mr. Wright surprised me by picking up a pencil and stating, "This is what we are going to do." Within a few minutes, he had sketched a pyramidal canvas tent, including dimensions, in the lower right-hand corner of my drawing. He then rose and walked from the room. I took a second look at his drawing, and of course noted that his new tent was to be supported from within by poles.

A TALIESIN REFLECTION : : 26

Among the Taliesin apprentices was a likeable Canadian, Ron Salisbury, from British Columbia. He didn't own a car, so he often rode along with me on "town day," our half-day off each

Monday. On one occasion, Ron asked if I'd like to go horseback riding with him in the desert. He missed riding horseback, and had noticed a stable that rented horses near Camelback Mountain.

For some reason I agreed, although I had only ridden horseback once when quite young. This had occurred by Lake Strawberry in the California Sierras, where my friends' parents had a cabin. The two other boys had decided to ride horseback so I went along, reluctantly, for the ride.

After our horses' saddle and stirrups were adjusted, my two friends sprang into action and mounted their steeds. One of the ranch hands was about to assist me when I noticed my horse was blind in one eye. I said no thank you, we would be going on some steep trails, and I wanted a horse that could see on both sided of the path.

I was given another mount and we were on our own. Shortly after leaving the stable, the horses refused to move, no matter how much they were prodded, they were reluctant to stray from their food supply. They had done this before and knew the procedure well. After a half-hour of coaxing, we decided to turn back. This only prompted them to hasten their pace. Soon, I was pulling at the reins, trying to keep my horse from galloping ahead. Within a few minutes, I had developed a cramp in one leg, causing me to fall from my horse. When one of the boys reached me and asked if he should return the horse to me, I declined. "No thanks," I said, "I'll walk back to the ranch."

This was the tale I related to Ron. This time, he reassured me, things would be different. Not only were there no mountain trails to navigate, he would make sure I was given a gentle horse.

After Ron explained to the stable hand that I was a novice and should be given an "easy" horse, we mounted up and walked our horses from the stable. For awhile, everything went fine. Ron and I talked as the horses wandered trails lined with giant saguaro, prickly pear, cholla, barrel, and other desert cacti.

In a short while, my horse began quickening his pace. Although this began gradually, pulling gently on the reins didn't change his cadence one iota. He picked up speed, and I tugged some more. When Ron noticed I was too far ahead and proceeding too fast, he spurred his horse on to close the gap. I believe my horse heard Ron's horse getting closer, and my mount took off like a racehorse. At this point, I could no longer hold him back, and he galloped even faster. I have no idea why what happened next happened, but this mammoth monster that I was on suddenly made a right-angle turn, and I went flying off. As I did, I also turned upside down. Before my inversion took place, I could see I'd be heading straight for patches of cholla cactus, and the hairs on the back of my neck stood out. Luckily, I landed flat on my back between two large chollas without suffering much damage. One cholla ball was imbedded in my arm, which Ron removed later at the car. He couldn't stop beforehand, as he had been chasing my horse. After catching it, and bringing it back to me so I could ride back to the stable, I told him, "No thanks, I'll walk back."

Both of my horseback riding episodes I had in my entire life ended in the same way, and believe me, that was the last time.

ACTOR CHARLES LAUGHTON

In January, 1953, the theater marquee in downtown Phoenix announced a forthcoming attraction: the reading of John Brown's Body, starring and directed by Charles Laughton, with co-stars Tyrone Power, Dame Judith Anderson, and Raymond Massey. The tour, which opened in Santa Barbara's Lobero Theater, eventually played in forty states and three Canadian Provinces, with the cast traveling over 30,000 miles by bus. Although the tour had barely started, Charles Laughton was pleased that the Wrights invited him to stay at Taliesin prior to the Phoenix opening.

During the week of Laughton's arrival, I happened to be working in the family kitchen, so I served him and the Wrights at their formal dining table. After conversing with the Wrights following dinner, Laughton volunteered to perform an evening of readings for the fellowship.

The Cabaret Theater was decorated for this affair, and I had set up the dining table for the Wrights and their guests, including Charles Laughton.

Laughton was introduced on stage; however by this time everyone at camp knew that the gifted actor would be delivering his readings. These were both humorous and serious literature and were well received by the fellowship. Laughton was pleased by the reception, and as a friend of Wright's, he offered another evening of readings. In all, he delivered three readings, which were well received.

In appreciation, Wright decided to give Laughton an overnight picnic at Schnebly Hill near Sedona, Arizona. This was the Wright's favorite spot for both quiet time and to marvel at the surroundings.

Whenever Wright wasn't involved with work including a time frame—or a multitude of guests—often he would suggest that the fellowship prepare for a picnic. He loved these outings, and his favorite picnic spots were near Spring Green and Scottsdale.

Beyond roasting a pig, lamb, chicken, or hamburgers at these affairs, the fellowship looked forward to asking Wright any question at all. A well-read man, Wright could expound on various subjects, much to the fellowship's delight.

This grew into the well-established Sunday morning talks, that would sometimes begin during breakfast, or mostly would begin upon completing breakfast with a subject he hoped the fellowship would consider. "Well, boys," he'd say, "what shall we talk about this morning?" Always, someone would quickly respond with a question.

Apprentice Bruce Brooks Pfeifer began recording these Sunday morning talks, and many have been transcribed into book form or on tape, and can be located at bookstores.

On Thursday, an advance party from camp left to prepare the picnic site honoring Charles Laughton, and to create a place for roasting the lamb the following evening.

By Friday, Mrs. Wright was not well enough to attend, so she and several others remained in camp. Wright and Mr. Laughton were in the lead car, and the remainder of the fellowship followed. There was a great deal of marvelous scenery to absorb along the route.

At the picnic area, I spread out blankets and cushions, also tableware for Wright and Mr. Laughton, Wes and Uncle Vlado, (Mrs. Wright's brother). Lamb, roasted to perfection, was served. After dinner, someone built a fire, and all gathered around to hear the chorus sing the better part of an hour. Then we spread our sleeping bags and retired for the night.

Wright decided that Laughton should not sleep on the ground, so Wes drove them to a nearby motel for the night.

The next morning, Wes returned with Wright and Laughton for a breakfast of hamburgers over an open fire. After breakfast, the campsite was cleared, and we followed Wes along backcountry roads, where a few cars proceeded to become stuck in the mud. Several of us muscled them out of their predicament. Over the years, Wright had grown accustomed to these predicaments. Not so, Mr. Laughton. Still, he took it in stride.

CONVERSATION WITH FLLW

During my second year at Taliesin, I was fortunate to become engaged in a one-on-one conversation with Mr. Wright.

I was on family kitchen duty that week and I had served afternoon tea to the Wrights in the desert alcove adjacent to the garden room. I was just coming from the little kitchen with more hot tea in case either of the Wrights would care for more, when I heard Mrs. Wright say she would be going to her own quarters to write some letters.

She passed me at the entrance to the room and I asked Mr. Wright if he cared for more tea. He declined, but he asked me to sit at the table with him.

Earlier he had spent three hours in the drafting room, which is where I found him to join Mrs. Wright for tea. I suppose he felt everything was under control with Jack in the drafting room or surely he would have gone back, but he seemed to want to talk.

He asked me if I was getting along all right, and if I had any problems with anything. I answered everything was more than I had expected within the world of Taliesin, and I couldn't be more pleased.

We spoke of some of his buildings in general, and then we came to the Kaufmann house, *Fallingwater*, and how Mr. Kaufmann was on his way to meet with Mr. Wright while he was actually drawing the plans for Mr. Kaufmann's acceptance.

Mr. Wright was always at controversy with the architects who believed in and followed the International Style, and would argue the point for Organic Architecture at the drop of a hat. He went on to say he had finally had it with them, and with the Kaufmann commission he said, "We're going to beat them at their own game."

I was fascinated by his statement, which has never left my memory. To make a point clear, he would never say, "I am going to" . . . etc. He always used "We."

He got around to things I heard him say at Sunday breakfast in front of the entire fellowship also, but it was nice to hear these things while I was the only one in the room. He also again stated on of his favorite expressions: "Organic Architecture is where the part is to the whole as the whole is to the part." Since it was directed directly at me, it had an unsettling but beneficial effect.

He also referred to getting started on the outside in architecture by saying "borrow from me," and "use my name." He was always on top of things and knew what was what.

One sort of chilling remark he made, out of the blue, was "Remember, Death is a great friend."

A TALIESIN TRAGEDY

At Taliesin I became friendly with a talented couple I had admired from the beginning of our friendship. Bob and Ann Pond, together with their baby son, were at Taliesin when I arrived. One could immediately tell this pair was imbued with the fellowship spirit of jumping in, at a moment's notice, with whatever needed to be done. Both were artistic, and Ann had another talent, writing poetry. Following our time at Taliesin, we kept in touch over the years and met at fellowship gatherings. In 1997, Ann sent me her book of poems, inscribed, "To Earl: Affectionate regards, Ann." This collection included poems from 1950 to March 1985.

Ann Wetmore Pond was born in 1925. She graduated from Hillsdale College in 1948 with a B.A. in English and Science. She married Robert Pond in 1949. Ann belonged to the Taliesin fellowship from 1950 to 1954. She raised three children and lived in Greenwood, Indiana for 32 years.

Robert Pond completed 2 years of college at Otis Art Institute, in Los Angeles, California, now known as L.A. County Art Institute, before becoming an apprentice to Frank Lloyd Wright.

The Ponds' first child, Roger, was born at Taliesin. He was about eighteen months old when the fellowship was saddened by his drowning in the triangle pool on the south side of the drafting room. All of us had followed this lovely little man's growth from his days in the playpen to finally standing and learning to walk. A delightful, friendly child, Roger was interested in whoever would stop and give him recognition.

Later, he wandered about the apprentice's court where folks would stop and talk to him. One day, I noticed he had wandered from the court and was stomping about, fully clothed, in the reflecting pool outside the Kiva Theater. The pool, designed to hold approximately six inches of water, served as a mirror for the seven-foot rock placed as a focal point for the adjacent walkway. A few apprentices were standing about watching, laughing at the youngster having fun in the water. I was almost compelled to snatch him from the pool, and give him a spanking for what he was doing. Although I felt strongly, I didn't want the Ponds to think I was interfering with their child's discipline. Should I have taken charge when Roger's parents weren't there? Over the years, I have agonized about that.

Several weeks later while reading in my tent, a terrible scream pierced the Sunday calm. Soon an ambulance, with siren screaming, arrived in camp. Attendants tried, in vain, to resuscitate little Roger, who had been found by his mother, face down, in the triangular pool.

Loved by the entire fellowship, Roger would be missed by all. His death cast a pall over the camp. The Wrights, together with Bob and Ann, agreed to continue with the formal Sunday evening, in which Bob and Ann participated in the chorus. The program provided support and comfort to the bereaved parents.

Apprentice Kelly Oliver stayed up all night to construct a small redwood coffin for Roger.

On the afternoon of the following day, the fellowship gathered at the base of the hill behind camp for Roger's services. Apprentices John Geiger and Curtis Besinger brought desert flowers to decorate the site.

The chorus sang Bob and Ann's requests while Curtis and John Amarantides provided music. Wright read a section from a Walt Whitman poem selected by Ann. Following the reading, Wright asked for a moment of silence to consider our thoughts. The entire fellowship was quietly standing there when an apprentice, who happened to be a good friend of mine, Duke Johnson, from Piedmont, California, had the alarm go off on his new

wristwatch. He fiddled with it for what seemed like an eternity before he was able to terminate the sound.

This tragedy occurred at one of the most prolific periods of Wright's life, when he had many projects on his mind, yet he was so humble he would take the time to support a friend, or in this case, apprentices.

In a later letter to me, Bob reflected on his loss of Roger, and stated:

"I cannot think of a better place to be during such a crisis. Mr. And Mrs. Wright, and the fellowship, were so kind and understanding. When we returned to Taliesin, Ann and I asked Mr. Wright if we could put Roger in the chapel cemetery.

He located the spot and said this will be the Fellowship Row. The row has since filled up with other than Fellowship members.

Curtis and I went up to the quarry and cut a stone to use as a grave marker. I spent hours shaping the stone to get the corner's square, etc. I cut Roger's name in Taliesin Style letters and filled them with gold leaf. The stone deteriorated over the years due to the weather and mowers.

Now I have two more stones: Douglas, who Ann was pregnant with when Roger died, was killed in a mountain climbing accident, and Ann is with her two boys.

Earl, you taught Roger to speak his first sentence, "There they go," while holding him in the back seat while on a trip to Oak Creek Canyon, one of those great picnics.

Earl, I have just been thinking back and writing it down. I am sorry you felt guilty about any of this, you shouldn't.—Your friend, Bob."

I wrote to my mother and Mary Lou, whom I had been corresponding regularly, about the lamentable loss of little Roger, and how the entire fellowship was saddened by his demise.

:: :: ::

Following is a poem written later by Ann.

WORK CONTINUES

This was one of the most prolific periods of superlative creation by Frank Lloyd Wright. During this time, the drafting room had the following work on its boards: 1) the George Lewis residence at Tallahassee, Florida; 2) the Luis Marden residence at McLean, Virginia; 3) the Frank S. Sander residence at Stamford, Connecticut; 4) the R. W. Linholm residence at Cloquet, Minnesota; 5) the Archie Boyd Teater studio at Bliss, Idaho; 6) and the Ray Brandes residence at Issaquah, Washington. There were also additions and revisions to be made to the working drawings for the Price Tower and the Guggenheim Museum.

Although the fellowship was busy with many drawings to complete, one could also feel a pall in the drafting room. For many weeks, the loss of little Roger was felt by all.

Wright asked Kenn Lockhart to create a model of the Price Tower. The Prices had requested a model of their building to be displayed at a petroleum exposition, where plans for the tower would be displayed. This would be a huge task, considering the time involved; so Kenn requested Curtis Besinger's assistance, as Curtis had already completed many of the working drawings for the building. Apprentice

Kamal Amin was also called in to help finish the tower model as time was running out.

Joe Price came to Taliesin to photograph the model, which had not been completed at the time of his arrival. A few weeks later, the finished model was shipped to the Prices in Bartlesville.

The fellowship then packed drawings and other supplies, required for our return to Wisconsin, and after arriving, we continued with the reconstruction of the theater that had been damaged by fire.

Wright traveled to New York City, where he received the National Institute of Arts and Letters' *Gold Medal for Architecture*. After returning to Taliesin, he again made the trip to New York; this time regarding an appeal for a building permit for the Guggenheim Museum. Several times during that summer, his presence was required in New York—always with respect to negotiations for the museum.

Soon, discontent crept into the fellowship that divided our activities into two camps. On one side were those who remained loyal to Frank Lloyd Wright's idea of building organic structures, also his current plan to hold his International Exhibition in a temporary building, yet to be constructed beside buildings owned by the Guggenheim Foundation in New York

City. The other camp consisted of those following Mrs. Wright's plans to hold a demonstration of *Dance Movements* in Chicago.

Although there was diffusion of thought and energy within the fellowship, Wright did approve of special costumes and sets to be designed by Gene and Wes, which would be used in the forthcoming Movements.

The Wrights argued about this, as Wright planned to send Kenn Lockhart and Tom Casey to New York to help construct and set up his exhibition. Mrs. Wright did not want those chosen to participate in the Movements presentation to leave Taliesin; however, Kenn and Tom did leave for New York within a few days.

Following that, Wright learned the exhibit building was progressing too slowly; so additional apprentices were sent to assist in the project.

Models of Wright's work had arrived at the New York docks from Mexico, where they were last viewed. Several models and exhibit panels had been damaged and were brought to the Guggenheim site for repairs.

Meanwhile, Wright's exhibition was generating publicity in New York magazines and newspapers, and through radio and television broadcasts. He was interviewed in a TV studio showing his new model of the Guggenheim Museum, and later by celebrity interviewer Jinx Falkenburg on radio.

Wright had also designed a house to be viewed along with models and photographs displayed in the temporary exhibition buildings, both being constructed by Contractor David Henken. David and his wife, Priscilla, had been apprentices at Taliesin in the mid 1940s, and they helped organize Usonia Homes, Inc., a cooperative housing project near Pleasanton, New York, for which Wright had designed the site plan, as well as residences for Sol Friedman, Edward Serlin, and Roland Reisley.

The press opening was held on October 21, while work was still underway for the formal opening set for October 23, 1953. Following

a successful opening, those apprentices who had worked on the project were returned to Taliesin.

During early November, the performance of Dance Movements was held in Chicago, to the relief of many. Once again, the fellowship would be united in carrying out Wright's architecture.

With so many working in New York for such an extended period of time, little had been accomplished on the rebuilding of the Hillside Theater. More hands would be available, but completion must wait until the following year, as soon we'd pack the trucks for the caravan to Arizona.

THE WINTER OF 1953

Following the stake truck's arrival at Taliesin West and the unloading and storage of drawings and canned goods, the drafting room became as busy as it had been in Wisconsin.

Wright continued traveling to New York to discuss revisions in the Guggenheim drawings.

More supplementary drawings became necessary for the Price Tower, soon to be built. Wright then designed a marvelous house for his own son, Llewellyn, and family in Bethesda, Maryland. In addition, the senior Prices requested that Wright design their future home in nearby Phoenix.

Everything at Taliesin West was proceeding well, which was not the case concerning my mother. Although her letters arrived on a regular basis, I could read between the lines. Working full time as a dietitian at Hewlett-Packard's Palo Alto plant, was, I felt, too much for a woman of 58; so I decided to return home and relieve Mom of her labors.

LEAVING TALIESIN

Sometime during mid December 1953, I asked Gene to schedule an appointment for me to see the Wrights together. This would eventually be one of the most difficult tasks to perform in my young life of 27 years.

I was asked to meet the Wrights in the garden room. When I arrived, they invited me to sit with them. I knew they had experienced this situation many times in the past, which still did not make it easier for me.

Immediately, I explained that since my father's death two years prior, the task of sending me money had become increasingly difficult for my mother. Only on occasion had I asked for funds to tide me over; still I felt uncomfortable doing so when she was in a financial bind. I'd decided to leave the fellowship, return to California and find a job to help with the family situation.

When I'd finished speaking, Mr. Wright looked at his wife, then said, "If it would help, you would no longer have to pay the annual tuition."

I thanked them profusely, as their offer meant they'd considered me a good worker;

also that Mr. Wright himself had appreciated what I'd accomplished at both Taliesin locations. However, concern for my mother's situation won out, and I explained I would simply have to leave.

Mrs. Wright must have appreciated my work during the past months, as she stated that, should my home situation change, I would indeed be welcome at the fellowship.

This produced tears, which I quickly sniffled back while saying, "Thank you so much for what you both have given me." With that I stood, thanked them again, and sadly walked from the room.

After bidding goodbye to my closest friends, I packed my possessions into my car for the long drive back to California where I would be spending Christmas with my family, and Mary Lou.

Frank Lloyd Wright (photographed by Mr. Wright's personal photographer, Pedro E. Guerrero) instructing John Geiger, on tractor, regarding work in progress, while author waits to converse with the master
:: 1951

CHAPTER FOUR : :

ON MY OWN

CHRISTMAS 1953

The coming months brought mixed emotions, as I agonized over my decision to leave Mr. Wright and return home. Still, I was delighted to be on familiar ground again, and my mother was happy to have me home for Christmas.

I was scurrying around, buying gifts for the family and Mary Lou, when my brother announced we should have Christmas dinner at his house. Not only would this be easier for Mom, who was still working, as memories of our dad would not be as strong at Harry's home, and I was very pleased with his decision.

After the holidays, I contacted an architect friend for interim work. Soon, I was drawing plans for a small grandmother's cottage to be constructed on a large estate in Los Altos. Upon finishing those drawings, I did various jobs for him until the spring of 1954 when I began work on Cabaña Tanglewood.

CABAÑA TANGLEWOOD

My first building commission arrived "on a silver platter," (so to speak,) from my very good friend, James Moore, whom I had known since junior high school. What Jim wanted to build was an inexpensive, two-bedroom, weekend and vacation cabin. Before leaving Taliesin, I had viewed the site in the Santa Cruz Mountains

and had done most of the working drawings in my tent at night. Jim offered that if I assisted with the construction, I could use the cabin on occasion, sort of an "early-model time-share."

The site had a marvelous view of a few miles to the south looking towards a ridge of redwoods. Due to the sloping ground and extensive vegetation, if the front part of the cabin were cut into the hill, neighboring houses

My good friend, Jim Moore, Willow Glen, CA
: : 1943

RIGHT AND BELOW
"Cabaña Tanglewood"
for James Moore.
Poured Masonry and
redwood. Santa Cruz
Mountains, CA :: 1954

"Cabaña Tanglewood" Living room and dining area with kitchen beyond : : 1954

would not be visible. A few pine trees could be seen, but a large portion of land was overgrown with manzanita. The first time we walked the site, machetes were used to clear our way. In doing so, I realized that much of this rugged land would need clearing to accommodate the septic tank drain field.

Because of the extraordinary amount of manzanita compared to the small cabin, I named it "Cabaña Tanglewood." The living room's poured masonry walls were oriented to collect heat from the sun during the day and to radiate heat into the cabin at night.

We discovered a rock quarry about a mile away where we could hand-select some of the

Photo of author by his mother while supervising "Cabaña Tanglewood" : : 1954

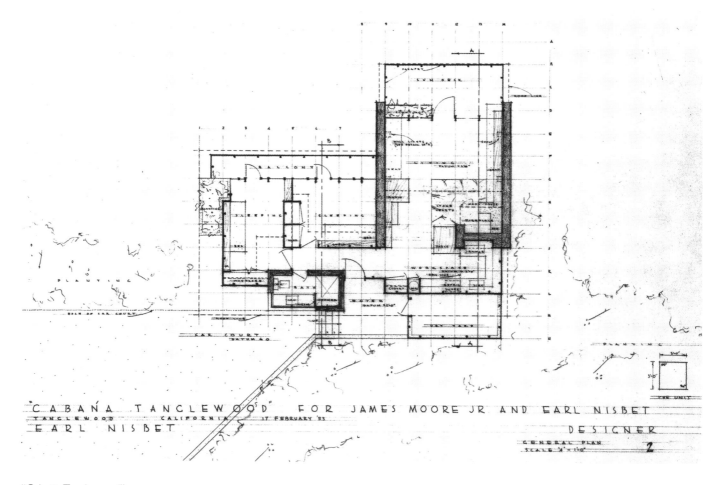

"CABAÑA TANGLEWOOD" FOR JAMES MOORE JR AND EARL NISBET
EARL NISBET   DESIGNER

"Cabaña Tanglewood",
Santa Cruz, CA. General
plan :: 1953

FACING PAGE, TOP
"Cabaña Tanglewood"
for James Moore.
View from Southeast.
Santa Cruz Mountains
:: 1953

FACING PAGE, BOTTOM
"Cabaña Tanglewood"
View from Southwest
:: 1953

rocks to be used for the poured masonry. From a mutual friend's sawmill, (with a very good price), we obtained straight-grained redwood to be used for walls, shelves, doors, posts and furniture.

Much privacy was obtained by cutting the massive fireplace wall, workspace, dry yard, and entrance walls into the hillside while making it easy to look out—except from the bathroom. There, the windows were perforated into patterns one might see looking through pines or redwood trees. Because the bathroom faced the street, car court, and entrance, the window glass was sandblasted for privacy, which also contributed to creating a room similar to a lantern when lit in the evening.

The living room contained built-in seats along each wall with metal planters behind each seat. Special wall lights that shone up, down, and through were built in for reading. Lighting for mood illumination was installed on the walls. Poured stone masonry used for the fireplace also wrapped through to the work-space, where it vented the kitchen stove. A small table was built next to the fireplace to accommodate four diners.

All of the wood walls were of single-wall construction, lapped one inch outwardly for every ten inches vertically, allowing rain to run off to the ground. Both bedrooms had virtually the same view, as did the living room, and the fenestration was job-built with perforated

VIEW FROM SOUTHEAST

"CABAŃA TANGLEWOOD" FOR JAMES MOORE JR AND EARL NISBET
TANGLEWOOD CALIFORNIA 17 FEBRUARY 55 DESIGNER
EARL NISBET

VIEW FROM SOUTHWEST

"CABAŃA TANGLEWOOD" FOR JAMES MOORE JR AND EARL NISBET
TANGLEWOOD CALIFORNIA 17 FEBRUARY 55 DESIGNER
EARL NISBET

boards adjacent to the tall glass exterior doors. In order to keep the cabana small, a three-foot unit system, (grid), was used instead of a more typical four-foot unit.

Balcony railings were constructed with the same lapped board detail with vertically cut-in mullion-type struts, spaced at three-foot centers for stability. Planter boxes of poured masonry were planted with native shrubs for low maintenance.

Constructed in 1954, the cabana was featured that year in a special issue of *Better Homes and Gardens* magazine.

HEMICYCLE FOR HARRY

Some years earlier, I'd been fortunate enough to purchase two lots, back to back, in the foothills about three miles west of Stanford University. At the time, I was too busy with other endeavors to consider building on either lot. Later, though, my brother, Harry remarked that he'd considered moving to that general area.

After showing Harry the two lots (each facing different streets), I suggested designing a house for myself on one lot and another for Harry's family on the adjoining property. He liked the idea and said he would give it some thought.

When Harry saw a photograph of the Jacobs' hemicycle house, (a two-story curved structure constructed of stone walls, wood, and glass. A berm of earth is packed against the stone walls, opposite the view walls, for insulation purposes) designed by Frank Lloyd Wright, he became so interested in the design, he asked if I would draw plans for a hemicycle home for

Hemicycle house for Mr. and Mrs. Harry Nisbet. General plan
:: 1954

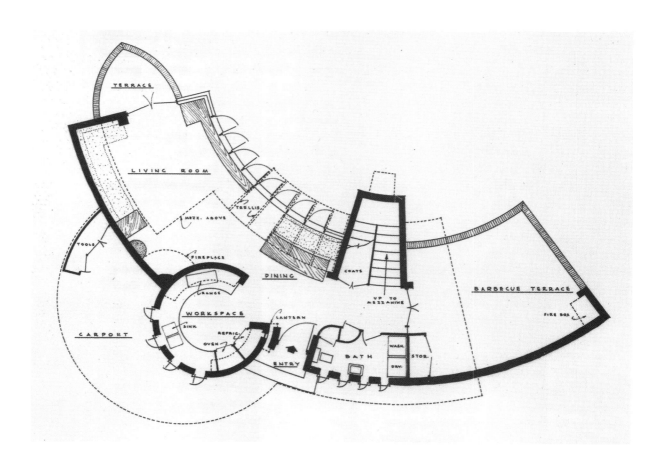

HOUSE IN BROOKSIDE PARK
WOODSIDE CALIFORNIA   2 NOV. '54
EARL NISBET   DESIGNER.

he and his family. Although Harry had seen photos and designs of many Wright houses, he seemed stimulated by the idea of living in a hemicycle house. Actually, the site would be appropriate for that particular shape because of the existing White Oak trees, and the slight slope of the ground. It also had a great sun orientation, plus a magnificent view to the south of a range of oak trees.

I asked my brother if he'd spoken to his wife about the possibility of living in a hemicycle. Responding that he "would talk to her soon," but not until I'd rendered a few drawings which, hopefully, would help her accept a house of such an unusual shape. I replied that we'd bet-

ter cross our fingers on that one, but that I would start work on the drawings.

After considering what would satisfy a young family on a limited budget, I soon had the plans ready for presentation to Harry. He could then tender the plans and perspectives to his wife (and good luck!). Still, I was skeptical about one of a pair deciding on plans for their future abode. Had he not been my brother, and being so elated about a hemicycle, I would not have been involved in this trying situation.

Harry liked what the drawings revealed about the views from the living room, dining room, and the master bedroom. He appreciated having two bathrooms, and was overjoyed

"Hemicycle for Harry".
View from Southwest.
Brick and redwood
boards
::1954

NEAR LEFT
Model of 3-piece con-
crete garden lantern
with author's logo for
openings
:: 1955

UPPER RIGHT
Base of 3-piece concrete
garden lantern with fin-
type legs. Constructed by
author as gift for clients
:: 1955

UPPER MIDDLE
Base and hexagonal
lantern portion of 3-piece
concrete garden lantern
constructed to interlock
:: 1955

LOWER MIDDLE
The hexagonal top of
3-piece concrete garden
lantern
:: 1955

LOWER RIGHT
Composite 3-piece
concrete garden lantern.
The completed lantern
is dove-tailed and held
together by gravity
:: 1955

with the terrace for relaxing and for barbecuing
on weekends. Neither his wife nor his young
daughter drove, so a one-car carport with storage area was sufficient After viewing my presentation, he hugged me, saying that he'd call
when he received affirmation from "the boss."

Although Harry had loved the drawings—to
the point of hiring a professional model builder
to construct a model of their future home—
somewhere along the way, his luck ran out. His
wife would have none of it. From the start of
this project, I'd felt that Harry's wife would veto
the drawings. She came from a prominent family and until she'd eloped with my brother, had
lived in a tastefully decorated Victorian house.
Sadly, I also felt that Harry would have been
quite happy in his hemicycle.

A GARDEN LANTERN

Sometime during the mid-1950s, I decided to
design and build a wooden form for the construction of concrete garden lanterns. This
would be one that I could reproduce and use
as gifts to clients for whom I'd designed buildings with appropriate gardens. I had been helping a friend redesign a new house he had under
construction, and I was able to complete the
forms in an extra carport space.

Up to this point, I'd had a negative feeling about the design of classical oriental garden lanterns with their hexagon-shaped top and round, or sometimes hexagonal, body perched on four legs. I didn't feel the four legs were appropriate to support a hexagonal lantern; so I worked out a design based on three legs shaped as fins, which gave the lantern better support.

The following photos show: (A) The fin-type-legs, (B) The hexagonal lantern, (C) The hexagonal top, (D) The completed lantern—dovetailed and held together by gravity.

BLOIS HOUSE AND FALCONER HOUSE

Before leaving for Taliesin, I had purchased two small lots in Portola Valley, California, from my carpentry earnings. I'd planned to build a house for myself, with an adjacent drafting studio for showing prospective clients my previous work.

The house would also contain an extra bedroom for my mother, should she choose to move from her home.

An article in the *San Francisco Chronicle,* about the Cabaña, changed all that. Richard M. Blois, an old friend from San Mateo High, had read the article and wished to meet with me. He was now an attorney, and he wanted to build a house for he and his wife near his office in Palo Alto. During our conversation, he learned about my property in Portola Valley. Soon, he convinced me to sell the lots to them, and design a small house on the property.

During the time I began work on the Blois house, I heard from a contractor in Palo Alto. He too had read the Cabaña article, and he asked that I meet his friends in Santa Cruz who wished to build a house on their property. After seeing photos of Cabaña Tanglewood, he felt sure they would ask me to design their house. A meeting was arranged with Mr. and

Blois House. Balcony off living room. Portola Valley, CA
:: 1955

Blois House. All habitable space above carport. Concrete block and mahogany : : 1955

RIGHT
Blois House. Living room and balcony over carport. Concrete block and mahogany : : 1955

Blois House. Bedroom wing. Concrete block and mahogany : : 1955

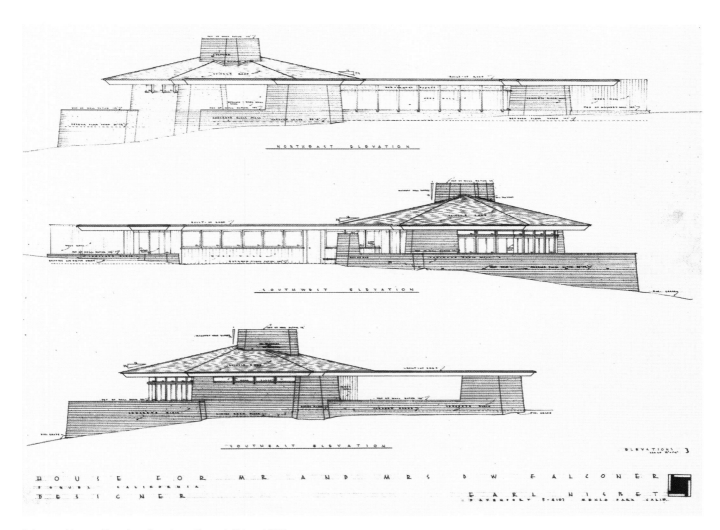

Falconer House. Exterior elevations. Soquel, CA :: 1955

Mrs. Donald Falconer; we visited the site together, and later discussed the project at their home. Soon, the contract was signed and several meetings followed before I decided to proceed with the drawings.

Having two clients at the same time was great. After completing a portion of the Blois house, we'd meet to discuss their work. I'd then proceed with drawings for the Falconer house, followed by meetings with them, and so on. I supervised the work on both houses, which were completed within weeks of each other.

ON ABSTRACTING FROM NATURE

Let me begin with a quote from Frank Lloyd Wright: "All natural forms are aggregates of simple elemental forms, geometric units, and subject to abstraction."

When an artist visualizes an impression of his inner feelings and conveys that impression in tangible form through his own medium to the observer or listener, this is the basis of organic design through abstracting from nature.

The main purpose of abstraction is to simplify natural forms, visualizing their underlying

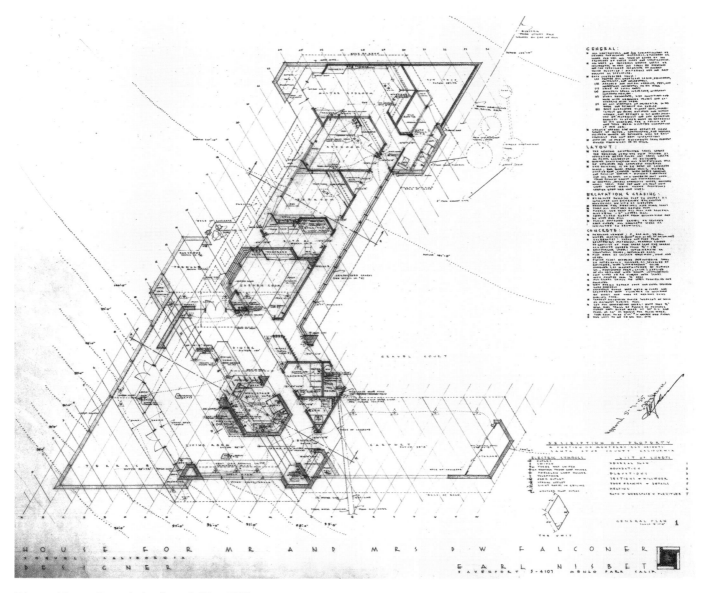

Falconer House. General plan. Soquel, CA :: 1955

attributes and assimilating the impression into the conscious mind. The designer is thus able to convert his mental images into abstract ideas as the inception for his design.

Human creativity demands freedom of the mind and the abstraction process begins by analyzing nature in the overall form, then proceeding to visualize the various parts that make up the whole. The abstracted parts, or units, give inspiration to the artist to produce a creative work more original than nature itself.

Frank Lloyd Wright found that natural ornamentation, natural materials, and natural colors contribute to, but do not in themselves make organic architecture. Mr. Wright first saw the desert in 1929 when he had a commission to

Falconer House.
Bedroom on left,
leisure room and
dining room, living
room and terrace
on right. Soquel, CA
:: 1955

BELOW
Falconer House.
View of bedroom
wing from carport.
Soquel, CA
:: 1955

Falconer House. View
from below. Soquel, CA
:: 1955

Falconer House. View from across canyon. Soquel, CA :: 1955

Falconer House dining
room, kitchen behind
shutters
: : 1955

design San-Marcos-in-the-Desert (a resort
hotel) for the Chandler, Arizona area. In 1937
he designed his own Taliesin West by way of
abstracting from its site, and nature, then generating the form of the buildings necessary for
his work. This new insight into creativity freed
him from the lingering traditions of Europe
and even freed him from his earlier mid-west
architecture.

   Designers must develop their own methods
to formulate organic design in architecture. It is
preferable to understand how Wright arrived at
his design than to simply copy his work. Once
you understand the underlying principles, there
is no end to the possibilities of variation. Some
design with an enormous number of sketches
and drawings, while others design in their mind
as Mr. Wright used to do. He was asked where
he came by all of his designs, and he stated he
simply shook them out of his sleeve.

   A final quote from Frank Lloyd Wright: "God
is the great mysterious motivator of what we

Falconer house. View from
leisure room past dining
room to living room
: : 1955

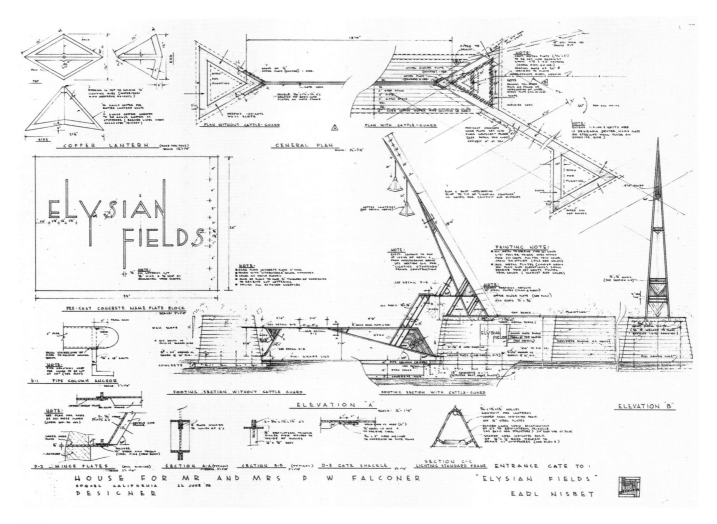

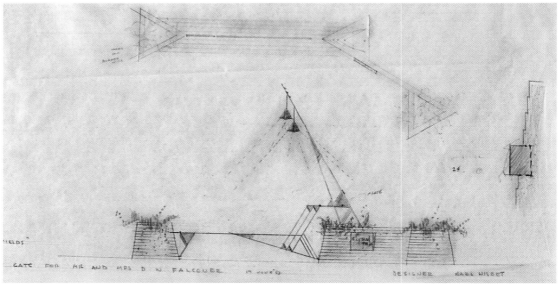

Cattle guard with plant
boxes for entrance to
Falconer House
:: 1958

Entrance gate and cattle guard for "Elysian Fields" named by the Falconers for their estate. Soquel, CA :: 1955

call nature, and it has been said often by philosophers, that nature is the will of God. And, I prefer to say that nature is the only body of God we shall ever see. If we wish to know the truth concerning anything, we'll find it in the nature of that thing." If a thought from me might be beneficial, remember also: Architecture is the art of being lucid with nature.

FALCONER'S OTHER HOUSE

In 1955 I first met with Mr. And Mrs. Donald Falconer to design a house for them, but they were undecided as to a site for their residence.

They owned 42 acres of land, which contained many possibilities for building, but they could not decide on a specific location.

I agreed to walk the acreage with them to offer suggestions as to ease of construction, sun control, etc. Together we narrowed the selection down to two sites, which of course, had their own amenities. Even with only two locations to consider, they still could not chose one over the other.

They had requested certain requirements for their house, and I mentioned to them each would be different because of where it would be constructed on their land.

Since they mulled it over for two weeks without a definite decision, I told them I would design a house for each site for them to consider.

Presented here is the house they did not choose to build.

Falconer House, Plan B. Floor Plan :: 1955

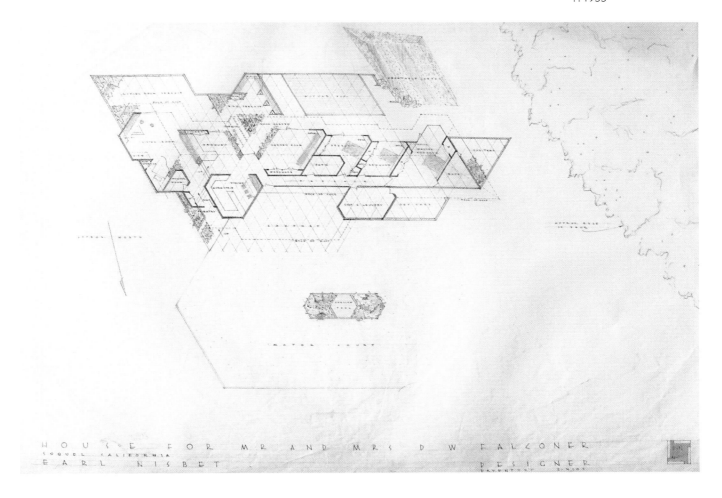

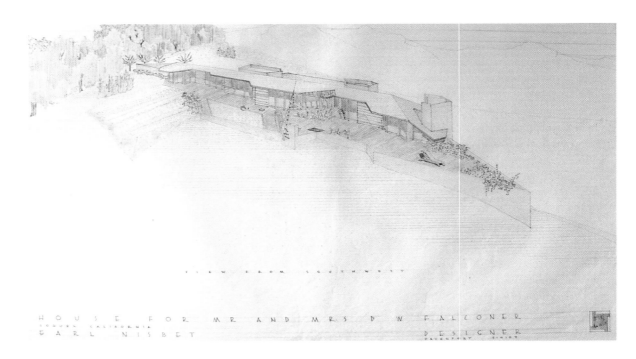

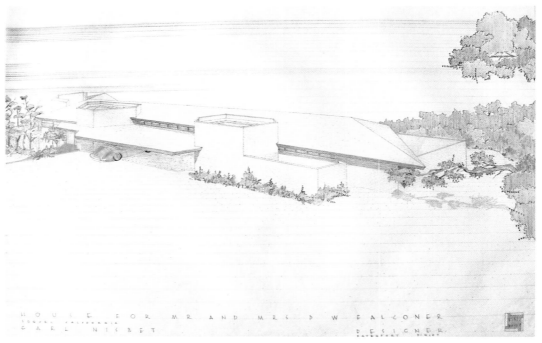

Falconer House, Plan B.
View from Southwest
:: 1955

Falconer House, Plan B.
View from Northeast
:: 1955

WOODEN MURAL FOR
MR. AND MRS. DON FALCONER

When the Falconer house was nearing completion, I presented Mr. And Mrs. Falconer with one
of my concrete Garden Lanterns as a "House-
warming" gift.

I also made a wooden mural for them to
hang at the entryway to their house.

What you see is a preliminary drawing, for

the development of scale drawings, for the execution of the mural in several different woods.

The colors you see here were only used as a study to indicate "depth" in the mural. The selection of woods were left in their natural state, but were of different colors, and shades of color to fabricate a mural which was more effective visually.

CANYON HOUSE

"Canyon House" was designed for a site in Los Trancos Woods, California, which is approximately eight miles west of the Stanford University campus.

Ted Bekins and his wife had seen drawings of the Blois house and asked me to design a

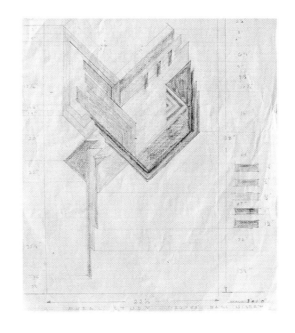

Preliminary drawing for wooden mural for Mr. and Mrs. Don Falconer

"Canyon House."
View from Northeast
:: 1954

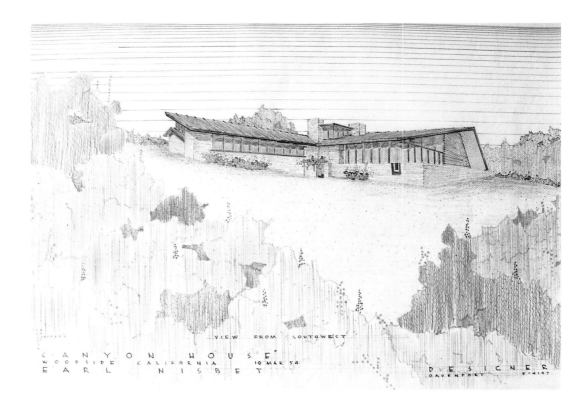

"Canyon House"
View from Southwest
:: 1954

Floor Plan for "Canyon
House" for Mr. and Mrs.
Ted Bekins. Los Trancos
Woods, CA
:: 1954

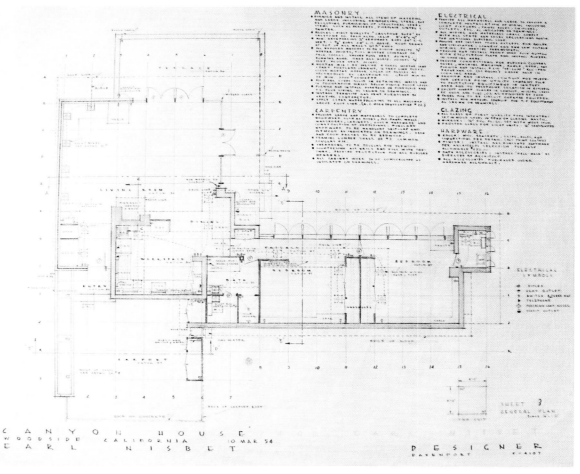

The accompanying drawing shows the development of a sketch of a fuchsia blossom, abstracting its main elements, and finally, developing a design for a copper hanging lantern based upon the reality of the original bloom : : 1954

small house for them situated among a cluster of white oaks.

The tranquil setting had a good orientation and the views were superb. They also did not require a great deal; therefore it did not take long to formulate what you see on page 109.

DRAWINGS AND COMMENTS

In order to help elucidate how the following drawings came into being, I feel a brief statement is in order.

Roger Gores, brother of mystery writer Joe Gores, was predisposed towards living in fascinating Carmel Valley, California, and for one reason or another, he asked me to develop something for him on two occasions, for two different parcels.

Jack Newman, owner of a photographic store in Burlingame, California, asked me to design a house for his small family on a superb 10-acre site. His requirement was to have few

Depicted here is the first of two studies for Joe Gore's brother, Roger Gores, who contemplated building on either of two sites, Carmel Valley, CA : : 1965

Second study for house for
Joe Gores' brother, Roger Gores.
Carmel Valley, CA
:: 1965

BELOW
"Skyline House" for Mr. and
Mrs. Jack Newman. General plan.
Owners requested as few interior
doors as possible. La Honda, CA
:: 1954

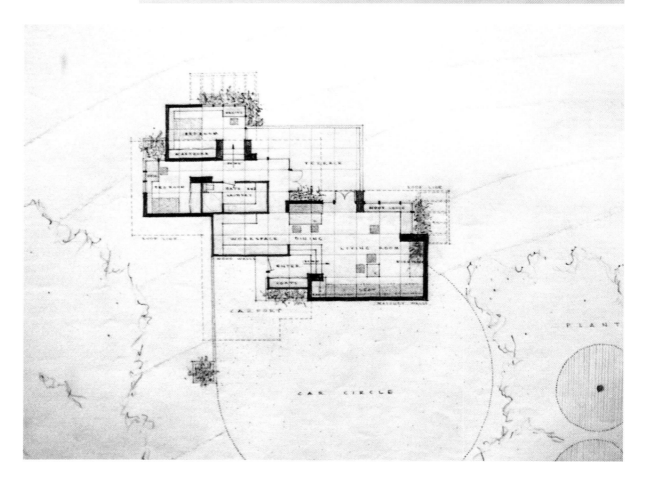

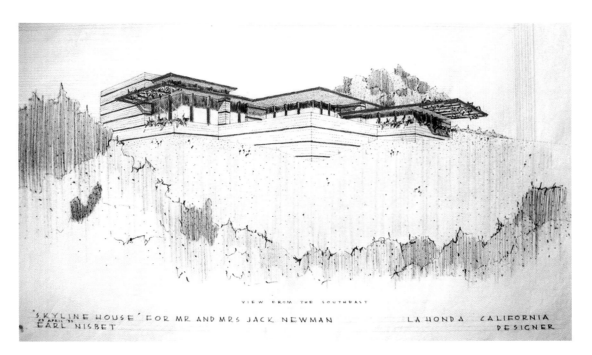

"SKYLINE HOUSE" FOR MR AND MRS JACK NEWMAN
EARL NISBET

LA HONDA CALIFORNIA
DESIGNER

House for Mr. and
Mrs. Jack Newman.
View from the
southeast. Concrete
block structure
with horizontal
shadow lines
:: 1954

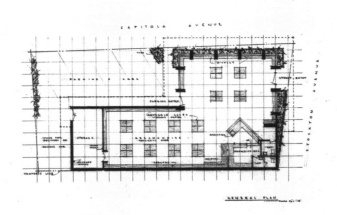

PHARMACY FOR DR AND MRS SEDGWICK
CAPITOLA CALIFORNIA   16 DEC 55
DESIGNER

EARL NISBET

Pharmacy for Dr. and Mrs. D. Sedgwick. General plan. Capitola, CA :: 1955

Pharmacy building
for Dr. and Mrs. D.
Sedgwick. View from
the southeast.
Capitola, CA
: : 1955

BELOW
House for Mr. and
Mrs. Roscoe M. Smith.
Los Altos, CA
: : 1955

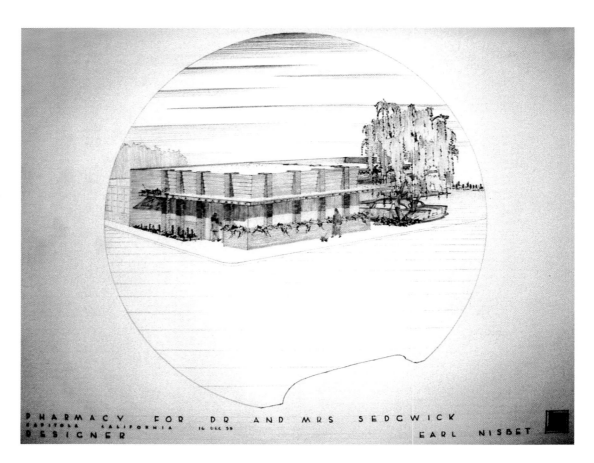

PHARMACY FOR DR AND MRS SEDGWICK
CAPITOLA   CALIFORNIA   16 DEC 55
DESIGNER   EARL NISBET

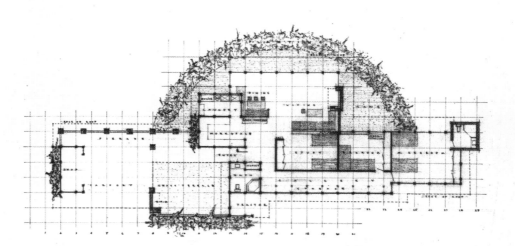

HOUSE FOR MR AND MRS ROSCOE M. SMITH
NEAR LOS ALTOS CALIFORNIA
EARL NISBET DESIGNER   DAVENPORT 5-4107

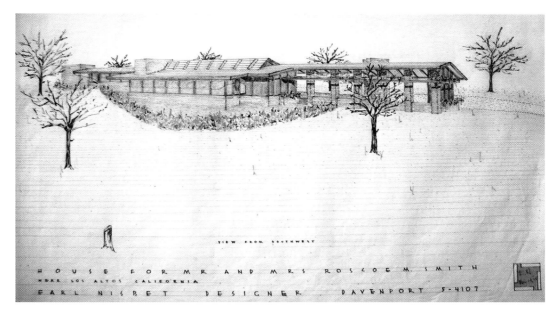

House for Mr. and
Mrs. Roscoe M. Smith.
View from the southwest
: : 1955

BELOW
Plan of house for Mr.
and Mrs. Harry V. Spade.
San Mateo County, CA
: : 1955

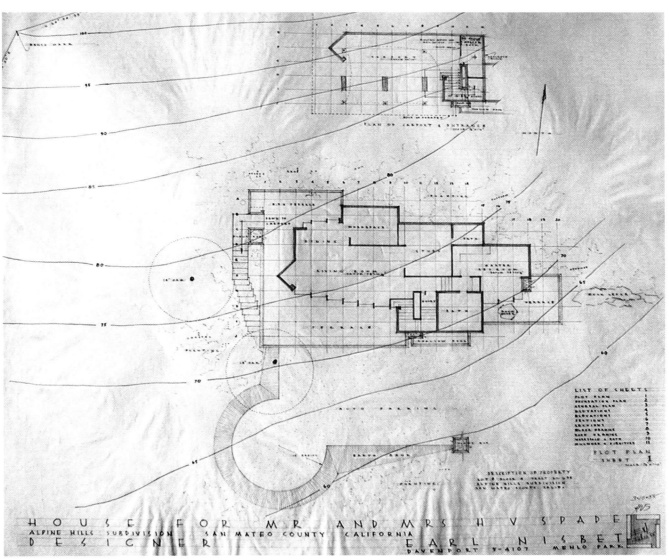

HOUSE FOR MR AND MRS H V SPADE
PINE HILLS SUBDIVISION   SAN MATEO COUNTY   CALIFORNIA
DESIGNER   EARL NISBET
                                   DAVENPORT 5-4107   MENLO PARK

House for Mr. and Mrs. Harry V. Spade. View from the southwest. Concrete block with horizontal shadow lines. Alpine Hills, CA ::1955

doors in the house, but keep the interior as open as possible.

Dr. Darrel Sedgwick owned a very small corner lot in the village of Capitola, California. He desired a small efficient pharmacy building with as many parking spaces that the site would allow.

Mr. and Mrs. Roscoe M. Smith had a lovely corner acre in Los Altos, California. The already constructed homes in the area were quite large and expensive. With their limited budget, I stretched the design of the house, in order to make it appear larger than it actually was.

Mr. and Mrs. Harry Spade, both realtors, had a corner site with a westerly view, in the foothills behind Stanford. To help with sun control, I set back the living room supporting posts

and provided their living space on the second floor level, allowing for a better view.

Mr. and Mrs. Fred Tate planned to produce skylights for dwellings and wanted their residence to become a showcase for their products.

Mr. and Mrs. Robert Michelson asked me to design an entrance gate, with light, for their residence in Atherton, California. They also requested a design for a glass and wood screen, which they would have fabricated for their living room and family room.

MY BROTHER HARRY

Although we were the best of friends, through the years my brother Harry and I had a constant mental battle running between us. We

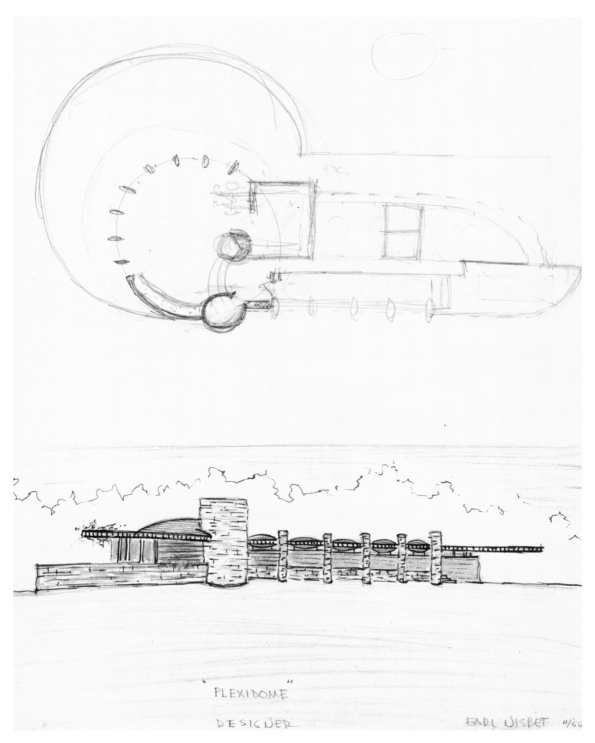

"PLEXIDOME"

DESIGNER   EARL NISBET 11/56

Preliminary drawing for Mr. and Mrs. Fred Tate. They desired to construct a dwelling using his company's skylights as a showcase for his products :: 1956

Mr. and Mrs. Robert Michelson of Atherton asked author to design a wood and glass screen for their living room and family room. They also wanted a lockable gate and light for their driveway entrance : : 1954

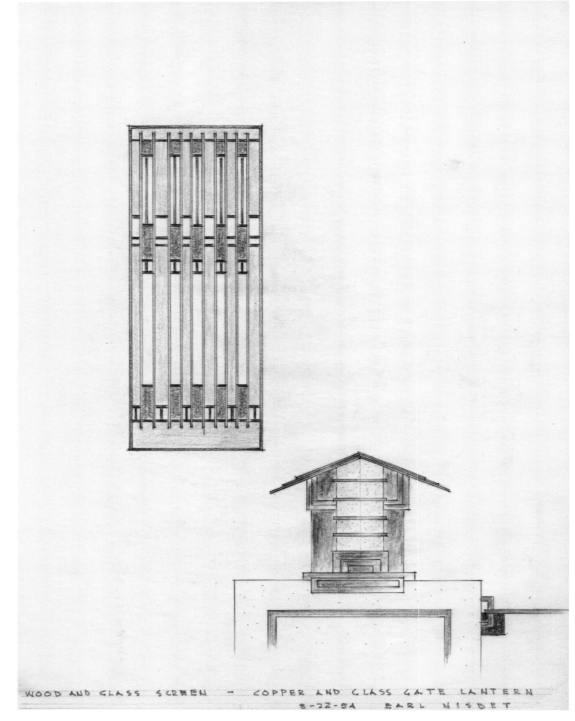

WOOD AND GLASS SCREEN - COPPER AND GLASS GATE LANTERN
8-22-54   EARL NISBET

were each tenacious in trying to devise an embarrassment to play upon the other, preferably while he would be in the company of relatives, or friends. These incidents were not meant to harm, just to make the other feel uncomfortable, embarrassed, or ill at ease for the moment.

We sometimes put our heads together to subject a friend to a portion of our particular type of mayhem. This particular event was actually directed at my brother's boss. They too, were good friends and lived just a few doors from each other, and shared carpooling to work.

My brother's boss had just purchased a new Volkswagen and was assiduously keeping records of the gas mileage on each of his trips to work and back. He would tell my brother he was getting thirty miles per gallon on the highway, and twenty-four in towns, and so forth.

I visited my brother and his family frequently, and I happened to be there when Harry's boss came to the house and stated he had just switched brands of gasoline and he anticipated better mileage because the engine seemed to be more powerful with this new fuel. He showed us his journal of his various trips and the mileage derived from them.

After he left for home I suggested to Harry we present his boss with a gift. Harry thought it would be a wonderful idea; so when the boss and his family rode off in their larger car, Harry and I walked to his bosses' house and proceeded to put a half-gallon of gasoline in the VW's tank.

I wasn't there, but in a few days, the boss called Harry excitedly on the telephone to tell him to be sure to purchase the new brand of gasoline for his car because the VW was now getting forty-four miles per gallon.

Harry was very patriotic and believed in the United States of America with every ounce of his energy. When World War II brought us into the fracas, he immediately tried to enlist, but a medical problem thwarted his aspirations.

He contributed to various causes, especially when it benefited service personnel, and he continued to help, where he could, long after the war was over.

I happened to visit him and his family one day after an appeal had gone out across the country for private citizens to contribute money for the refurbishing of the Statue of Liberty, which had fallen into disrepair. A neighbor was also there as he showed us a wall-sized Certificate of Acknowledgement for the generous contribution he had recently made on the statue's behalf.

He extolled the worthiness of the project, as a beacon to all the people in the world to look upon the United States as a haven for the oppressed. He went on and on until his neighbor and I said we would contribute to the noble cause.

A few weeks later there was enough money contributed to the cause, and the construction of the rebuilding started, with metal scaffolding surrounding and reaching the top of the lady with the torch.

A large photo of the statue and her scaffolding was published on the front page of a local newspaper. I cut the picture out of the newspaper and mailed it to my brother with a drawn arrow to a specific piece of scaffolding, near the top of the photo, which I labeled "Harry Nisbet's contribution."

I know he received the picture because he didn't speak to me for several weeks.

HARRY'S GOLF BALLS

My brother and his family decided to purchase a very large existing house on a half-acre site that was closer to his job. One evening, he called my mother to tell her they had finally moved, and settled into their latest real estate conquest and invited the two of us to spend the following weekend with them.

I drove us to their suburban house, which was in a subdivision of flip-flop floor plans; the main characteristic of the buildings was they were all painted white with gray trim. The only thing setting them apart from their neighbors was their street number.

We were shown through the house and garage, and we placed our overnight bags in our rooms. Since it was a Friday evening and past 5 pm, my brother brought out the vodka for the occasion. My mother was never one to drink alcohol of any type; so both my brother and I would serve her screwdrivers with half the vodka, and she thought the orange juice was delicious.

After downing a few, Harry took us to a nice restaurant for dinner and more conversation. The subject of golf came up and he told us he had purchased some special practice balls made of cotton, which you could hit as hard as you wanted, but they would only travel about twenty feet. He had been practicing with them already in his back yard, that was mostly a substantial lawn with a border of perennials planted next to the fence for low maintenance.

After dinner we went back to their new estate to retire for the evening. In the morning we told one another we had a good night's sleep while heading for the breakfast table. Soon after breakfast was over, Harry was anxious to show me the practice golf balls he thought so wonderful. He brought a dozen out from the garage, with some clubs, and lined the dozen up about eight inches apart. I noticed at that point that he could almost use regulation balls, since his lawn was about 120 feet across.

He was demonstrating how hard the balls could be hit when his wife called to tell him he was wanted on the phone. As he was leaving, he suggested I hit a few while he was gone. I took a swing at one of the practice balls, which looked quite similar to a regular golf ball, but when he went inside to answer the phone, I picked a green walnut from one of their trees and rushed into their garage where previously I noticed a shelf of spray paints. I grabbed a can of white paint and sprayed the walnut with a glorious white finish. It was still wet when I placed it in line with his practice balls,

but unless you got very close to it, you couldn't tell the difference.

I waited a bit and Harry rejoined me and I handed him his club. I had hoped my mother and Harry's wife would come outside with him, but there was just the two of us to witness what happened next.

He swung as hard as he could, and the practice balls landed about 30 feet away, but he was also trying to get them to land close to each other as part of his practice. When he got to the walnut I had painted, he again swung with all his might and the walnut exploded into a thousand small particles, and my brother's jaw dropped a foot as he looked at me while his eyes looked as large as saucers. When I started laughing, it didn't take him long to realize he had been had.

Neither he nor I mentioned it over the weekend, and I didn't tell my mother until we were on our way home.

The next afternoon was Sunday. Harry and I were imbibing a bit in chairs under a large umbrella at the rear of the house, and he decided he was going to mow the lawn, and he wanted me to see his new gasoline-powered mower that pulled itself over the lawn, no pushing required.

He brought it out from the garage, and after explaining its numerous features, he started the monster and proceeded to cut the errant grass. In a few minutes of watching him walk back and forth, back and forth, I could see the futility of the situation. I went over to him and had him shut off this new and powerful implement because I wanted to talk to him. After conferring with him for a few seconds, he brought out two small portable tables and we placed one at each end of the lawn with our chairs and our drinks. Now we were in business, he started the machine up again, and pointed it at me. It truly was a wonderful workhorse as it plodded along cutting a swath in the tundra all the way to my table where I turned it around and pointed it at Harry, who after sipping his drink, got to his feet and turned it around and pointed it at me. In forty-five minutes we were finished with the lawn, no sweat.

TAHITI

After completing Cabaña Tanglewood, the Blois house, and the Falconer house, I worked for the next three years in two architect's offices. One of them told me of a wealthy banker from New Zealand he had met during World War II, and wanted to help him open an office in Auckland, but his wife said she would not leave California and therefore he would not be going. I had worked for this architect for approximately two years, and we had become friends. He liked my work and said he would telephone the banker and recommend me to open an office down under. It seems the banker would provide loans on houses his builder friend would construct, but they wanted someone to design California-style houses. In a few days, I

had a letter of introduction to the banker, with his business and his residential address.

I informed Mary Lou of my plans to hopefully do well in Auckland, and at a later date, I would send for her. I felt it would be best for us to live apart from in-laws, but she was not at all happy with this turn of events.

Since there was no definite date I should arrive in Auckland, I thought I would route the trip through Tahiti, as that was a place I had always wanted to see.

I had to get a passport, so I drove to San Francisco to begin the processing, but I found out that they wanted a U.S. citizen to witness my signature. Joe Gores had been living and working in San Francisco, so I went to see him at his apartment.

I told Joe about the architectural possibilities in New Zealand, and when I mentioned I wanted to visit Tahiti on the way, he said, "Where's Tahiti?" He hadn't heard of Tahiti at that point in

Joe Gores observing author practicing his "abandon-ship drill" aboard the S.S. Wairuna to Tahiti. Los Angeles Harbor : : 1957

The nefarious Quinn's
Bar, Papeete, Tahiti
: : 1957

RIGHT
Tahitians dancing at the
nefarious Quinn's Bar,
Papeete, Tahiti
: : 1957

his life, so I suggested we go to a travel office
and pick up some brochures; I had left mine at
home. When he read the literature, he decided
he would go with me; he could take some time
off of the "repo" work he had been doing.

At this time in his life Joe had done a lot of
writing, and had submitted several articles to
various magazines, but he hadn't sold much. He
said, "Why don't we do a couple of articles on
Tahiti while we are there?" I'll do the writing
and you shoot the photos." "Fine," I said, and
he mentioned he would send queries off to
several magazines. Soon we had the affirmative
from *National Geographic*, *True* magazine, and a
travel magazine.

When we planned our trip, one could only
get to Tahiti by private yacht or commercial
freighter. We checked the yellow pages and
saw an advertisement stating that a New Zealand freight line took passengers on their ships
bound for the South Pacific. We went to their

was crammed with drawings, instruments, pencils, pens, triangles, etc., for the future office.

While on board the freighter we met the captain and the other four passengers. Joe and I strolled the decks and we would occasionally see a whale spouting in the distance. When we went to the bow of the ship, we would see porpoises swimming adjacent to the bow, and swimming as fast as the ship. Then, on occasion, a flying fish would sail out of the ocean and land on deck. They would look so helpless, just flapping about, so we would fling them back into the sea.

We arrived at Papeete, Tahiti at dusk, and we were told the captain would not be taking passengers ashore until the next morning. We were excited to be there, although we could not see much, even as the lights of the town began to come on.

I had wanted to go to Tahiti for such a long time; it was difficult for me to go to bed that evening. Both Joe and I set our alarm clocks for an early rise and we were on deck again just before the sun came up. When it did rise, it shone over the top of the mountain that was the backdrop for Papeete. I took a great picture of Papeete with the sun rising just behind one

office and found out that the passenger capacity for their two different-sized ships was either six or twelve passengers. When we selected the day for our departure, we found we would be sailing on the smaller six-passenger ship.

I brought with me two footlockers for the trip. One was filled with clothing and the other

Papeete police chief Luis Babo, with vahine, dancing in Quinn's Bar, Tahiti :: 1957

of the masts of the ship, and the entire shoreline was in an ethereal misty atmosphere. Later on, Joe sent it in to a magazine that was having a photo contest for money, but it was stolen, and we never got it back.

Soon a motor launch came to bring the passengers ashore. I made arrangements to temporarily store my footlockers at the freight company's office while Joe and I perused the town. It was only a few blocks long, and in a couple of hours, we had seen quite a bit of the area including having beer at the well-known nefarious bar called Quinn's Tahitian Hut. We ordered two beers at the bar and sat down at a table close to the front door. We had just touched the glasses to our lips when two girls came up to us and asked us to buy them beers as they proceeded to sit with us. Joe immediately went to the bar for two more cold ones while I was trying to comprehend their names. The girls spoke French and Tahitian, but English, my only language, limited me considerably. Joe

An interisland seaplane prepares to land at Papeete, Tahiti. Yachts are tied to the quay in front of the island's main hotels. :: 1957

had taken French in college and he was able to keep our conversation flowing.

After re-introductions, Joe told me my girl friend's name was Delphine and his was Claudette. He then told the girls our names, but neither of them could pronounce my name. It seemed simple enough, but as hard as they tried, it never came out quite right. Frustration was beginning to set in as they tried a couple of times more, and they both began to frown.

Finally I told Joe to tell them my name was Jimmy, like the name of my best friend in California. Jimmy wanted to come with us, but he could not leave his new and growing business without losing everything he had ventured for the past three years. Immediately, both girls gave us angelic smiles that shone from ear to ear. They were happy they could pronounce Jimmy. So for the rest of my stay in Tahiti, I went by the name Jimmy.

A few beers later, Delphine and Claudette literally pulled Joe and me to the dance floor because Tahitian dance music had just started

Author and his vahine Paulette and friends. Tahiti :: 1957

PHOTO: JOE GORES

on the nearby jukebox. The music was exciting and made you want to dance, but even men's hips must sway to and fro with the beat of the music. It was fun to try, but I was never able to accomplish the necessary motion.

Joe told me the girls had been good friends all through their school years and now they

Papeete harbor, a relatively "sleepy village" in 1957 as seen from the Stuart Hotel Balcony

Skipper Tony Armit and author viewing Cook's Bay, in Moorea, from an adjacent hilltop
:: 1957

My Tahitian vahine Chiro
:: 1957

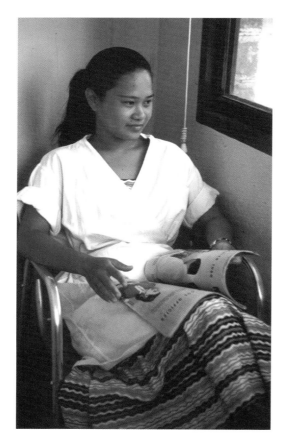

spent most of their time in and around bars, drinking and dancing. We downed another round of beers and the girls told us to come to their room with them. We only had to walk a few blocks to a two-story building where they had been renting sleeping space on the second floor; they did not have rooms, they had part of a room. A large open space had been partitioned off with hanging rugs separating the dormitory-like bed areas. It was cool and clean, but it seemed a bit odious to not see the dozen or so beds in the space, but you could hear clocks ticking.

The next morning they showed us one of their favorite places for breakfast, and it was actually nice to have some solid food to compensate for the beer we indulged in the night before.

We checked the prices of the hotels near the waterfront and decided we would go to an inexpensive hotel we heard of just a few blocks away from downtown Papeete.

After dinner in town, we walked to the hotel we had been told about and checked into our

Tahiti's masses arrive to see the first Matson passenger liner dock at Papeete. The begining of the end of tranquil days :: 1957

rooms. Joe's room was on the second floor, as was mine, about six doors away.

After reading some literature I had picked up in town, I went to sleep. About three o'clock in the morning, I woke up to see a very large native holding a very large club over his head. It seemed as though he wanted to hit me, but fortunately there was an old grandmotherly woman with long white hair holding onto his arm, as though she didn't want him to club me.

I spoke up in English, "What do you want? What do you want?" as I backed into the corner of the room while sitting on the bed. Neither of them spoke a word; I was spooked by then and called out, "Joe! Joe, come here!" In a short time I heard Joe running toward my room, and by the time he got there, both the native with the club and the grandmother were gone. The next day we found out, in Tahiti, they call these visions of people *tu pow pow*, or ghosts.

The hair was still standing out on the back of my neck, and I continued to shake even after Joe put the light on, and all was bright. I dressed and we went to Joe's room so he could dress, then we left the hotel to go down to the water where we sat on an overturned pirogue and talked about the experience till dawn.

I dreaded going back to that hotel again; so we looked around town and found another hotel later in the day. The price was about four times the cost of staying in the first hotel, so we decided to keep looking for something cheaper.

The next night we went to Bar Lea, one of the local bars, for refueling of beer and peanuts. On the way back to our new hotel, we were walking in the street and we noticed a car that came slowly up to us from behind. We both looked over our shoulders and saw it was a police car. We thought we might not need our new hotel as we might be thrown in jail for streetwalking. We soon found out it was the

TOP
Author's Tahitian vahine Lois

BOTTOM
Photo used in *True* magazine (July 1959). Article by Joe Gores : : 1957

police chief of Papeete and he just wanted to talk to us. He saw we were larger than most men on the island and asked us if we worked out with weights. We said we did, and he said he thought so because of the size of our shoulders. He said he too worked out with weights and just wanted to talk about the sport.

We became good friends with Chief Luis Babo, and we went to a gymnasium with him from time to time. Later on he even lent us his private automobile so we could drive around the island to take pictures.

We mentioned our experience with the two hotels we encountered and that we needed less expensive quarters. In a day or two he gave us a ride in a police car to a small two-bedroom thatch-roofed house which we could rent for sixty dollars a month. That was great; we could stay in Tahiti for several weeks at that rate.

After moving into the small house, we purchased two used bicycles to ride back and forth to town. We also purchased two underwater Tahitian spear guns in order to snorkel for fish. On the house property there was a lime tree at the kitchen window, a breadfruit-tree, bananas, papaya, and a large grapefruit tree; so we had access to a great deal of free food. Rice was inexpensive, and while riding our bicycles to town and back, we would see people selling coffee, bread, honey, brown-sugar, and so on at reasonable prices.

Joe started to write three articles, and he told me the kind of photos he would like me to try and shoot to accompany each of them. I took pictures of several areas of the island that might work well for National Geographic with lakes, mountains, trees, flowers, waterfalls, horses, buildings, boats, people working, playing and so forth. By this time we had met a nice young man, part Tahitian, part Chinese, who ran a small photo shop, and he would process our colored photos while I developed and printed the black-and-white shots.

We would also talk to skippers of small boats at the pier from time to time. We became friends of three young men from Vancouver, B.C. who invited us to sail with them on their yacht, a twenty-six-foot ketch, for a trip to Moorea, which was only about eight or ten miles away; the overcrowding would not play a major difficulty for such a short trip. They had named their boat *Jopeda*, taking the first two letters of their own names. John, Peter, and David.

MOOREA

It is said that the island of Moorea, with its trident shape, was formed from the water about three million years ago. It now is the home of 12,000 inhabitants concentrated in the many villages located seaside. Because of the short distance to the Island of Tahiti, Moorea sometimes is referred to as the Sister Island. The name Moorea means yellow lizard, from a legend where a large yellow lizard swished its tail and opened two bays.

Moorea sometimes has been described as a gigantic garden with tropical scents, vanilla being the most prominent, and an abundance of trees, cool rivers and waterfalls. It is also surrounded by a barrier reef with twelve passes, allowing ferries and pleasure craft admittance.

The first European to explore Moorea was Captain James Cook in 1769, but he didn't visit the entire island on that voyage.

A famous building, the octagonal Ebenezer Church at Papetoai, was built on the site of the ancient Taputaputuatea Marae, a temple for the local religion, in 1827, making it the oldest building in the South Pacific.

We accepted the boy's kind offer to sail with them, and in a couple of days we anchored in Cook's Bay, and we were truly amazed at the beauty of the high cliffs seemingly growing out of the water. The five of us dove into the clear, blue water and swam for a short time. The rest of the crew had gotten back aboard the Jopeda and I was swimming in the bay by myself, when I saw a very large school of small white fish coming toward me. I submerged a few feet below the surface to see what would happen if I just stayed in place as they got closer. When they got close to me, they reminded me of a crocheted veil, and then they opened up and swam past me before closing ranks. It was a thrill I will never forget, and in the eight months that followed, I never experienced that circumstance again.

The boys had their own bicycles aboard the Jopeda and Joe and I borrowed them one day to bicycle around the island. Every mile, and every turn we encountered, was filled with breathtaking beauty.

We stayed a few more days in Moorea before sailing back to Papeete.

WILLARD BASCOM

Willard Bascom was born in Bronxville, New York in 1916 of a single mother. He was described as an ocean engineer, diver, and ocean adventurer as well as a maverick innovator, and passionate about art and science. He studied poetry, music, painting, photography, cinematography, and underwater archaeology.

In his teens, during the great depression, he worked on the Delaware Aqueduct Tunnel project. He then studied mining at the Colorado School of Mines. He subsequently worked as a mining engineer in Arizona, Idaho, and Colorado.

His career in ocean science began in 1945 when he joined John Isaacs to work as a research engineer, first at Berkeley and later at Scripps Institute of Oceanography (SIO). He lived in Monterey after the war and was a good friend of John Steinbeck. He was a member of John Isaacs' scientific party during the Bikini Atoll atomic bomb test.

Willard Bascom's career was like a many-faceted polished diamond; he had many interests, and he was very successful in the many feats he performed.

In 1954, he joined the staff at the National Science Foundation, where he organized and directed the first phase of Project Mohole, the first effort to drill in deep water through the earth's crust. He began this in 1961, and they drilled at depths of 11,000 feet near Guadalupe, Mexico. They collected samples of the earth's second layer, and measured the temperature increase 600 feet below the bottom of the seafloor. Steinbeck wrote an article about it for *Life* magazine.

He pioneered undersea exploration for diamonds, discovering about 20 million carats of gem diamonds for De Beers Diamond Company. He also found lost objects and ships on the seafloor. He was also responsible for the recovery of salvaged airplane parts and bodies from two jet planes that crashed in the ocean near Los Angeles, California. He then discovered a long-lost sunken galleon, Nuestra Senora de las Maravillas.

Bascom continued with undersea search in Greece, finding a wreck off Cape Artemision that yielded three high quality bronze statues for the Greek National Museum. He was also involved in the successful search and recovery of gold treasure from the Civil War sidewheel steamer *Brother Jonathan* that sunk off the northern California coast in 1865.

The thatched-roof house where Joe and I were living was located between Papeete and Point Venus, which is the most northern portion of the island of Tahiti, and we were only two blocks from Matavi Bay that had a beautiful white sand beach; the fish for snorkeling were plentiful.

One morning we had walked to the beach in order to obtain some fish for dinner, and we happened on an American who was also about to do some spearfishing. He introduced himself as Willard Bascom, and we discovered that Willard Bascom was a highly intelligent man with a great deal of knowledge on many subjects. That was the beginning of a close relationship with him and his wife during our stay in Tahiti.

The Bascoms would invite us to dinner at their house, which was on the beach, and quite close to ours, and we would reciprocate when the fishing was exceptional.

Willard's wife, Rhoda, let Joe and me know that she was going to have a surprise birthday party for him in a few days, and we were invited, along with several of their friends. It just happened that the day before the party was to occur, Joe and I were doing some spear-fishing in shallow water. Joe speared a small octopus and he could neither retrieve his spear from the creature, nor could he get it loose from the coral it was attached to. He called to me to help him, so I shot my spear into the organism and we both tugged for some twenty minutes before we conquered it.

Since it was going to be Willard's birthday the following day, I suggested that we give it to him as a present. We found a magnum-sized bottle with a large opening and cleaned it and removed the labels. We then stuffed the octopus into the bottle, careful to have all of its suction cups showing against the glass. We next melted wax to act as a stopper and gift-wrapped it, placing a large red bow on the top. It looked as though he would be receiving wine or rum for his birthday.

When he opened the bottle on his birthday, he started laughing and we thought he would never stop.

The next evening Joe and I were invited to an octopus dinner, which Rhoda had cooked in coconut milk, and it was so delicious that I still think of it now and then.

Since the Bascoms had an automobile, Joe and I would occasionally go into Papeete with them for dinner, or just go bar-hopping and dancing. No matter where we found ourselves, we always had a great evening.

The island of Tahiti is divided by an isthmus at the village of Taravao, which separates Tahiti Nui, containing about two-thirds of the land area, from Tahiti Iti, containing the other third of the land area.

Since we were able to borrow Luis's automobile, Joe and I drove around Tahiti, including Tahiti Iti, several times in order to obtain various photographs. We wanted to sell to *National Geographic*, because they always included several photos in their articles. We even climbed Mt. Orohena, the tallest mountain (7352 feet) on the island, in order to find interesting views.

On one of the drives around Tahiti I was alone, because Joe wanted to stay at the house and write, and I happened upon the lake where Gauguin had painted a famous scene containing a white horse. What made the hair on the back of my neck stand out was the fact that there was a white horse standing in approximately the same location as in the painting.

One night Luis, the chief of police, invited us to go to a boxing match with him as he was going to referee the bout. The two combatants were welterweights and both were native Tahitians. Luis explained the rules to the fighters and round one began. They seemed to be equally matched for about the first six rounds, but one man started to tire, and his adversary got a heavy punch through the exhausted man's defenses; he was out on his feet, and he fell, rigid as a board, backwards hitting the back of his head on the floor; he was out like a light.

Smelling salts were administered without success and water was splashed on his face with similar results. Finally an ambulance was called and he was taken, still unconscious, to the hospital and x-rayed. The doctors found out the fighter had been in the French Navy, and upon receiving a head injury, the surgeons had placed a metal plate over his brain. He never should have been fighting, but he loved the sport, and he felt he should let the devil take the hindmost. He lived, but we have to assume that was his last fight.

QUINN'S BAR

When Joe and I arrived in Tahiti, Papeete was a sleepy seaside town with a few yachts tied to the quay along the main street, which was across from the best hotel in town, the Hotel Stuart. There were low buildings everywhere, forming the nucleus of Polynesian society in an extraordinary land and climate. Near the Hotel Royal Papeete, large banyan trees cast their shade throughout the park, which has a public water tap by the village washhouse, where women come to wash their clothing and pareos of many-colored designs. And you can listen to them chatting to each other in French or Tahitian. You become enchanted by this most engaging mood, and obviously friendly conversation.

Walking from the washhouse, on the dirt street, past the Hotel Stuart around the corner on the wooden walkway, one arrives at Quinn's Tahitian Hut, the wicked, wicked bar. Sometimes during the day, it looks quite respectable, with few clients, since the wild times usually begin later in the evening.

During the first three weeks living in hotels, in town, sometimes you would go back to your room and find women in your bed that you had never seen before. They were known as Quinn's girls or *town girls*. They were in a class all by themselves. They would throw themselves at you, wanting to be your vahine, (permanent girlfriend). If you happened to run out of money, they will do your laundry, con beer from tourists, find you a place to sleep, and even bring you food from time to time.

The town girls are well-known, and are the most available for most Americans, but nearly any girl in Tahiti, be they Tahitian, Chinese or French will be your vahine if she will go out with you at all. Tahiti has no professional virgins, illegitimacy doesn't exist, and there is no stigma attached to unwed motherhood.

You are never certain how Quinn's girls will act in different circumstances. You might see three or four of them wrestling, kicking, and biting a French sailor, all the while being barebreasted, then a few hours later see them, including the French sailor they were fighting with, having a beer at some bar.

Once, a bearded Englishman gave two town girls a bad time and he would not buy them breakfast the following morning; so later in the afternoon, when he was sleeping, they went into his hotel room and cut off his beard on just one side of his face. It was only when he saw himself in a mirror in Quinn's Bar a few hours later that he realized why everyone was laughing.

Quinn's could provide you with beers from around the world, but the beer most patrons drank was a local beer called Hinano, which never got a chance to age, since it was from a small brewery; therefore it was usually green in color. If you drank too much of it, for too many days, it might catch up with you and give you a bout of Montezuma's revenge, South Pacific style.

Of course no matter what brand of beer you have been consuming, sooner or later you would have to excuse yourself to go to the bathroom. At that time Quinn's bar had a lavatory like I had never seen before. There was only one room for both sexes. As soon as you opened the bathroom door you saw a long, stand-up stall for the men on the left side of the room. At the rear of the room were a few closed stalls for women, or men, if gentlemen were serious about what they were there for. I believe some women tourists went back to their hotel rather than experience the washroom.

As far as the men were concerned, they had to be careful while relieving themselves. If it happened to be a Quinn's girl, or town girl, they might reach around you to help you direct your stream, then run laughing into a stall.

One evening, we had been drinking Hinano with our new vahines, Marie France and Doris. As we were going out the front door of the bar, the two girls, wearing nothing above the waist, grabbed Joe's bicycle and rode up and down the street in front of the Stuart Hotel for an hour and a half, laughing like crazy. They continued falling over every few yards until their elbows and knees were raw and bleeding.

The next morning, after breakfast, Joe and I decided we needed a day of rest; so we told the girls we were going to take them into the country for a swim and to lie in the sun. They liked the idea, and after packing some food, we hired a driver who had a large Chrysler convertible for the day. We went to a delightful freshwater pool where we could dive and swim. Joe's vahine danced a hula wrapped in a sarong, until it fell off and she made a fast dive into the water. Afterwards the girls gathered flowers for tiares and couronnes, splitting the tough-fibered grass stems and threading the blossoms on them, using reeds for needles.

Late in the afternoon, our driver took us back to town; he charged three dollars for the day.

We would see our friends from the Jopeda every few days or so to keep in touch. When they left Vancouver, none of them had ever sailed before, but they were heading around the world. None of them knew navigation and they didn't have a radio that worked. With all this against them, they somehow hit the Marquesas Islands after forty days at sea, they planned to take on supplies and stay there a week. Some four months later they set sail for Tahiti. They expected to lie over for two weeks, but they were still in Papeete after five months, and broke. They sold everything that they could from the Jopeda so they could be off again. I even purchased a portable typewriter from David to help with their financial situation.

Joe and I had a farewell beer with them, which started in the morning that continued into the afternoon, and wore on until evening; finally the next day, loaded with tiares and couronnes, they set sail.

A few weeks later word came from the Cook Islands that the Jopeda had been demolished on a reef at Raratonga and sunk; it was a bit of hard luck. They all survived, and were disappointed at not getting all the way around the world, but at least they saw Tahiti.

Shortly after they left, Joe and I met two more friends, Tony Armit and Tig Loe, on their 28-foot ketch, Marco Polo, for another cruise to Moorea. They had been on a three-year world cruise and would soon be heading home to Auckland, New Zealand. We anchored in Pao Pao Bay, one of the most beautiful anchorages in the world. You would see fishermen in out-riggers working with lighted torches well into the night, and at the same time you would hear singing from the nearby village. We would talk on deck while the sun was setting, and shortly the moon would peek over the tall, sharp-faced mountain, which made the bay.

As we talked, Tony said, "I'm glad we met you chaps; sometimes we go six months with-out meeting anyone our own age."

Joe put in, "I thought there was a lot of guys knocking around the world."

Tony shook his head and continued, "Not as many as you'd think. Too many chaps want security, marriage, house, and a car; they don't want to take a chance after that."

Two weeks later the Marco Polo was off on its final 3,000 miles for home where they plan to sell the yacht and purchase a larger one to sail the South Pacific indefinitely.

MOVIES IN TAHITI

In the past, movies were hard to come by and there were so few in Tahiti, the same movies would be shown time and time again, and of course the patrons would get bored knowing what was to happen next. Finally the projectionist had a brilliant idea on show-ing an old western which everyone had already seen a dozen times. The night Joe and I happened to be in the audience to see this western, everyone was screaming at watching the cowboys jumping off their horses and running backwards. Of course, the film operator was running John Wayne in reverse.

Announcements had been posted all around Papeete for one and all to come to a free movie which had just arrived. The movie people were invited to see was a new release of the 1935 film Mutiny on the Bounty, directed by Frank Lloyd and based on the novel by Charles Nordhoff and James Norman Hall.

Charles Laughton played Captain Bligh, the evil and sadistic tyrant who has his men flogged, keelhauled, etc. at the drop of a hat. Clark Gable played first mate Fletcher Christian, portrayed as a fair and magnanimous officer who is involved in the mutiny, and sets Bligh and his followers adrift in a boat with little food and water rather than appeasing the mutineers who wish Bligh killed.

The movie was filmed in Tahiti, and it was being shown with subtitles so everyone could follow the story. You could hear the audience groan when a seaman was being flogged or some such sadistic act was taking place.

Neither Joe nor I nor some of the American sailors in the audience could understand the outburst from the audience in the scene where Bligh and Christian and some of the crew had come ashore to meet the white-haired King of Tahiti, and offered him an alcoholic beverage when they sat down to eat. The old gentleman, with striking facial features, holds up both hands in protest and says he doesn't approve of alco-hol because it is bad.

At this point, everyone in the audience burst out laughing at his remark, and we didn't find out what caused the eruption until after the film. It seems Hollywood had hired this hand-some old man to play the Tahitian chief, but in reality he was the town drunk.

JULY 14: BASTILLE DAY

Joe and I could hardly wait until July 14 arrived, as that date, in Tahiti, is much like the Olympics in America. It happens each Bastille Day when the entire South Pacific competes with one another in Papeete. There are native dances, races, pirogue racing with men and women competing, spearing coconuts atop a thirty-foot pole, music contests, costume contests and several other competitions.

The Fete, as the locals call it, is supposed to last for four days; however if everyone is still enjoying himself, it goes on longer. The year we were there, it lasted fifteen days. There is a great deal of biere Hinano consumed during the festivities, and after fifteen days, everyone was spent.

It is quite majestic with everyone wearing colorful pareos or grass skirts with tiares and couronnes adorning the heads and necks of the contestants. Music may begin at any moment, and soon you will see undulating hips of both men and women in competition for prizes.

When the daytime events are over, most of the attendees move to one of several bars in and around Papeete to drink, sing, dance, and drink to the beat of the music; mostly, they drink! Surprisingly, when the bars finally close in the wee hours of the morning, approximately 20 percent of the transients then board Le Truck (bus) to be driven to Lafayette, another dance hall out in the country, that never closes. Joe and I only went to Lafayette once; it was much too exhausting for us, and we didn't even have to get up in the morning to go to work. Yes, it's true, some people in Tahiti actually have jobs and have to work for a living.

Once in a while meandering the streets of Papeete, Joe and I would run into an old salt from bygone days, who'd jumped ship and decided to spend the rest of his life in Tahiti. He was known locally as New Zealand Jim, and must have had some pull with some local government official, because he had already been here for years. Usually the police intervene and put you on a boat if they catch you overstaying your welcome of six months.

Joe and I sat with him in a Chinese restaurant one evening while we were having noodle soup with one hand and pushing away hungry cats with the other. When our conversation drifted to women, he said, "The thing about Papeete is the girls, laddie. That's the truth. I'll tell 'em, if you stay with old Jim, it's a hundred

francs in the morning and a pack of cigarettes and bugger a thing more, and they'll stay. If you're a bloody millionaire and don't suit 'em, it's to hell with you. No sir, I say, stay here and get all you can while you're a young buckó it's a crazy, bloody world outside."

He told us about a honeymoon couple from Hawaii who had a room next to his at the Stuart. The bride arrived starry-eyed but inhibited; a week later she flew back to Hawaii-for a divorce. "She couldn't stand the competition," he explained. "Tahiti turned that buck into a bloody wild man, laddie, it was two months after she left before his money was gone."

Joe and I saw another couple from California who tried to honeymoon in Tahiti, but in this case the groom sometimes didn't even get back to his hotel room for two or three days. His new wife left for home within the week.

If the girls don't like you, they don't like you. The movie actor Edmond O'Brien made reservations to spend a month at the Stuart. He arrived while we were there, but he had a difficult time obtaining a vahine. For some reason or another, they did not find him interesting, and a movie star in Tahiti is just another person. In any event, after five or six days, he returned to Hollywood.

Phillip is another American who lives up in the hills with his adopted daughter and a Tahitian named *Cigarette Carton*. He was then past eighty, but he would still make the trip into Papeete on his motorcycle, once a month, for a night with a vahine. His comment on American females: "They're women with hearts of stone, son, hearts of pure stone."

OCTOBER 4, 1957

On October 4 I happened to be in the shop of my Chinese friend, who was listening to the radio announcer, speaking in French, telling those who could hear him in the South Pacific, about a historic event happening at that very moment. The Soviet Union successfully launched Sputnik 1. The world's first artificial satellite was about the size of a basketball, weighed only 183 pounds, and took 98 minutes to orbit the earth on its elliptical path. We were told that launch ushered in new political, military, technological, and scientific developments. This of course marked the start of the space age and the US-USSR space race.

Going back to 1952, when the International Council of Scientific Unions decided to establish July 1, 1957 to December 31, 1958 as the International Geophysical Year (IGY), because the scientists knew that the cycle of solar activity would be at a high point then. It was in October 1954 that the council adopted a resolution calling for artificial satellites to be launched during the IGY to map the earth's surface.

Then in July 1955, the White House announced plans to launch an earth-orbiting satellite for the IGY and solicited proposals from various government research agencies to begin development. In September 1955, the Naval Research Laboratory's Vanguard proposal was chosen to represent the U.S. during the IGY.

Obviously the Sputnik launch changed everything. As a technical achievement, Sputnik caught the world's attention and the American public off guard. Its size was more impressive than Vanguard's intended 3.5-pound payload. The public feared the Soviet's ability to launch satellites also translated into the capability to launch ballistic missiles that could carry nuclear weapons from Europe to the U.S. Later, the Soviets struck again, on November 3, Sputnik II was launched, carrying a much heavier payload, including a dog, named Laika.

[The two preceding paragraphs are from the NASA Web site; for more information, go to www.hq.nasa.gov/office/pao/History/sputnik.]

There were many heated discussions in Tahiti following that day in October 1957.

PROGRESS?

When Joe and I arrived in Tahiti by way of a New Zealand freighter, that and sailboats were just about the only way to get to Tahiti. There were also seaplanes that flew in on a biweekly basis, but they originated their flights from Suva, Fiji. How you got to Fiji was up to you.

After several months of living in Tahiti, we saw the first Matson passenger liner dock in Papeete. They were scheduled to call every six weeks thereafter. A few months later when Joe and I decided to leave Tahiti, they were just starting to build a jet airstrip on the outskirts of Papeete. The jet planes and passenger liners seemed like the forthcoming of doom for those beautiful islands in the South Pacific.

MATSON NUMBER TWO

Joe and I were in Tahiti as the afternoon heat built up, so we ducked into a nearby bar, and while in the process of quaffing a few beers, we noticed two young American girls sitting at a table near us. We began a conversation with them, and we found out they were college girls who had signed on for a trip with the recently docked Matson liner. I believe they were from the second passenger ship Matson had sent to Tahiti.

Somehow we got onto the subject of what Joe and I had been eating while we were living in Tahiti. Since I did most of the cooking, I told them we didn't have much money left, so we ate a lot of beans and rice, and breadfruit, which we could pick and roast on our lot. I said there was a great deal of free fruit around the house. We went spear fishing for most of the fish that we consumed. I also told them the raw meat for sale in Tahiti was not refrigerated; so I never purchased any to cook.

Before the evening was over, we found out they worked serving passengers meals, and they invited us to come aboard for lunch the next day. They said there would be few passengers on board that time of day and they could place us at a table where we could choose what we wanted to eat.

Joe and I had been wearing shorts for months, but this day we wore trousers and flower print shirts, disguising ourselves as Americans, and marched up the gangplank and on to the dining room. The girls saw us and placed us at a table where they too could sit occasionally. We each selected what we wanted from the buffet and sat down. Joe started to thank the girls for what wonderful food was available; how long it had been since we had such marvelous nourishment available to us, and how nice it was presented on the table; how wonderful it smelled, etc. By this time I was half way through my meal, so I said to him, "Shut up and eat." He got the message.

One day I was in Papeete, on my bicycle, to purchase some vegetables to cook for dinner that evening. When I swung my leg over the bar of the bicycle, I caught my shorts on the seat and one of the buttons on my fly popped off. I already had one button missing, and now with two gone, the front of my shorts didn't want to stay closed. I picked up the errant button from the street and went to a very small shop where they made shirts and other garments. The problem was it was a Chinese shop and they only spoke Chinese and French; so I gestured to the old woman who ran the business; this button needs to go here, pointing to my fly. She nodded yes several times while she grabbed a needle and thread. The place was so small; I wondered where I would be able to remove my shorts. It didn't take too long for me to perceive there was no such place in her shop as she dragged me outside of her shop and had me sit on a chair on the sidewalk. As I was sitting there, fly ajar, she kneeled down in front of me, grabbed my fly, and began her trade on the button I had retrieved.

Here I was, sitting on the sidewalk where all and sundry could pass by and see my predicament. I was quite embarrassed by what was happening to me, this nearsighted old lady about six inches from my fly, sewing away. It seemed like she would never finish, but when she finally did finish, I was more embarrassed than ever; to cut the thread off, she used her teeth.

THE NEXT WEEK

One afternoon, while snorkeling and attempting to spear a fish for dinner, I was swimming along the edge of the reef when I felt a slight prick on the middle toe of my left foot. It surprised me, and I looked over my shoulder to see if I had hit a fish of some type. Nothing was obviously close to me; so I surmised it was a piece of coral that I must have brushed against. I didn't give it much thought and I stayed in the water until I speared a nice-sized jack and went back to the house to cook.

A couple of days later my foot started to bother me so much I couldn't stand on it without feeling pain. The next day it swelled and turned reddish in color, so I decided to bicycle into town and see a French doctor whom we had already met at a party.

We were about six miles from his office in Papeete and I had to place my left leg on the handlebars and pedal with only my right foot. It was slow going, but if I lowered my left leg the pain was almost unbearable.

When I arrived at the doctor's office, he looked at it and gave me a shot of penicillin. He told me in the past many people died from their cuts on coral, but penicillin had changed all that. I felt somewhat comforted and pedaled on home.

Joe and I had met Lee and Anne Gregg, of the yacht *Novia,* a couple of months earlier and had dinner and drinks with them from time to time. They left San Diego in 1950, and had sailed Mexican, Central and South American, and Hawaiian waters. After their layover in Tahiti they were about to depart for Pago Pago, Sydney and Auckland. They would be leaving in a couple of days and they invited us to sail on the Novia with them to Huahine, Raiatea, and Bora Bora. We would have to take an inter-island boat back from Bora Bora, but we jumped at the chance to be with them for another two weeks.

It probably was only about 15 or 20 minutes after the Novia had its course set for the outer islands that I felt I had made a grave mistake. I loved boats, but I know I never was cut out to sail one, possibly sell one, but not sail one. I started to feel squeamish and the skipper told me to lie down. He knew he would not get any work out of me in my condition. Not only was I getting seasick, but also my toe had started to darken.

I was sick to my stomach all the way to Huahine and my foot started to throb again.

When we arrived at the quay in Huahine, Joe tied the Novia securely and we went into the village for a couple of beers and dinner. After a night's sleep, we cruised around the island before we set the rudder for Raiatea. By now my toe was a light shade of black, and when the skipper saw it, he said, "My God, you need a shot." He asked Anne to bring the first-aid kit, and he too proceeded to give me an injection of penicillin.

When we arrived at Raiatea, it was pretty much the same thing, beers and dinner. I was hobbling most of the time I was on my feet, and the pain was awful. We sailed around Raiatea before we headed for Bora Bora. I was flat on my back, or hanging over the rail, while everyone else was working, and I felt terrible about it, but Lee just chuckled and told me not to worry, they could handle everything.

We were only hours away from Bora Bora when my toe became so infected that it literally split open. Lee saw how bad it had become, and as soon as we tied up in Bora Bora he asked for a doctor. He was told there were no doctors on Bora Bora, but there was a Tahitian nurse who had helped American wounded during the war. We all went to where she lived. When she saw how bad my toe had become, she gave me another injection of penicillin, but this one was quite powerful. The shot she gave me contained one million units of penicillin. That one finally did the trick, and needless to say, I was extremely cautious around coral after that.

Joe and I saw the Novia off for Pago Pago and we stayed until the following Monday to leave for Papeete; we had heard about the incredible singing that took place at a certain church on Sunday, on Bora Bora, and we wanted to attend and hear the chorus. It certainly was well worth the extra time in Bora Bora to realize that experience.

When we were again in Papeete, we checked our mail at the post office, and Joe found out he had to report to his local draft board; he was being called into service for his country. The news sent a chill through me and I was glad all that was behind me.

We started to tell all the friends we had met we would be leaving Tahiti. We had a few farewell dinners with couples, and biere Hinanos with others.

The French Government would only let you stay in Tahiti for a maximum of six months. You had to leave for at least thirty days, because they did not want to let foreigners compete in business with the local French citizens and native Tahitians.

We had been lucky to become friends with the chief of police, as he was able to pull some strings in our behalf. We were in our ninth month in Tahiti, but our money was about gone. I didn't have enough to follow up on my letter of introduction to the banker in Auckland, so I made reservations for a one-way trip to Hawaii to see what those islands were all about.

Joe "I'm never going back" Gores made reservations for Minneapolis, where he was finally inducted into the army; he spent a great deal of time in Washington, D.C.

We both left Tahiti the same day on an inter-island seaplane bound for Apia, Samoa. After we landed we found out we would have enough time to hire a guide and visit the grave of Robert Louis Stevenson. I don't know if it is any easier now, but the day we were there we could only drive to the base of Mt. Vaea, where Stevenson's grave is located. We had to hike the rest of the way to the site.

After paying our respects to such a prolific writer who only lived forty-four years, we went back to the airport to connect with our next flight.

Joe and I said our good-byes to each other at the airport in Samoa and wished each other good luck. Joe would soon be in the army and ordered to Fort Lewis, Washington, where he would spend some time before being reassigned to the Pentagon; there he was delegated to the news branch, and in time would be writing biographies of Army generals.

He started to sell his writings soon after and was the first American writer to win two Edgar awards in one year (1970); one for Best First Mystery Novel by an American Author, *A Time for Predators*, and one for Best Short Story Mystery, *Goodbye, Pops*.

Over the years he would go on to write dozens of short stories and become best known to mystery readers of the world for his D.K.A. series, which features skip tracers and repo men and women working for Dan Kearney and Associates. All are great stories and are the closest anyone has ever come to a private-eye version of the famed 87th Precinct.

He would also turn out television plays for "Kojak," for which he won another Edgar in 1976; "Kate Loves a Mystery," "Columbo," "Remington Steele," "Mike Hammer," and "Magnum, P.I."

He also would write and rewrite screenplays for several movies, and a successful movie was made from his novel Hammett. A not too well known book of his, *Marine Salvage*, is one of the best books I have read by any writer.

I have watched him work from time to time, and have to admit he is certainly a dogged writer. In the beginning of his writing career, just about everything he put in the mail for possible publication came back to him. In one year he got 300 printed rejection slips, and papered the walls of his San Francisco bathroom with them.

I was nearly out of money, which thwarted my plans to continue on to Australia and New Zealand. I decided to fly to Fiji and then make my way to Hawaii to look for work. I wanted to acquaint myself with that part of the Pacific for a few months before returning to California.

I could have flown directly to Hawaii from Samoa, but I had read some stories by W. Somerset Maugham describing the most luxurious and sumptuous hotel in the South Pacific, and that would be the Grand Pacific Hotel, in Suva, Fiji. I had also heard it was so elegant that everyone dressed for dinner; there were two waiters for each table, and the place settings included five pieces of silverware on each side of your plate. There were water glasses, and stem glasses for wines and glasses for cognac, besides the teacups, and cut flowers for the centerpiece for each table. I just had to go there to see it for myself.

It was close to lunchtime when I arrived by taxicab. I walked through the arch-way past the Chinese vases on each side of the entrance for the temporary storage of fine Malacca canes and ladies' silk umbrellas, to seek out the maitre d' hotel, to inquire about a table for lunch.

He looked me up and down and decided to seat me even though I was not wearing a jacket, but I was wearing a tie. I know I would not have been admitted for dinner, dressed as I was. He proceeded to seat me at a table near the center of this great dining room; it was nearly filled with people by then, and all the tables near the windows were brimming with people buzzing in conversation.

Everyone looked fit and proper, which made me feel a bit uncomfortable, even though I was in traveling dress. A waiter took my order for lunch and soon I had forgotten about the men in ties and the ladies in silk.

The fish dish I ordered was splendid for the first two or three bites. Suddenly something was wrong as I felt a sharp pricking feeling in my throat which startled me, as it not only hurt it was making me gag, and I started coughing until dozens of pairs of eyes were looking in my direction. My waiter came up to me and after finding out about my situation, had me eat some bread to see if the impediment could be extricated in that manner.

It could not, and the waiter and the maitre d' escorted me to the darkened barroom adjacent to the great room. They had already called out, "Is there a doctor in the house?" and an elderly gentleman took charge by having the bar cleared and had me lie on it, on my back, while some of the diners watched it all from their tables. I turned out to be the floorshow, and I was still coughing as the doctor asked for two spoons and a flashlight.

He had the bartender hold the light on my open mouth as he proceeded to look at my situation. I was pleased he was not going to play a tune with the spoons, but rather, he used them to try to remove the piece of bone that had pierced my esophagus. He was finally suc-cessful in turning the obstruction in my throat, but lost it when he tried to remove it with the spoons, and it went down. It felt as if I had swallowed a broken teacup.

When I finally stopped coughing, the doctor had me eat a few more pieces of bread and drink about three glasses of water. That did the immediate trick, but I was apprehensive with what might happen the next day.

I thanked the doctor, and the maitre d' asked if I cared to finish my meal. I politely declined and they didn't charge me anything for my embarrassment.

That was my encounter with the grandest of the grand in the South Pacific; the next day I would be landing in Honolulu.

CHAPTER FIVE:

SETTING UP PRACTICE

THE CREST: A HOUSE IN HAWAII

Looking back, I believe I was quite fortunate in meeting the couple I met before opening my office in Hawaii.

I had just come from a nine-month stay in Tahiti, and some friends there suggested I look up some of their friends in Hawaii; they had already been told about me and would be glad to help me get started in architecture.

I was going to proceed slowly, by working for a local architectural firm if possible. I called a few architects about working for them, and one asked me to bring some drawings to his office, and after I showed him some of my work, he said to come back to work for him the following Monday. I arrived on Monday, early, and the architect was not there, but he had told his chief draftsman about me, and for him to get me started. The chief showed me to a drafting board located directly behind his, and he assigned something for me to do. A couple of minutes later he lit up a long cigar and the awful smoke passed right over my board. I saw how that would be so I told the chief to tell the architect I would not be able to work there. That was difficult to do as my money was running out, and I would have to seek another job. The architect called me that evening and was incredulous I would not

work for him because of his chief's addiction to cigars.

A couple of days later some money arrived from California from an article published in *True* magazine that Joe Gores and I had done while in Tahiti. I felt it would be enough to last me a few months, so I bought a newspaper

July 1959 issue of *True* magazine with article by Joe Gores and photographer Earl "Jimmy" Nisbet

and began to look for office space. I found
something I could remodel, in the heart of
Waikiki. It had been a second-floor dress shop,
with two rows of sewing machines running
along the walls in a narrow, but long space. A
lighted show window, adjacent to the main
entrance on Kalakawa Avenue was included
with the office space, and another entrance to
the office was on the street around the corner;
so I tri-sectioned the space and used one-third
for my dwelling and two thirds for the office.

I immediately knew what I could do to make
the office portion attractive for visitors, and
maintain privacy for my living room.

BELOW LEFT
Storge cabinets in author's Waikiki office

BELOW RIGHT Author's office in Hawaii constructed
entirely with hand tools

ABOVE
Author's Waikiki office while living in Hawaii :: 1958

An abstraction by the
author to be displayed
in his drafting room
: : 1953

Although I had done a great deal of carpentry in the past, my tools were in my mother's garage in California; so I would have to purchase some new tools. I didn't have enough money to purchase power tools, but I could afford some basic hand tools.

I went to a lumber company and ordered some mahogany plywood and redwood boards for fascias and trim, and I selected some tools, such as a hammer, a $4.95 handsaw with three blades, a nail set, hand plane, level, square, screwdriver, and a few more small items. The saw was one that had a wooden handle with a slot in which to change the blades that came with it. One blade was for ripping wood, one was for crosscutting, and the third was a keyhole blade for cutting circles or getting into tight spaces.

I didn't feel I should spend any money on sawhorses; however I had located two

Author during interview
for *Honolulu Advertiser*
newspaper article
: : 1958

wooden boxes in an alley where I usually parked my car, and I borrowed them for the job.

After cleaning the room, and painting the ceiling and certain walls, I started to install the plywood for the walls, ceiling, and partitions that would conceal my living room from the office space by the installation of a hidden door. I next devised a storage cabinet, that would not only hide some of my books and drawing materials, but would also become a backdrop for displaying my drawings for prospective

clients. I didn't have enough cash for nice hinges, so I designed the cabinet doors with a sloping front that would allow them to stay in place by gravity.

There was a small kitchenette at the main entry, which was not at all attractive; so I constructed a mahogany partition around it with a semi-concealed doorway.

The floors were a terrible mess of various-colored vinyl tiles, and looked as though the installer enjoyed local Hawaiian beer. That, of course, would not do, so I went into Honolulu

"The Crest," House for Mr. and Mrs. S. C. Doo. Black Point, Oahu, Hawaii. View from shoreline :: 1958

S. C. Doo house.
First sketch. Black
Point, Oahu
: : 1958

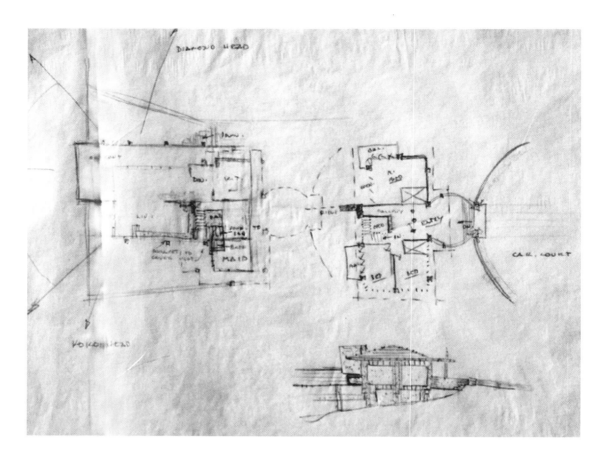

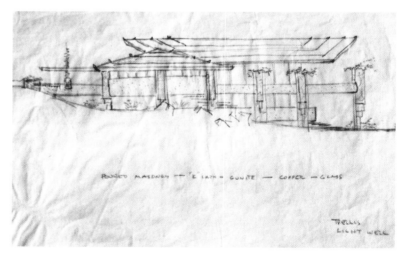

LEFT
Preliminary sketch of "The Crest" as seen from the shoreline : : 1958

ABOVE
S. C. Doo house. First Elevation sketch : : 1958

Living room and terrace of the Doo house at the edge of the Pacific Ocean, Hawaii :: 1958

RIGHT
"The Crest," A house
for Mr. and Mrs. S. C.
Doo. Black Point,
Oahu, Hawaii
:: 1958

BELOW
Bird's eye view of
"The Crest," before
a roof change and
the koi pond is
designed
:: 1958

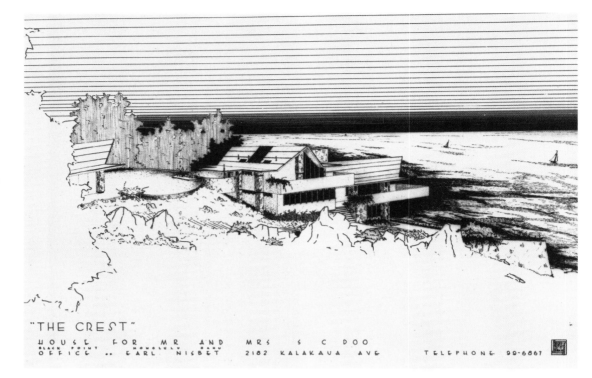

"THE CREST"
HOUSE FOR MR AND MRS S C DOO
BLACK POINT   HONOLULU OAHU
OFFICE of EARL NISBET   2182 KALAKAUA AVE   TELEPHONE 99-6867

and found a Japanese store selling beautiful rolled-straw matting, which I used to cover the tile.

Next, I made a few pieces of mahogany furniture for the interior office space. I had been using 1/4" plywood for the walls, so I glued two sheets together to make the chairs and a table; it was quite a bit cheaper than purchasing 3/4" plywood, and the pieces would be lighter to handle.

After I was satisfied with the remodel of the space, I asked the friends of friends in for tea. After seeing my work, they seemed to be impressed, and said it was probably newsworthy and would call one of their friends, who happened to own the *Honolulu Advertiser.* A couple of days later I was photographed and interviewed for an article, which was published a few days later.

One person who read the article was Sai Chow Doo, a prominent attorney who asked

S. C. Doo house. Entry doors constructed of copper. Overhead lighting in deck. Stained concrete floors to match copper patina.

"The Crest." Doo house koi pond and outside dining terrace : : 1958

Dining area of Doo house. Solid teak walls
and furniture designed by author :: 1958

Copper nameplate
attached to poured
masonry mail and plant
box at entrance to S. C.
Doo house.
:: 1958

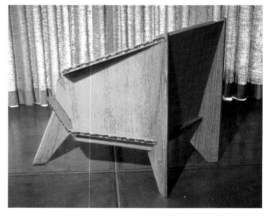

LEFT MIDDLE
Entry right of fireplace above. Dining room to left. Teak furnishings
designed by author. :: 1958

LEFT BOTTOM
Doo house. Poured masonry walls. Stucco exterior. Copper vents
and lights :: 1958

RIGHT MIDDLE AND BOTTOM
Solid teak living room chair. Front, back, and side
views :: 1958

Doo house. Solid teak dining room chairs
:: 1958

Doo house. Oahu,
Hawaii. View from West
:: 1958

his wife to also read the article. They discussed the situation, and the following day they put their house up for sale; they had decided to have me design a house for them. This was told to me during our first meeting, and I was both pleased and flabbergasted that they were both so impetuous to list their house without us having first met.

They had already seen a site that they liked, but it was quite steep, and possibly there might be too much lost land to make it worthwhile.

Mr. Doo drove me to the site in his Porsche Speedster to ask for my thoughts. About a third of the lot was level and the other two-thirds dropped away quite rapidly towards the ocean. If the slope was not utilized it would be nearly useless. It was right at the edge of the Pacific, and it had a natural basin in the rocks that would work nicely for fishing. I said I believed I could work something out for them as they had already told me some of their requirements. The Doos purchased the lot and we

RIGHT
S. C. Doo house.
Carport as seen from
house entry. Stained
concrete steps lead
down to main entry
:: 1958

BELOW
Perspective drawing
of "The Crest," a
house for Mr. and
Mrs. S. C. Doo
:: 1958

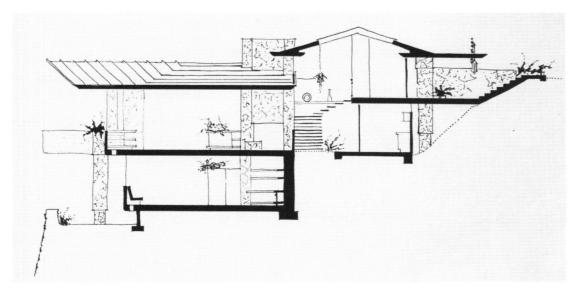

LEFT
Doo house.
Longitudinal section.
Oahu, Hawaii
: : 1958

BELOW
"The Crest." House
for Mr. and Mrs. S. C.
Doo. General site
plan, section/elevation.
Black Point, Oahu,
Hawaii
: : 1958

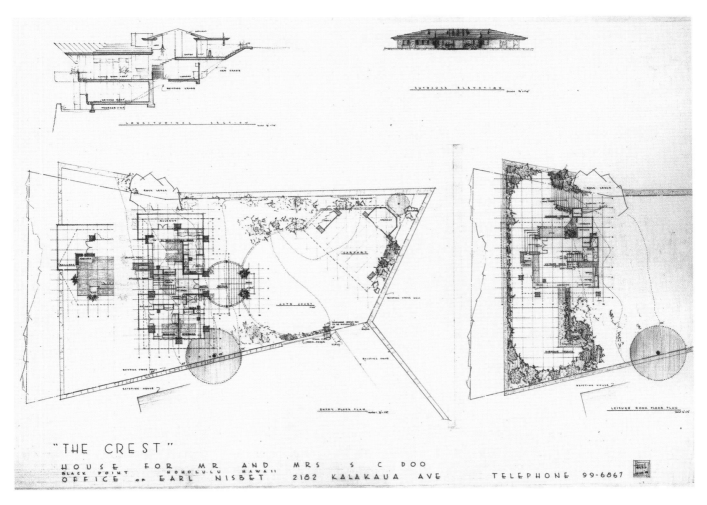

"THE CREST"
HOUSE FOR MR AND MRS S C DOO
BLACK POINT   HONOLULU   HAWAII
OFFICE of EARL NISBET   2182 KALAKAUA AVE   TELEPHONE 99-6867

THE CREST

HOUSE FOR MR AND MRS S C DOO
OFFICE EARL NISBET 2182 KALAKAUA AVE TELEPHONE 99-6667

"The Crest" for Mr. and Mrs. S. C. Doo. Birdseye view from the Pacific Ocean after the addition of the koi pond, outdoor dining area, and change in roof lines
:: 1958

signed a contract, and we began to have several meetings, at my office, at restaurants, and at their house, where I learned that Mrs. Doo was a gourmet cook.

After our contract was signed I would go to the site to get the feel of it in the evening, early morning, in the rain and also in windy weather. A few weeks went by and one day Mr. Doo called me to see what I was going to propose. His office was also in Waikiki just two blocks away, and I told him to come on over, but I hadn't done any drawings up to this point; so I started a small sketch of what I had been thinking. What I showed him in that sketch is just about the way the house was built, with the exception of changing the roof line to get a bit more shade where it would be helpful.

The Crest was designed for a family of five, including two small girls and a grandmother, and

about twenty "Koi." Both of the Doos said I would have to do something nice for their colorful fish; it was paramount over all other requirements. I worked out a long swim for them with a wide shaded area under some concrete steps so they could escape from the direct sun.

The carport and storage rooms are on the auto court level with descent over a rounded bridge to the entry foyer. Three bedrooms and baths are located on the upper of three floors with balconies projecting toward a marine view.

Open stairs lead down to the second level, which houses the dining area, workspace, powder room, laundry, maid's room with bath, and the living room space, terminating in a balcony overlooking two terraces and the Pacific Ocean.

Another stairway leads down to the third level that contains a leisure room with a bath and a kitchenette; this area is also utilized as a guest suite from time to time. From there, an outside stair leads to the two barbecue terraces, the koi pool, and a circular sitting area, lending variety to outdoor dining.

The house was designed as an all-steel framed building because of the ravenous termites in the area. The termites are so horrific that in a few weeks the batter-boards sometimes become loose and fall over. A special soft-copper tubing had been previously been drilled at 10" on center, allowing for the periodic infusion of chemicals from outside of the dwelling to treat the under slab portion of the building. This system might have been a first in Hawaii in the annual control of ground termites within the foundation of a house.

The Crest is an integral part of its environment, a rocky sloping site; it is not simply perched on it. It is, also, a house with a single unifying theme throughout. It establishes its difference from its neighbors by its forward thrust on the lot to encompass an almost 180-degree view out over the sea. To anchor the house to the steep slope, The Crest was designed using a dendriform technique, that is, putting down outside "roots" of poured concrete masonry for better stabilization with the earth. The unify-

Doo house on the cover of Don Over's *Pacific Builder's Report* :: June 15, 1959

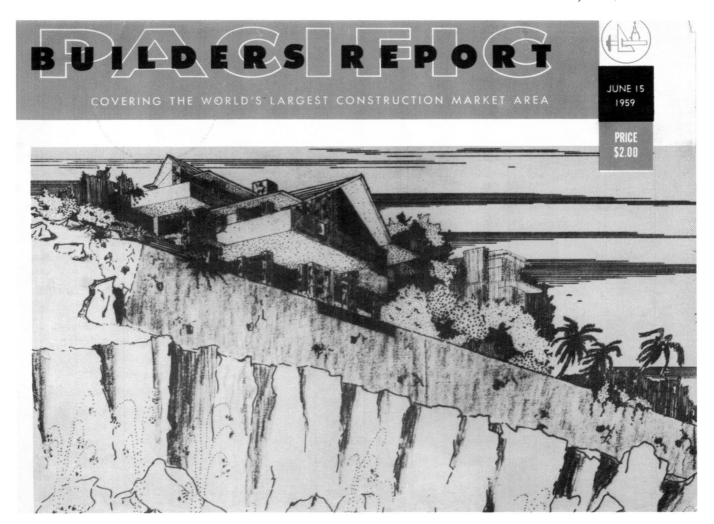

ing theme that reads throughout to make it one harmonious unit is the solid teak board and batten brought from Hong Kong and rubbed with oil to give it a lustrous richness. When plaster is used, it has been finished the same color throughout. A wooden carved strip, of my design, is also of solid teak from Hong Kong, and is carried from room to room, on shelving and furniture edging, and even to the kitchen stove and cabinetry.

This is an uncommon house for a family of uncommon interests. Mr. Doo is knowledgeable in art, music, and philosophy and he also collects books and Ming dynasty art. His extensive collection of tapes demanded an exceptional stereophonic installation and special cabinetry for their storage. It was with him that James Michener conferred on Chinese culture as it developed in the islands while researching his book Hawaii.

Mr. and Mrs. Doo invited me to dinner several times at their house, and on a few occasions also attending were their friends, Mr. and Mrs. James Michener, who the Doos had known for a few years. During after dinner chatting, it didn't take long to discern the insight of the minds of both Sai Chow and James who could seemingly discourse on any given subject. I was truly in awe of both gentlemen.

Mrs. Doo is an outstanding cook, so special attention had to be paid to the kitchen. Since she frequently cooks with a Chinese wok, a seven-burner stove was designed into the stainless steel counter with a raised ring for the distribution of even heat, radiating to the wok. The stainless-steel shelves above the stove are used for the pots and pans while in various stages of cooking, and the controls for the burners were placed above the stove in a shelf fascia so the two small children could not reach them.

The concrete floors have an integral patina color to harmonize with the treated copper roofing, doors, vents, grilles, light boxes and lanterns. At times the wind comes in hard over the ocean, so some ventilation was provided to enter the house from below the cantilevered floors, and sliding grilles within the rooms control the flow of air.

TAHITIAN PARTY

On February 11, 1959 I left two copies of the Doo house working drawings at the Hawaiian Builder's Report Pacific office, which was owned by Don Over, as most of the architects on the island had done for bidding purposes. Contractors would come to their office to see if any contemplated buildings would allow them to bid on part or all of the building, depending on their type of trade.

Don usually looks over each set of drawings that comes into his office. After looking at the Doo house drawings, and noting it was to be an all-steel residence, probably the first in the islands, he came to my office to discuss publishing it in his Builder's Report magazine. Of course I was pleased that he wished to publish it, and I quickly agreed.

While we were discussing life in general, in Hawaii, he learned I had spent nine months in Tahiti, and was surprised; he had spent a great deal of time in Tahiti himself, and knew the French were very strict about not letting visitors stay more than six months.

I told him I had met the chief of police in Papeete and we had become good friends, and he was the one who pulled some strings in order to let me stay longer. He then told me he too was able to stay for long periods of time in Tahiti as he had married a Tahitian girl, who allowed him that privilege, and he too was a personal friend of the chief.

Soon James Michener's name came into our discussion, and when he found out I had been with the Micheners socially, he invited me to his house for a Tahitian party. There was to be many Tahitian dancers and musicians in attendance, all friends of his wife, who also dances. He was inviting several more notable personalities from around the islands, including the mayor of Honolulu.

Besides the Micheners, he had also invited Gregory Peck, the movie actor, who was vacationing for a few weeks.

Don had a very large house, constructed on a long lot that had a massive rear garden, and a lawn that ran down to the beach. Near the median, Don had carpenters construct a wooden platform for dancing among the flowers and the swaying palm trees. For diversion, you could also go to the swimming pool or sauna for relaxation.

Next week, the night of the party, I drove up to Don's house to find several cars already there, and it sounded like the party was already in full swing, with the rhythmic Tahitian music reverberating along with the gentle swishing of the Pacific surf.

Don, the perfect host, answered my knock at his front door, along with a sweet Tahitian girl holding a tray of various alcoholic beverages. After meeting Don's wife, I was soon swept up in the exultant atmosphere of the evening.

James Michener and his wife, Mari, were already there, and I chatted with them for a time. I saw another friend whom I had met in Tahiti, and moved on over to talk to him. He told me he was thinking of opening a chain of hot dog stands around the islands, and would I design something that would be distinctive, but reasonably priced? I said I would be glad to talk to him about it when he was closer to the project's realization.

The Tahitians were dancing up a storm, and I happened to be near the front door, talking to Don, when a knock was heard. Don opened the door and a tall, well-known man in a gray suit offered his hand. It was Gregory Peck, with three of his friends. Don welcomed them to his home and proceeded to introduce me to Mr. Peck and friends. Don stood there talking to his guests, and the sweet Tahitian girl arrived with her tray of refreshments.

Meanwhile, the music hadn't missed a beat, and everyone who could do Tahitian dancing was on the dance floor. I saw a Tahitian girl I

James Michener, right, playing instrument at "Tahitian Party," Hawaii :: 1959

LEFT
Mari Michener, "up front," observing Tahitians dancing :: 1959

had met in Tahiti next to the musicians, so I excused myself and went over to her.

Everyone at the party had gathered around the dance floor, keeping time with the music, and keeping refreshments of some sort in a free hand, while appreciating the female dancers in their native costumes. It was quite lively, so much so that I noticed no one broke away from the dance floor to approach Mr. Peck.

I could see by his reaction that Peck had expected to be the most imposing person at the party, and when no one even asked for his autograph, within fifteen minutes he had gathered his friends together and was gone.

JOHNNY HILL IN HAWAII

I am not certain of the exact date, but I believe it was in July of 1959 that Johnny Hill came to Hawaii for a corporate meeting about his work on *House Beautiful* magazine. Someone in the organization met Johnny at the airport and told him of the Doo house under construction near Diamond Head, and after some discussion brought him to the site.

Johnny was staying at a hotel close to my office and gave me a call early that afternoon. We talked on the phone for a short time, and he decided he would come to see me to talk more about the Doo house and he also wanted to tell me something special he was doing for *House Beautiful*.

I answered the questions he asked about The Crest, and he told me he would only be in Hawaii for two days, but he wanted to show me his design for a Pacesetter House (a *House Beautiful* feature) that would be published in the magazine soon.

We went to dinner at one of my favorite restaurants, located between his hotel and my office, and after dinner we walked to his hotel room where he unrolled his plans for a delightful house, to be built with a great deal of natural stone. It was truly an organic beauty; anyone would be proud to live within its walls. I was glad he had shown me drawings, and it was nice to see it published later.

After his scheduled meeting the next afternoon, we went to dinner at another fine restaurant, and we said goodbye to each other; he was flying back to New York City early the next

morning, but it was nice to see him after so many years.

LONGEVAR

I was preparing to open the front door of my office on April 23, 1958, thinking of phoning my brother on his birthday, when two gentlemen, Mr. John Brooks and Mr. Aaron Evans, were approaching.

After being seated, they told me someone had recommended me to attempt to help them devise a way to sell their several acres of lightweight, floatable *pumice* they recently acquired on the big island.

An important contractor's trade show was scheduled to open on May 17, and they wished to exhibit examples of how contractors might use their pumice material.

After a couple of hours discussing the strategies of moving the material to various Hawaiian Islands, and the distribution thereof, I suggested a way of using their material by manufacturing pre-fabricated decorative panels. Carpenters would be able to construct dwellings of various sizes, which would provide insulation, be fire and termite safe, and eliminate the need for repainting. The sum of these qualities required a special name for future structures built in this manner. I called the system, "*Longevar*."

They hired me to produce a display for the upcoming show, and I was inclined to enlighten the general public that a variety of house designs could be implemented by using these basic manufactured panels with integral ornamentation. Two or three men could easily handle these two-foot wide panels of varying heights because of the extreme lightweight.

Midglen, had been constructed of 12" × 12" concrete blocks, based on Mr. Wright's *textile-block* houses constructed in Southern California, where 16" × 16" decorative concrete blocks were used to make walls visually attractive.

By manufacturing 2' × 8' sections of wall in metal forms, rather than individual blocks, it

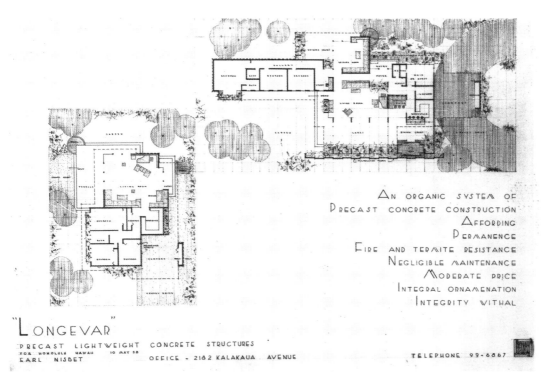

AN ORGANIC SYSTEM OF
PRECAST CONCRETE CONSTRUCTION
AFFORDING
PERMANENCE
FIRE AND TERMITE RESISTANCE
NEGLIGIBLE MAINTENANCE
MODERATE PRICE
INTEGRAL ORNAMENATION
INTEGRITY WITHAL

"LONGEVAR"
PRECAST LIGHTWEIGHT CONCRETE STRUCTURES
FOR HONOLULU HAWAII 10 MAY 58
EARL NISBET   OFFICE - 2182 KALAKAUA AVENUE   TELEPHONE 99-6867

"Longevar" for partners John Brooks and Aaron Evans. A new system of lightweight concrete residential construction for Hawaii
:: 1958

BELOW
"Longevar" large house. View from southwest
:: 1958

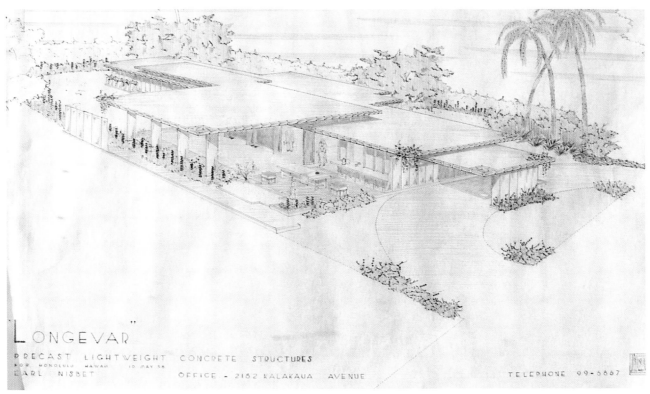

"LONGEVAR"
PRECAST LIGHTWEIGHT CONCRETE STRUCTURES
FOR HONOLULU HAWAII 10 MAY 58
EARL NISBET   OFFICE - 2182 KALAKAUA AVENUE   TELEPHONE 99-6867

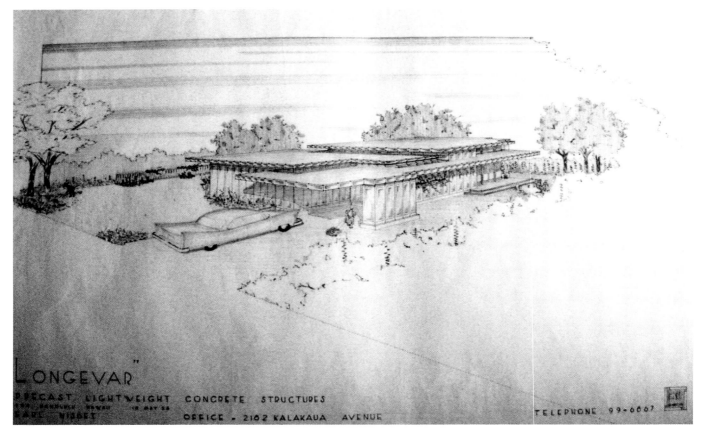

"Longevar" for partners John Brooks and Aaron Evans. Small house. View from northeast. : : 1958

would be much easier to have a professional looking countenance upon completion.

The following drawings show examples of using these panels for a small house as well as a more luxurious dwelling.

STEVE OYAKAWA

Stephen N. Oyakawa was born in Kahaluu, Hawaii, and had been at Taliesin for three years before I arrived. He and I worked together on a few projects, including the birdwalk at Taliesin and some carpentry at Midway, and soon we became friends.

After I departed Taliesin, he stayed on for another ten years before he left to start his own architectural practice in Hawaii. I had lost contact with him and didn't realize that he was in Hawaii at the same time I was.

One day I received a telephone call from him, and he came to my office to reminisce about Taliesin. After chatting for some time, I took him to lunch, and over the next several months we saw each other several times.

He invited me to meet his family at the opening of an apartment house he had designed for them. It was a very nice building of about eight units, as I recall.

On March 9, 1959 he invited me to lunch to tell me he had married Kay Davison; although she was in the states at that time, she would be coming to Hawaii soon.

A few weeks later, Steve, Kay, and I went to dinner one evening, and during conversation Kay said to me, "Do you know they are still talking about your driving the dump truck and reading the newspaper at the same time?"

I didn't know how to answer her; I had completely forgotten about it, and if I was going to be remembered for something, I would rather be it be about some work I might have done, not reading a paper. I just answered, "Oh?"

MOTHER'S BIRTHDAY

While I had been working on the Doo house drawings, I had also been corresponding with my girlfriend from Atherton, Mary Lou Esposito, who mentioned she was thinking of flying to Hawaii to see me. She also mentioned she might look for work and stay in the islands for a time.

In a couple of weeks, after my writing to her stating I thought it a splendid idea, she arrived, and I picked her up at the airport, garnishing her with a dozen leis. There were so many around her neck she could hardly see the sights on the way to her hotel. I insisted she wear all of them into Waikiki, but when she checked into her hotel, she carried half of them in her hand.

During the following three days, I drove her around the island and we had meals at some of the more interesting restaurants. She liked what she had seen and decided to look for work and live in Waikiki for a while.

At her place of employment she met a girl she liked being with, and she accepted the invitation to move into her two-bedroom apartment and share expenses.

Mary Lou had her family ship some additional clothing and other items that we picked up at the Honolulu Harbor.

She was now established in nice living quarters; a few months had passed, when she received a letter from her mother saying that she and my mother and my aunt were planning to come to Hawaii for a week's visit. The dates were set so we could meet them at the airport and bring them to Waikiki.

Mother's birthday party, June 1, 1958. Mother, Aunt Margie, Mary Lou and her mother

LEFT
Author's mother, May Nisbet, enjoyed her woven Hawaiian hat while visiting Waikiki :: 1958

It just so happened their arrival date was on June 1, 1958, which was my mother's birthday. I asked Mary Lou if she could get permission from her roommate to throw a surprise party for my mother. It was OK, so I purchased some balloons, confetti, and streamers, along with a birthday gift, and we proceeded to decorate the apartment.

When they were due to arrive at the airport, we were there waiting to drive them to their hotel in Waikiki. We hugged and kissed, and presented them with leis after they got through the gate, and after obtaining their luggage, we managed to get the most recent visitors to their rooms.

Mary Lou and I had decided we would not mention my mother's birthday until she came to see the apartment.

After the girls settled into their rooms, we took them to lunch before going to Mary Lou's apartment. As soon as we opened the door, we arranged for my mother to enter first, and as she did, we shouted, "Happy birthday!" By then it was quite a surprise and my mother acted as giddy as a schoolgirl, and she was pleased as Punch. It certainly made my day.

MAY NISBET'S PHOTO GALLERY

After my discharge from the army, I returned home to find my mother's interest in photography had accelerated dramatically. She had purchased a 35mm Kodak camera, and had taken an evening course in darkroom techniques at a local junior college. Since she was so invigorated with her hobby, I helped set up a darkroom for her in one of the family bathrooms.

Developing film and enlarging black and white photographs energized her more, I felt, than singing and playing the piano.

I am pleased to offer a few examples of her work on pages 161 and 162.

FALCONER'S PHONE CALL

During early June, 1958, I received a telephone call in my Kalakawa office from Don Falconer saying that his wife, Eunice, had named their house and land, *"Elysian Fields."* He asked if I would design a combination entrance, cattle guard, and gate, with a name-

plate. Following a brief discussion, I told him I'd follow through and the drawings would be sent post haste.

Using the same type of masonry block that had been used for their home, I added overhead lighting, also some planter boxes. The electrified gate could be operated from one of their cars, with the nameplate *Elysian Fields* cast in Trinity White concrete.

The drawings were completed and sent to the Falconers, with my compliments, on June 22, 1958.

BAD DAY AT BLACK ROCK

Thursday, April 9, 1959 started out like any other day for me in Hawaii. I got up and had a shower before I walked two blocks for breakfast at my favorite restaurant on Kalakawa Avenue. They served the best Kona coffee for miles around, and it was within walking distance from my office.

After returning to my drawing board to finish some larger shop details for some copper work that would be going on the Doo house, I was listening to some classical music, as was my custom. I rarely listened to the news over the radio, and I only caught a bit of the news on television at friends' houses, as I didn't own a television set.

In a half-hour or so there was a knock at my door, and I was a bit surprised to see Mary Lou. She said she had called in at work and arranged to take the day off. She had heard a news report earlier in the morning stating Frank Lloyd Wright had passed away after surgery at a Phoenix hospital, and she didn't want me to find out without her telling me.

Of course I was devastated, and I felt empty inside. Mr. Wright had changed my life in many ways and I appreciated my time with him. I couldn't think right, or want to do any more drawing that day, so Mary Lou and I drove around the island at a leisurely pace. It was difficult for me to drive as my eyes welled up with tears, but on we went.

Mother's portrait of a swan. Author called it "Mother's Goose," which was not too well received. : : 1957

RIGHT
Portrait taken at a party by author's mother while on a visit to Hawaii : : 1957

ABOVE
Hawaiian Wood Rose : : 1957

LEFT
Gray day for the incarcerated orangutan : : 1957

A coming storm
:: 1953

A neighbor's cat :: 1954   Out of Africa :: 1954

The "Sunbeam Talbot" I had while living in Hawaii :: 1958

Portrait of author by his mother during her visit to Hawaii :: June 1, 1958

Portrait of author taken by his mother during her visit to Hawaii. One of her favorite photos :: 1958

Later that day, when we wound up in Honolulu, I drove to the Western Union office and sent the following telegram to Mrs. Wright and the fellowship:

"Words are inadequate, but for we who loved the Master more than a son can love his father . . . he lives on."

PROJECTS

During the last several months of my living in Hawaii, there were several possible jobs that came to my office, but for one reason or another, none of the following came to fruition.

MARCH 23, 1959: A possible client himself, Frank Beatty, brought the sister of Buster Crabbe, the swimmer and movie star, to my office as she was interested in building a hotel in Kauai. She wanted to see some hotels I had already designed, but I never had the opportunity to design one at that point in my profession. She seemed disgruntled that Frank would waste her time, and I never heard from her again.

APRIL 14, 1959: I met with Mr. and Mrs. James Michener to discuss designing a house for them. Since they had already seen the Doo house they seemed confident that I would produce a dwelling where they would feel at home. I mentioned I would help them select a site if they cared to have my help, but a couple of weeks later, James called to say they had decided to move back to Bucks County, Pennsylvania.

JUNE 23, 1959: Larry Garret, a very nice chap I had met in Tahiti, came in to see me about designing some hot-dog stands we had previously discussed. I told him I would work something up to show him the following week. I did some work on the project, and when I called him to tell him to come in to see what I was proposing after our discussions, he told me he had to call it off because the financing he was expecting didn't come through. He did invite me to another one of his parties the following

Saturday, and he showed me a new hat he had purchased that same day. He told me to try it on, and I told him I didn't wear hats. He insisted and placed it on my head. After I adjusted it, he looked at me and said, "You keep it. It looks better on you than it does on me."

JULY 16, 1959: Mr. and Mrs. Altiery came to my office to discuss building a house at Waimanelo Beach. I met them at the site and had dinner with them later, but that was the last I heard from them.

NOVEMBER 12, 1959: Mr. Doo called to tell me he had recommended me to a Mr. Yamamoto to design a bowling alley for him, but I did not hear from Mr. Yamamoto himself.

APRIL 27, 1960: A Bob Hankins came to my office to discuss my designing a golf driving range and a putting range at Waialai, but Mr. Hankins didn't follow through.

MAY 14, 1960: Realtor Eve Lynn came to my office to ask if I would participate in building a hotel complex. I told her I would be pleased to

New hat presented to author by client Larry Garret. Shirt designed by the author : : June 30, 1959

Author's rendition in oil of Mt. Olomana. Windward Oahu, Hawaii :: 1960

do so if the site warranted it. She drove me to a site at Laie, but I could not see the value for that site, so we drove to an open waterfront site at the Glover Estate, on the windward side of the island. I recommended it to her and she said she would recommend it to the backer. She called me a week later to say the funds had dried up.

JUNE 1, 1960: Eve Lynn came in to talk about designing an apartment house, but nothing came of it. She did bring a set of oils and an easel which she wanted me to have, as she had recently given up painting. I declined the oils as a gift, but I did borrow them to paint an oil of Mt. Olomana on the windward side of the island.

JUNE 6, 1960: Eve Lynn asked me to design a brochure for a subdivision she was going to do on the Big Island. After some discussion I agreed, and I named her subdivision Tiki

Gardens, which she loved; she said when I completed the brochure, I would receive one of the five-acre lots for my work. She got the brochure, but I never got the lot.

Another project, which might have worked out, was from Sai Chow Doo himself. He was extremely pleased with the house I had designed for him, and he wanted me to design a hotel right on Waikiki Beach. It seems he was a partner with some other businessmen in an existing hotel on the beach. Not only was it old, it was also too small for the site; Sai wanted to tear it down and have me design a larger one, but when it came up at a meeting with the other partners, his idea was rejected.

SOMETIME IN JUNE 1960, some personal friends of the Doos came to my office to ask me to go before their architectural committee to propose my ideas for a church their congregation would be building soon. Mr. and Mrs. Shimura

RIGHT
My abstraction to show a Japanese church committee how I would design their building, next to the sea, using concrete, copper and glass for minimal upkeep
:: 1960

BELOW
Office building study for the Doo Conglomerate, Honolulu, Hawaii. Mr. Doo wished to convince his partners to construct an office building and restaurant in a downtown Honolulu location and asked me for a quick plan
:: 1960

had seen the Doo house on several occasions and were extremely pleased with all aspects of the dwelling and they both thought I would do an imaginable church. I thanked them for their support, but I told them I had not designed a church before. I went on to say at least two architects would probably appear before their architectural committee to show plans and photographs of their church designs, and their committee would select an architect who had at least designed one church.

I did agree to discuss building a church before their committee, however, I already assumed a negative outcome. If the Shimuras hadn't been so thrilled about the possibility of my designing something for their group, I wouldn't have accepted the opportunity.

By the time of my appearance before their committee, I had drawn an abstraction to try to explain the materials I would propose using for their building, because of the salt spray from the nearby ocean. I told them I had never designed a church before, but should I have the opportunity to design their building, I would use concrete, copper, and glass for the structure; each material would be a low maintenance item and there would be a significant savings over the years.

Needless to say, an architect who showed them photos of one of his painted churches obtained the commission.

THE CASTLE

When my work on The Crest was finished, I had a long talk with its owner, Sai Chow Doo, who had become my friend as well as client, regarding my leaving Hawaii. I informed him I was contemplating going back to California to be better able to look after my mother, who was quite healthy, but was getting on in years. I said I was a bit disillusioned because his business partners had decided not to raze their existing hotel in Waikiki in order that I design a new and larger one, which Mr. Doo had proposed to them in order to compete in the ever-expanding tourist trade.

He already knew I had been selected to design a hotel that was to be constructed on the other side of the island, but at the last moment funding for that resort was turned down. He was well aware that his friend James Michener and his wife were leaving Hawaii to again live in Bucks County, Pennsylvania; that meant I would not be designing a house for them in the islands, as they had recently requested. At that point in time, it would be a definite struggle to keep my office in Waikiki open since other proposed work was not coming to fruition either.

Jim Moore, my Cabaña client and longtime friend had been writing to me all the time I had been in Tahiti, as well as during my three years in Hawaii. The first telephone call I received from him was well appreciated, but long overdue. We had a pleasant conversation for many minutes when he finally asked, "When are you coming home?" My reply was instantaneous, "Tomorrow," I said. His rejoinder was, "Holy cow, I could have saved eight bucks on this call!"

Mr. Doo tried to encourage me to stay a bit longer with the hope something would materialize for me, but I didn't feel that it would work, and in a few days I had dinner with him and his wife to say our farewells. When I left the island, they drove me to the airport and placed so many leis over my head, it was difficult to see through all those fragrant flowers. I was sad to leave those beautiful island and my many good friends I had gotten to know, but I felt good about being close again to my mother.

I moved into my mother's house and opened an office in Los Altos, which was less than ten miles away. It had been the former office of Architect Goodman Steinberg, when I had worked for him. I enjoyed the small town atmosphere and relative slow pace, plus the price was right.

I don't recall how it actually came about, but somehow I was interviewed about The Crest, also known as the Doo House, and it was subsequently featured in a Sunday supplement in the *San Francisco Chronicle*.

A week or two later I received a telephone call and had a meeting in my office with a most delightful couple, the Elwoods.

Wayne Elwood had recently retired from more than thirty years in international business. He was vice-president of FMC Corp. and president of FMC International. Both he and his wife, Catherine Crary Elwood, were Stanford graduates and long-time Palo Altans. She, being a modern medievalist, had an intense interest in the history of the twelfth century.

In the past, the Elwoods had traveled extensively, making over seventy-five trips to Europe, and they had indulged Catherine's love of history in small objets d'art and an occasional period piece. She tempered the comfort of contemporary upholstered pieces with fabrics reminiscent of medieval tapestries.

It was in Europe that Mrs. Elwood's fascination with the medieval years began. In the late 50s her husband, Wayne, was sent to Brussels to represent a large U.S. corporation, and Mrs. Elwood used the two years spent there to provide their two sons with educational sightseeing.

To bring more knowledge to their adventures, she (who insists she hated history in

San Francisco Chronicle

Sunday BONANZA

HOUSE IN HAWAII - A MANY-FACETED GEM SET IN ROCK . . PAGE 8

Cover photo of S. C. Doo house as published in the *San Francisco Chronicle* newspaper
:: 1965

school) did perceptive research into early France and the area that is now Belgium. Being as fluent in French as in English made library research easier, but she found it wasn't quite enough, so she taught herself medieval French.

In the deeper research this afforded she ran into several historical mysteries, and some solutions, and back in the United States she started writing a novel to present her theories.

Being so steeped in history, the Elwoods decided to build a retirement home on a lot bordering a 1400-acre wilderness park, to fit into Mrs. Elwood's time element.

After seeing the site, and after many discussions regarding their requirements, we had a meeting of the minds, and later Mrs. Elwood

said, "Nisbet brought my medieval thinking completely into play in the house, it was a perfect translation of my historical interests into the language of contemporary architecture." At this point, I must acknowledge I did not name their house The Castle. Over time, friends and visitors began to refer to it as such.

It has been said this modern-day castle is unabashedly contemporary, built with glazed tile floors, anodized aluminum window sashes, and all the other accoutrements of minimum maintenance.

The first view you get of the house is its high round tower, which suggests a medieval character. It's not just imagination, it's part of the plan, and the design captures the solidity and beauty of Romanesque architecture, without the romantic Gothic features. The completed effect is artistic, but very practical, according to Mrs. Elwood.

The wheat-colored stone walls designed to blend into the golden hillside in summer, look as though Norman stonemasons might have carved them. The building blends into its oak-studded acre as agelessly as the ruins of an ancient castle, and the pale green concrete tile and fascia match the lichen on surrounding trees.

Inside the two-bedroom structure, the walls are similar to those of the exterior. The tower makes a round and very efficient kitchen, but before you reach this room, you walk through a spacious loggia, one wall of which is the edge of the tower. This shape provides interesting angles that allow a powder room and guest closet off its wide entryway. Round stone columns nearly three feet in diameter on nine-foot centers buttress the major walls throughout.

The two-level master bedroom suite looks out on treetops, and it provides the luxuries of a library, sitting room, study, and bedroom combined. The living room has cathedral ceilings and a large fireplace; an angular nook created especially for the grand piano leads your eye across the room to high windows opening northward onto the concrete terrace.

From the terrace there is a view that encompasses most of Santa Clara County, and below is a lake on a golf course and Stanford University. Thirty-five miles to the north is the skyline of San Francisco. The view is similar to the one seen looking toward Paris from Henry IV's chateau in St. Germain-en-Laye.

None of the trees on the site were destroyed during the construction, though a few branches were cut back. On both sides of the house there are terraces and patios, "A place to sit no matter the time of day, the season of the year or the weather conditions," Mrs. Elwood has stated to friends. One of the living areas opens to an oval pool, which happens to be the favorite spot for the family.

Catherine Elwood is an author of historical and mystery novels, and since the death of her husband no longer lives in her medieval-modern castle, but it was a great help to her in keeping the ambiance of her novel.

Over the years Catherine and I have kept in touch with each other by way of lunches and correspondence. In a later Christmas card she included this note to me,

"Dear Earl,

Can you believe it's 17 years since we built the Castle on the hill? I'll always think of it as the loveliest house anyone ever had, with good wishes,

Catherine Elwood."

I still cherish the months we worked together seeing The Castle come alive.

The present owners of the house use the house as their home base when they are not living in their native Philippines, where they have a home their neighbors also call The Castle.

ENTER CLARENCE P. CHAN

The Elwoods enjoyed the house I designed for them in 1968, for several years, but in 1980 Wayne Elwood passed away and his wife, Catherine, found it difficult to maintain since she was now alone.

Elwood House. Concrete block walls, concrete tile roof. Living room and terrace on left. Circular kitchen and entry. Master bedroom suite to right. Garage below bedroom. Palo Alto Hills, California :: 1965

LEFT
Elwood House living room and terrace. Entire house designed around seven oak trees, which were all saved : : 1965

MIDDLE LEFT
Elwood House. Two car garage below master bedroom suite, pool to right. Colored concrete steps lead up to main entrance. Roof and fascia of colored concrete tiles, walls are stucco : : 1965

BELOW LEFT
Elwood House. Pool adjacent to bedrom suite. Curved concrete blocks supporting columns : : 1965

BELOW RIGHT
Elwood House. Colored concrete steps leading to entry and kitchen tower : : 1965

She regretfully relinquished the house she was so comfortable with, and sold "The Castle" to a relative of Amelda Marcos, from the Philippines. Some additions were made to the house without integrity, and in a few years it was sold to a gentleman who purchased it with the thought of refurbishing, and subsequently re-selling for a profit.

In 1996 it was listed with realtors for sale, and a young man, who's parents lived a few blocks away in the same subdivision, had already coveted it as he drove past it daily on his way to his successful computer related business. The first day he saw the realtor's sign on the property, he made the purchase.

The woman realtor had called me to answer some general questions of hers, and she told the new buyer, Clarence P. Chan, about me.

A short time later Mr. Chan called me for a meeting to discuss enlarging the house to include a family room, which would better suit his needs.

I met with him and agreed to design a family room as an extension of the house, which would encompass part of the existing exterior patio. Clarence was very affable and we seemed to get along more like friends, rather than on a strict business basis.

I finished the drawings on December 7, 1996, and soon thereafter the addition was

Elwood House. Living room terrace, living room, circular kitchen and entry. Master bedroom suite beyond. Concrete block, concrete tile roof
:: 1965

completed to his satisfaction, and I was paid for my work.

Clarence had many grandiose ideas, which I tried to subdue, as I didn't feel everything he wanted would be in the best interest of the existing design, and things like a "mote" around "The Castle" on a hillside was not only not practical, but would have cost a fortune. To gain what?

He did come to me again as he decided he might make some kind of trade of something he had for a Russian helicopter, and what he wanted was a 5-car garage, but built strong enough to land a helicopter on its roof.

I designed the 5-car garage using all-steel-framing, which was attached to the existing house in such a way, it looked as though it was part of the original design. I presented the finished plans to him on March 30, 1997, and in a few months it was completed, and again, I was paid for my work.

In July of 1997 Clarence asked me to design a "bath, gym, and changing cabana," which would be appurtenant to his existing swimming pool. I designed a study, which he seemed to like, and I presented it to him on August 29, 1997. Soon thereafter he mentioned to me at one of our many luncheon meetings, he would put off building the gymnasium as he was thinking of adding a "larger bathroom" to his existing master bedroom suite. He also put off paying me for the work on the gymnasium, as he would include it when he would pay me for the bathroom addition.

At this point in time we were seemingly like very good friends, and on March 23, 1999, I presented him with complete plans for the bathroom addition, including all the necessary engineering drawings and calculations.

Clarence held onto the plans for a few months, and he called me for another luncheon meeting to discuss his newest idea. He decided not to do the bathroom addition, but rather, it would be included in his most extraordinary endeavor ever. He wanted to enlarge the existing dining room, enlarge the two existing bedrooms, and add 2 more bedrooms and 4 more bathrooms, plus dig a basement under the house; so he could have a shooting gallery.

I immediately advised him to join a gun club for shooting purposes as digging a basement under, and adjacent to load bearing walls of an existing house built with concrete block would be cost prohibitive.

He wouldn't listen, and he asked me to do the drawings for the 2 bedrooms and 4 bathrooms, enlarge the dining room and of course, add the basement.

I worked on it for a few months, which included several luncheon meetings, and finally presented him with the finished drawings. I included all the necessary engineering calculations in order to obtain a permit on December 31, 1999. I again mentioned the cost of excavation and shoring existing concrete block walls would be a very large cost factor for the overall project.

He said he thought they would start construction in the spring, but when spring arrived, he called me for another meeting. He decided he would go ahead with the construction, but he would like me to revise the plans and include another bedroom.

He said he was not in a great hurry at this point, and after a few more meetings, I presented him with the complete revision, which included the additional bedroom. He always liked the idea of my being associated with Frank Lloyd Wright, and he seemed proud to have the complete engineering calculated by my friend, and FLLW's engineer, Kamal Amin, who was my houseguest for a week.

On September 20, 2000, I presented him with the full working drawings, titled, "Dining Room and Bedroom alterations: also 3 Bedrooms and 4 Bathrooms + Basement additions for: Mr. Clarence P. Chan."

He intended to do the work on an owner-contractor basis, as he had done on the first family room addition and the 5-car garage addition, but it has been 5 years now that he has had the drawings and he has not begun construction. I believe when he discovered what the basement would cost he abandoned the project.

About this time, the telephone company changed the prefix in our area, and I had also received a new number. I tried to call Clarence to inform him of a change in my number, but he would not accept my calls.

I then sent a registered letter to him with my new number, but neither he nor his wife would accept the letter because, I believe, when they recognized my envelope they thought something else was inside.

His wife once answered my telephone call and asked who it was. When I mentioned my name, she said, "I'm trying to sleep," and hung up.

This was a surprise to me as they had invited me to their thanksgiving dinners as well as Fourth of July parties. They even invited me to their wedding, which I attended at a large gathering at a Pebble Beach country club. I even presented them with a Frank Lloyd Wright clock for their house, which they seemed to enjoy.

At this writing, Clarence's mother, Amy Chan, is the present City Manager for the City of Sunnyvale, California.

It seems as though, rather than pay me the thousands he owes me, it was easier to have one less friend than write a check.

THE LION IS KING

As business partners and friends, Jim Moore and I have been involved in many real estate transactions over the years. Occasionally, these involved unusual situations. None, however, was more unusual than circumstances involving a parcel of land we wished to purchase in Fresno County, California.

The seller's agent had shown us the acreage, answered our questions, and we had agreed to their terms. Anxious to begin work on the property, Jim and I waited for the necessary documents (still in escrow) to be signed.

When ample time had passed without response from the sellers, the Title Company gave us their address. Jim and I arrived at their home in Atherton—an exclusive area south of San Francisco—the following afternoon. The next few hours found us alternately ringing the doorbell of a large, two-story house, and awaiting the arrival of the home's occupants while sitting in the car. Toward nightfall, I grew worried that the local police, constantly on patrol in this affluent neighborhood, would start questioning our reason for remaining parked on this particular street. We had skipped dinner, having chosen to remain in the car instead of missing the homeowner's arrival. Eventually, we both fell asleep.

The next morning we awoke to the sound of a car passing ours. The vehicle then proceeded up the driveway to the house in question. We rushed to where he was parked and approached the driver.

After introducing ourselves and explaining our situation to him, we learned that he was the homeowner's son. We then heard this bizarre tale:

His parents and their friends had recently traveled to Africa on a big game hunt. A few days prior, his father had shot and seriously wounded a lion. Because the animal was bleeding profusely, the big game hunter insisted he could follow the trail and called off his guide. The hunter continued on his quest while the lion walked in circles, each rotation becoming continually smaller.

As determined later by those involved, the inevitable occurred. The wounded lion had attacked and mortally wounded the hunter. The unfortunate victim was found with much of his torso missing.

The son explained that his mother was so distraught she had remained with the group, and would return on the scheduled date.

Naturally, our real estate transaction could not be completed until the widow was granted permission by the court to sign the necessary papers.

Jim and I were both stunned by this gruesome and chilling tale.

GO-AHEADS?

Even as early as my preteens, my brother Harry and I were in daily mental combat with each other to see if one could make the other laugh at some absurdity. Although he was older, once in awhile I could get a guffaw out of him, as each tried to get the other to have, at least, a minor vexation at the dinner table where our mother or father would take sides.

This went on all the time in our years of growing up, but it was all in good fun. There was never any animosity between us, and being older, my brother actually looked after and protected me.

Several years later he and his wife came to my house, near the beach, to spend a weekend with me, and he was explaining to me some footwear that had just been introduced to this country from Japan, and would be extremely practical for use at sandy beaches. The sandal was just a flat sponge rubber sole with a strap beginning between the large toe and the second toe of the foot and connected midway along the sides of the sole. When worn, the rear portion was loose and would flap up against the underside of your foot, making a noise with each step; you had to be careful that they didn't come off your foot.

Harry, after his explanation, said that was the reason they were called "Go-aheads."

I immediately replied, "Why didn't they call them no-go-backs?"

I really don't know why he thought my comment was so funny, but he fell off the barstool and kept on laughing until he had to wipe the tears from his eyes.

TRAVEL TO SPAIN

Soon after the completion of the Elwood house (The Castle), I noticed a decline in new clients. The impetus was always there, within me, to try to solve problems for those who would seek my help, but fewer and fewer people came to my office with commissions for building. Mr. Wright had been asked where all of his buildings came from, and he replied he just shook them out of his sleeve. When you understand organic design, it is not a problem to be able to express yourself and realize your endeavor in many different forms. I considered the future and decided to call my best friend from high school days, Jim Moore (Cabaña Tanglewood). He had recently sold his business, and after some discussion, we decided to venture into real estate.

We looked for property to develop in the gentle rolling hills in northern California, and we bought and sold several parcels of land. We profited substantially and I decided to take eight months off to live, temporarily, in Spain. I spent a month in Madrid going to nightclubs to experience flamenco song and dance, which had fascinated me since hearing it in a few localities around the San Francisco area. While in Madrid I purchased a flamenco guitar from one of the best makers in Spain, Archangel Fernandez, and I took some private guitar lessons from a well-known guitarist, Juan Martin.

Madrid was quite exciting, and I wrote to tell my mother and Mary Lou about my exploits, meager as they were, but energizing for me. The *Pension* (small rooming house) where I was staying was a short walk to *Plaza Mayor*, the most important landmark in Madrid. This beautiful arcaded square was completed in 1619, during the rein of Felipe III, and a statue of him, astride his horse, is in the center of the plaza.

There are several cafes and bars along the perimeter that serve their patrons in the sun at outside tables. You might see students practicing *mime* or playing musical instruments, and passing the hat. Artists are to be found selling their paintings or will do a portrait of you while you wait.

I had already been to the *Prado Museum*, which is classified as one of the world's greatest galleries, and claims a higher concentration of masterpieces than any other museum in the world. It certainly impressed me as I walked through it to view works by Goya, El Greco, Velazquez, Ruben, and countless others.

Another impressive tour I enjoyed was walking through some of the 3,000 rooms that make-up the *Royal Palace*. The Spanish Royal Family no longer occupies the palace, and it has been open for visitors to experience. It is so vast; it even has its own lake adjoining the magnificent buildings.

I probably would have stayed longer in Madrid, but the weather had been very cold since the first day I arrived and it finally penetrated to my psyche as well as my bones; so I booked a flight to Mallorca, by way of Barcelona.

I had been told that Barcelona was Spain's second largest city in population, as well as area. Because it was situated on the shores of the Mediterranean, along the coast of the Iberian Peninsula, it sounded like a city worth experiencing, and my destination of Mallorca was only a hop, skip, and jump away. There is much to observe in any large metropolitan area, and I decided to spend a few days in Barcelona to become acquainted with some work by the Spanish architect, Antoni Guadi (1852–1926) whom I had become aware while in college.

By spending a day with an informed guide, I was able to visit the *Sagrasa Familia,* (The Temple of the Holy Family), and learned it was the most visited building in Barcelona, even though it was still under construction.

The temple was actually begun by another architect, Francisco de Paula del Villar, but he withdrew in the first year because of a dispute on how the columns were to be fabricated. Gaudi was appointed his successor when he was just 31 years old. This was a major turning point in his career, and he focused all of his creative energies into it, making it his life's work.

I was taken to another of Gaudi's works; an apartment house called *Casa Batllo*, which was

a remodel. Its dissimulation was an affront to the other structures on both side of the street.

Giant columns, with bulbous bases, are terminated at street level for the passer by to ponder. Looking upward you see a modified *Swiss cheese* type of facade in a multitude of colors, with appurtenances applied that resemble fish scales. Balconies weave in, and wave out, as you might observe an undulating serpent. This structure has been classified as both, *Expressionist* or *Art Nouveau,* take your pick.

There were a few other Gaudi structures I could have seen, but being impressed with the Sagrada Familia, I was disenchanted with his Casa Batllo.

I made arrangements to fly to Palma de Mallorca following my stay in Barcelona and I settled into this warm spot in the Mediterranean in a very short period of time. The first night I utilized a hotel room booked while I was still in Barcelona. The next day I contacted a real estate agent who showed me a third-story, walk-up furnished flat, overlooking the multitude of sailboats at the waterfront, and also in the panorama was the entire city of Palma de Mallorca, including the highly prominent, Gothic, Palma de Mallorca cathedral. One of the sailboats I enjoyed seeing while I was there, was Errol Flynn's schooner, the yacht Zaca. It was an especially well-designed-sleek-hull that would cut through the roughest waters anywhere in the world. Each time I walked near that yacht, I had the desire to try to go aboard, but in actuality, I had to realize, boats and my being on the sea with them are not compatible.

The flat I selected was one of three the real estate agent had shown me, and later I discovered the rear garden backed up to a wall of one of Palma's landmarks, "Castillo de Bellver," (Bellver Castle). The gothic castle, built in the 14th century, on a hill, in a circular configuration, for King Jaime II, has three circular towers with four floors. It was built as a defensive fortress and in the center is a parade ground and a courtyard is built over an underground reservoir.

On a tour, I noticed some slit openings, in the projecting walls above the main entrance, and a guide confirmed what I presumed was their use. If enemies were to storm the gates, the occupants would pour boiling oil on the intruders. When inside the castle, I saw a fireplace with a hood that was approximately 20 feet across, and it was quite near the openings aforementioned.

Another historic landmark worth visiting is the house where Father Junipero Serra (1713–1784) was born. This humble *casa* is approximately 24 miles east of Palma de Mallorca, in Petra, and is open to the public.

In 1750, Fr. Serra served the Franciscan Missions by sailing to Vera Cruz, Mexico, then walking to Mexico City, before beginning his life's work in Baja California.

He founded the first of California's Missions in San Diego, and eventually founded 21 missions between San Diego and Sonoma.

On August 28, 1784 Father Serra died at Mission San Carlos Borromeo del Rio Carmelo, and is buried there under the sanctuary floor.

In letters to my mother, I asked if she would care to fly to Spain and stay with me for a vacation, but she declined as a few years prior she had spent a month in Europe with her sister. Mary Lou was not interested in visiting Spain, at this time, as she had recently been hired by the paper-company, Kimberly-Clark.

My days in Mallorca settled into a somewhat routine in a couple of weeks. Upon arising, and having breakfast, I would practice guitar for a couple of hours, then dress for the beach, and then purchase a bottle of champagne and place it in a cooler in the "milk-butter-and-egg" store. I would then take a bus to the beach to sun and swim until the afternoon. When I felt I had enough sun, I would catch a bus to get back to the store and purchase a bag of roasted almonds. I'd pick up my bottle of champagne and walk upstairs to my flat, where I would take a shower and sit on the balcony to have my champagne and almonds. By the time I finished my snacks, the sun would be setting, and the lights on the cathedral and the waterfront would be coming on. After watching for a short period of time, I would go inside to practice guitar for an hour or so before going out for dinner. I would often attend nightclubs, after dinner; to hear some professionally played flamenco music.

The next day followed the next, and so on, until the end of my stay came into view, and I made plans to fly back to San Francisco.

I MARRY MARY LOU

I moved back to my mother's house and began seeing Mary Lou on a regular basis.

Very early in her life she had studied classical piano and was quite gifted in her playing. I enjoyed her music the several times I was fortunate to witness her mastery of the instrument.

I discovered, while I had been in Spain, she had been taking lessons with pianist Adolph Baller, who had recently become a Stanford faculty member. He already was an internationally renowned pianist known for his mastery of classical and romantic pieces.

Baller came to California in 1941 as a guest of the violinist Yehudi Menuhin. They formed a duo and performed all over the world for the armed forces.

Baller was already a founding member of the *Alma Trio*, and they immediately became known for their exquisite sound and balanced playing.

Mary Lou took lessons at the Baller residence in Palo Alto, but on occasion he would instruct her at her home in Atherton because he enjoyed playing on her Bosendorfer Grand Piano.

When Baller was performing in the bay area, Mary Lou and I made it a point to attend his wonderful performances. We were fortunate to have already seen him at a special show in Hawaii, and he was kind enough to invite us to his host's residence for a reception later in the evening.

I was enamored with Mary Lou since the first day of our meeting through the auspices of Joe Gores, some six years earlier. She had been in my thoughts a great deal of the time and I knew I did not want to lose her. With the hope that she did not want to lose me, I went to a local jewelry store and purchased an engagement ring with a matching wedding band.

On an appropriate occasion, I asked; she accepted; and the next four years would be written into history.

Although I was not a Catholic, in 1964 we were married in St. Thomas Aquinas church in Palo Alto, with Mary Lou's family arranging the wedding and reception.

My mother was quite pleased to be in attendance to witness the ceremony as my brother, Harry, had eloped with his girlfriend.

My brother was my best man, and Jim Moore agreed to be my *ring bearer*. By the way, if you agree to raise your children in the Catholic tradition, they give you dispensation to marry in a Catholic Church.

Mary Lou's mother wanted her only daughter to marry a Catholic, and I believe she thought I would come between Mary Lou and her becoming a renowned pianist. All this rubbed her the wrong way, and we never became friends. To this day, I have no idea what would have been the right way to rub her.

In 1966 we had a daughter, born on July 14th so I suggested we name her Michelle, for France's Bastille Day, *quatorzieme juillet*. That was apparently approved by the then heads of state, and the birth certificate so reads.

In 1968, the rubbed woman had her way by having her daughter divorce me. Mary Lou's mother advised her daughter in everyday choices for so many years on end, Mary Lou developed an immunity to think for herself.

As far as the mother-in-law was concerned, the quintessence of the relationship between

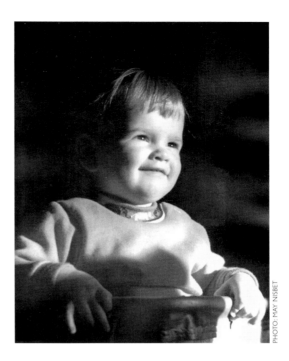

Author's daughter Michelle. Photographed by author's mother :: 1967

PHOTO: MAY NISBET

her daughter and myself was duly satisfied, in her mind, when I was asked to leave our house. The mother-in-law broached the subject with Mary Lou and I standing in the dining room, of all places. Finally I asked one question directed to my wife, "Do you want me to leave?" "Yes," was the answer, and noticing a grin on mother-in-law's face, I left. (I am certain you have noticed my lack of using *my* mother-in-law in the preceding sentences, because she was never *my* anything.

I moved back into my mother's house, and got together with Jim Moore. We continued to be successful in various real estate endeavors.

STUDIO FOR JOE GORES

On February 12 1979, Joe and Dori Gores asked my advice regarding the water seeping into their house in Marin County, California.

Their home was located on a side hill and the accumulated storm water could not drain from the uppermost foundation wall, causing the flooring to buckle.

I asked if they would prefer to sell the house and find another site in the immediate area. If so, I would design a new house for them.

They stated they preferred to stay in their present house, which had a magnificent view. I then drew a plan showing how to waterproof the foundation wall by hand digging a rock-filled drainage ditch, which would eliminate the water problem.

Joe also wanted me to design a combination writing studio and gymnasium for him, which would be appurtenant to the main house, and have a similar view.

The studio would be located on the upper floor with Joe's desk oriented toward the view and outside balcony. I detailed a glass railing, which would not interfere with the view. I also provided a concrete support, so their hot tub could be flush with the floor.

The work was completed by year's end, and Joe and Dori were pleased with the structure, as indicated by the following letter.

Appreciative letter from Joe Gores to author :: 1980

MY MOTHER'S DEATH (1968)

One morning I was having breakfast with my mother, and Christmas was only a few days away; she mentioned she didn't feel well, and she started to faint. I caught her so she wouldn't fall from her chair, and carried her to the living room couch. I immediately called for an ambulance that took her quickly to the Stanford Hospital, which was only a mile away. I fearfully followed in my car, but a doctor at the hospital told me she had expired in the ambulance.

My sweet, gentle, kind mother was gone. I went back to the house and saw the Christmas gifts she had wrapped for friends, relatives, and even some shut-ins who were too ill to get out and about.

She had even purchased and wrapped presents for my ex-wife and daughter, even though they never came to see her.

I once wrote in my journal one of the most genuine thoughts I have ever had: "I couldn't have asked for a better mother, I had the best."

I resumed working with my friend Jim Moore, and we went on to own a few mobile home parks and more real estate. We had a pleasant time working together at our own pace to put food on the table.

CHAPTER SIX ::

SETTLING DOWN IN CENTRAL CALIFORNIA

NEW HORIZONS

I had been living around Palo Alto and Stanford for the greater portion of my life, but the influx of people and more automobiles to the area, belching billions of tons of toxic gases into the air, and compromising our atmosphere, started me thinking about moving away. Smog had bothered my lungs each time we had gone to the Los Angeles area on one occasion or another. We had relatives near L.A., and we would visit between Thanksgiving and Christmas each year.

One time Jim Moore and I visited one of his relatives in Culver City, who worked in a high position at R.K.O. Studios. He had invited us to see how movies were being made and later in the day we were going to spend some time at the beach. We arose and had a lovely breakfast with our host and hostess in their air-conditioned house, but within a few minutes after going outside to our car, both Jim and I felt an uncomfortable tickling sensation in our lungs, which made both of us cough. With more and more traffic in the area, our coughing became worse.

We arrived at the movie studio in approximately twenty minutes, and our coughing began to subside in an air-conditioned building. We walked from set to set to see the various directors getting the most from the actors, but we

sometimes had to walk outside of the building to get to the next set. During our time outside, our coughing began to get more severe. Our host had seen the smog affect others, of course, and finally he suggested we not go to the beach, but stay inside the air-conditioned building until he was ready to go home for the day.

We had to agree this would be a better solution, so we basically spent the day watching the movie actor Claude Rains walking back and forth in an inside room studying his lines.

I mention this to clarify a point. I appreciate fresh air, and of course, I have never smoked anything. Impure air of any kind is the beginning of the downfall of the human body.

I was born and grew up in the Santa Clara Valley, which at that time was the most productive valley in the world for growing fruit and vegetables for world consumption. Field after field would be growing one vegetable or another. Ranch after ranch would be growing peaches, plums, apricots, cherries, apples, pears, and so on. I used to ride my bicycle past these orchards, and one could smell the different aromas when the trees were in blossom. One orchard bordered the next, and you could see blossoms for miles.

Some new businesses were coming to California and new buildings were being constructed around the fringes of the small existing cities south of San Francisco. They, of course, started to locate here because there were trucks or trains to carry their product to be shipped from ports in San Francisco and Oakland.

I was looking at this abnormal condition which, in time, could affect the valley demology; so I wrote a letter to the editor of the San Jose Mercury saying that the council should think about protecting the farmers and ranchers from the incursion that would soon be happening. I pointed out we should be building in the foothills and save our especially rich valley floor for the growing of food, for which it is best suited.

To my knowledge no one beat the drum, and the dollar and greed won out. What we have today is "Silly Cause Valley" with wall-to-wall asphalt and concrete with thousands and thousands of flat roofs thrown in for bad measure. Nearly all the farms and ranches are now gone because when expensive buildings were constructed adjacent to the farms and ranches, the city fathers did not protect them by way of lower property taxes. Their taxes went up and they were forced to sell to people who were willing to construct new buildings over prime vegetation, ad nausea.

I decided it was time for me to look for a piece of land around the Monterey Bay area to build a house, which would provide fresh air from the sea. I contemplated sites from Santa Cruz to Carmel; after about a year I settled on an existing lot in the pines overlooking the entire Monterey Bay. The view was due west and the view of sunsets over the water, priceless.

Soon after purchasing the lot. I got my building permit and hired a surveyor to locate certain points on the ground; I had designed the house to close tolerances regarding required setbacks. I then hired a man to help me lay out the building lines for the construction of the foundation.

Day by day the house was progressing, and sometime in the early stages I received a telephone call from Barbara Morrison whom

I had known from my early days at Taliesin in Wisconsin. Her husband Bill, Barbara and I became good friends; the friendship continued in California after the Morrisons left the fellowship.

Over the years Bill and Barbara had divorced, re-married and divorced the second time. During these trying times I saw each of them on one occasion or another. Bill and I even worked together in architect Warren Callister's office in Tiburon for a couple of months. Even after two divorces, Bill and Barbara were quite civil to each other, and I was still a friend with each of them. Sometimes Bill and I would go to dinner together, and on other occasions, Barbara and I would have a lunch or dinner together.

Somehow Barbara had found out I was building a house for myself, and she called me one evening to talk about it. After twenty minutes or so of conversation, she asked me if I

My brother Harry and Barbara at Christmas : : 1984

Barbara and author have just completed a project.—you may discern by the champagne in the glasses—during our house construction :: 1986

would like her to come down from Tiburon to help me in the construction. She had been working as a fill-in stenographer for a company that hired out people for a day, a week, or whatever, and she said a change would do her some good.

The next weekend I drove up to bring her, and some of her things, back to my abode, which was the beginning of many wonderful years together.

We didn't aspire to finish the house in the shortest period of time; rather, we both had time on our hands and we would go on trips and visit friends, reducing our construction to more of a lackadaisical endeavor, but we enjoyed ourselves. Instead of a few months to build a house, it took us a few years, but as I said, we enjoyed ourselves.

To illustrate, we both had lived in an area of California where exceptional wine is the norm, and we developed a proclivity to occasionally imbibe in champagne as a liquid of choice. This worked well for the two of us, and soon we would celebrate our construction accomplishments with a bottle of "bubbly."

When we finished pouring the house foundation, we drank a toast to concrete. When the wall framing was complete, and ready for the first-floor floor joists, another bottle was opened and readily dispatched. As we proceeded, and finished a major segment of the structure, we would have a cooler filled with ice and our favorite beverage at the ready. We framed window openings, and had our bottle and two glasses nearby.

When we completed our staircase, we opened a bottle of champagne for this outstanding achievement, of course. We proceeded by toasting the staircase at the top of the stairs. We then sat on each step while we drank from our glass and descended to the floor below.

We eventually finished an outside balcony, which was on the third level of the house, and from then on our objective was to see how far the corks would fly.

We finally finished roofing the house with our hand-made copper shingles. We then sat atop our abode, sipping away, and enjoyed one of the most spectacular sunsets we had witnessed to that point.

This might not have been the most prudent way to build our nest, but to us, it was delightful.

LAGINESTRA LETTER

After our separation from the army, my good friend Rocco Laginestra and I kept in touch for the first few years by mail, but somehow one of my letters had been returned to me by the post office stamped "No Forwarding Address." I found out the post office only forwarded mail for six months. Somehow Rocco overlooked sending me his new address when he moved away from Brooklyn.

From time to time I checked the Brooklyn phone directory, which was available in the San Jose library, but to no avail; he was no longer listed.

Finally, in May 1980 I happened to see his name listed as one of the prominent CEOs in Forbes magazine, and I wrote to RCA Records to see if indeed their CEO, Rocco Laginestra, was the same man I knew in the military police in Europe. I was thrilled to receive this letter from him.

R. M. Laginestra
May 12, 1980

Dear Earl,

You have, indeed, found the real Rocco, who spent, in retrospect, many fine months together with you in the army. I often wondered where you were, etc.

I am very happy that you took the initiative to send the card and letter. I really have fond memories of our association in the army. In my many trips to the West Coast, I would check the telephone directory for your name, and hopefully find the real Earl Nisbet.

I am, as you gathered from the address you used, working at RCA. Now that we have made contact, I hope that we will meet either on the West Coast or East Coast should either of us be traveling. I don't know what you are doing for a living, but you would make a great detective!

I look forward to seeing and hearing from you.

Sincerely,
Rocco

TO MICHELLE

It has been documented that nearly half of marriages in the US end in divorce, and it appeared I was helping to keep up the average.

I had no affront with Mary Lou, as the breakdown in our marriage was in reality because of her mother. She was determined what her daughter should or should not do. I acceded when she administered her will on Mary Lou, but I rebuked her opinions of what *I* should or should not do. This came to mean only one thing; I had to go.

Our divorce decreed that I was to have our daughter, Michelle, every other Saturday.

Mary Lou had moved back with her mother and father, and on my first scheduled Saturday with my two-year old daughter, everything worked out fine. Mary Lou came to the door with Michelle dressed warmly for the day. In early evening, after being with my mother for an early dinner, I returned Michelle to her mother. I suspected Mary Lou's mother had been away for the day, or surely she would have dictated the exact hour and minute I was to have our daughter back.

From then on it was impossible as Mary Lou's mother always answered the door, and she would tell me Michelle was sick and couldn't go with me, or variations on a theme for the next umpteen times. I attempted to see Michelle many times during the first two years, but the *dictator* won; so I quit paying child support until my attorney told me I would be put in jail if I did not pay. I paid.

In fact I paid until Michelle became 21 years of age.

Of course I had not known anything of my daughter's life during those two decades; so I finally hired a detective to see if he could find where she was living.

He reported Michelle was living in Sonoma County, California, which was a three and a half hours drive from where Barbara and I were living.

Barbara and I drove to the address we were given many times during the next three years. No one answered the door each of the times we were there, except the last time, before Barbara passed away. A man answered the door to say he had never heard of any *Michelle*, but an auto with Michelle's plates was parked in the driveway. With that rejoinder, we left.

During these previous years we sometime stayed with our friends, Alvin and Patty Badenhop, from Petaluma, who would accompany us on our mission.

Another friend that went with me to see if we could locate Michelle was architect Jackson Wong, whom I had known at Taliesin. He had been staying with me for a week, and was sympathetic to my cause, because he was having a similar family predicament in Oregon.

When we returned from our attempt to find Michelle, we discussed the lost years between father and daughter. He thought it might help if he wrote a letter to Michelle to enlighten her regarding what he knew I had been doing.

He later sent three letters to me for Michelle. These arrived after I came in contact with my daughter, and subsequently had a falling out.

My first meeting with Michelle came almost by accident as the Badenhops' asked if I would assist in photographing their son's wedding on August 2, 1997. I agreed, and the ceremony was held on a Pacific Coast beach.

After the reception, Patty Badenhop suggested we try to see Michelle as we were not too far away. Alvin drove us to the house and several cars were parked nearby, with one blocking the driveway as if someone was about to leave.

Soon a man and a woman came out and were talking at the woman's car. I quickly passed them and went to the door where a young lady was waiting. I asked if she was Michelle as I knew her mother, Mary Lou. She responded by saying that was Mary Lou getting into her car.

I went to the car and asked Mary Lou if she had time to come back into the house so we could all talk.

We chatted for nearly a half-hour and things seemed to go well as Michelle said she was thinking about hiring a detective to try to locate me.

After the meeting I did not see Mary Lou, but I did have the pleasure of seeing Michelle several times for picnics and dinners. We were getting along fine until she and her fiancée had a landlord problem in their hi-tech machine shop and she called me for some advice, which was taken the wrong way, and she hung up. I now ponder what might have been!

WONG LETTERS

In any event I offer Wong's "Letters to Michelle" to elucidate some Taliesin reflections which you might find interesting, and Michelle might someday read.

6-23-99

To Michelle:

Your Dad, Earl Nisbet, came to the Fellowship around the 1950s, and when I first saw him, he was out in the desert in his MG convertible, and when I asked him what he was doing, he said he wanted to know if his car would turn over with the fast way he was driving. I decided here is another strange apprentice; however he turned out to be an able apprentice, and does fine work. Another time when your dad was on laundry duty, a group of us were trying to set a roof truss upright, and we can not move it till Earl came along with a basket full of laundry, and with one hand he set the truss upright. That's how strong your dad was.

When we were at the Fellowship we were never very close; however our friendship grew when we left the school and we got in touch through an ex-apprentice directory. Our friendship grew and now we see and get in touch with each other often.

Your dad was assigned to take care of all the cars, and was at Taliesin so we did not see each other often.

We worked on several projects together. One was the now famous Bird Walk at Taliesin. With us was David Dodge, of the Dodge automobile family, and when he reached twenty-one, he inherited one million dollars.

8-19-99

To Michelle:

Here is another thought about your dad while he was at Taliesin.

When I was with Steve Oyakawa doing some plastering, he complained about his back that was bothering him. After a few days had gone by, he came on the job whistling and seemed to be in good spirits. When I inquired as to his good spirits, he told me that your dad had worked on his back, and he is feeling just fine.

I am sure your dad has helped many other apprentices, especially in the desert, as there we all gather large stones, with good-looking faces for wall construction, and there are many back problems.

Not only is your dad an in-house chiropractor, also he is the in-house automobile mechanic.

9-16-99

To Michelle:

Here is another thought about your dad. When he was out in the desert looking for stones with a good-looking face for the walls of Taliesin, he marked a couple of stones to resemble Indian Hieroglyphics and took them to decorate his tent site; however he left a few of these stones out in the desert, and an apprentice from Italy, named Franco, thought the stones were the real thing, and he gathered them up and shipped them to Italy. He could afford the shipping expense as he was a Marquee.

At that time, there was an uncrowned Prince from Italy, and when it came his turn to serve lunch and dinner, he absolutely refused to serve the Marquee as he was beneath his station; although he was not opposed to serving the rest of the fellowship.

Sincerely,

(Signed)
Jackson L. Wong

P.S. When I think of something else about your dad, I'll send it along.

BARBARA AND I PLAN SOME TRIPS

My fiancée, Barbara, began a tradition of taking each other to dinner on our birthdays with the celebrated choosing the place for the meal. When she asked me where I wanted to have dinner in June of 1983, I surprised her and said, "New York."

My plan was threefold as I wanted to see Rocco at RCA in New York City, and I wanted to purchase a new DeLorean sports car from a dealership in New York that was selling them for less that I could obtain one in California. Thirdly, I had known my wife's best friend was a minister in upstate New York, by the name of Bette Doty, and Barbara would be thrilled to spend some time with her.

I contacted Rocco who invited Barbara and me to have lunch with him at RCA headquarters at Rockefeller Plaza in Manhattan. As soon as we arrived, he came rushing from his office with a hug and at the same time, introduced his indispensable secretary, Dolores Dudo, who made us feel right at home.

It was great seeing him again after so many years had passed, and we had a nice time reminiscing our Army days over a sumptuous lunch.

After promising to meet again soon, Barbara and I said goodbye to Rocco, and we hailed a cab that took us to the DeLorean dealership. We made the automobile purchase and immediately headed for upstate New York, where we found Minister Doty's condominium, and had a pleasant stay of a few days.

I had brought enough maps along to chart our trip back to California by going through cities where Wright had constructed various buildings, which we intended to visit.

I called Rocco again to let him know we would be in New York again to see the Guggenheim Museum and to ask him to have lunch with us. He told me he would be flying to England in the morning to meet a Lord Gray on business, so we were not able to make contact with him again.

The next day we did take in the Hoffman Auto Showroom, designed by Wright in 1954, and the Guggenheim, which is quite an awesome building. It was nice to take the elevator to the top floor and leisurely stroll down the spiral ramp while viewing the artwork on display.

From New York City we headed for Pennsylvania where we saw the Kaufmann house, Fallingwater, and the Beth Sholom Synagogue, in Elkins Park. I had known Edgar Kaufmann Jr. at Taliesin, and he had invited me to stay at Fallingwater sometime, but I had never been close to the area before now, and he had previously given the house to the Western Pennsylvania Conservancy, which conducts tours of the buildings.

We next headed toward Chicago, as we wanted to see the many Wright buildings around Oak Park where he had established his own residence in 1889. We noticed most of the dwellings were well kept and the landscaping in perfect condition. Going through the Unitarian Church was quite a revelation, with the various but soft colors in evidence.

Before we left Oak Park, I took a photo of the new DeLorean in front of Mr. Wright's studio he had built in 1895, when horses were the transportation of the day.

Barbara and I were both impressed by one of Mr. Wright's most powerful designs, and it was uppermost in our minds to experience it on this trip. This was the Annunciation Greek Orthodox Church, which was built in 1956 at Wauwatosa, Wisconsin.

As we drove from Oak Park toward the church, the rains came down so heavily that the windshield wipers could hardly remove the water. We were close to the church at dusk,

but the rain was still pelting us, so I suggested we stop at a restaurant for some refreshments before we continue. By the time we finished our coffee, it seemed as though Wright had pulled some strings and made the rain stop. In a few minutes we were at the church, and without a tripod to steady my camera, but it was dry enough for me to lie on the ground for enough support to take some time-exposure photos. We both had the same feeling, when coming upon the building, which was so well lighted in the blackness of the night, of a space ship recently landed. Without a doubt, it was one of the most alluring buildings we had ever seen.

Following this extraordinary experience we drove towards Madison, Wisconsin to see the

TOP LEFT
Rocco Laginestra and author meeting in Rocco's RCA office after some thirty years of noncontact
:: 1983

TOP RIGHT
Barbara and Rocco Laginestra in his RCA office, 30 Rockefeller Plaza, New York, NY
:: 1983

BELOW
Our DeLorean parked in front of FLLW's Oak Park, IL studio
:: 1983

Author's DeLorean at
FLLW's Greek Orthodox
Church (constructed in
Wauwatosa, WI 1956)
:: 1983

Unitarian Meeting House and the Pew house,
both having been constructed in Shorewood
Hills.

The Pews were home and invited us in for
coffee (Barbara had known them from years
past), and they told us they would be selling
their house soon; they were both getting on in
years, and keeping a house up was too much
for them. It was sad; they had lived there since
it was built in 1939.

We next headed for Spring Green; we
wanted to see Taliesin again after having been
away for so many years. We arrived unannounced on the Fourth of July, and everyone
at Hillside was getting ready for a party and
some skits, which were planned for later in
the evening.

We spoke to an apprentice in the office at
Hillside about trying to see Johnny Hill, but she
said he had some malady and was not seeing
anyone these days, and in fact, he sometimes
would not come out of his room for dinner.

I finally persuaded her to call Johnny, at
Taliesin, and tell him Earl Nisbet and Barbara
Morrison would like to see him. After talking to
Johnny, the girl was surprised, but we were told
to wait, as Johnny would be right down.

He met us in the parking area and told us to
follow his car to Taliesin where we went to his
room to have tea with him, and a most interesting conversation. He said he knew something
was wrong with him, because he didn't want to

associate with people, but for some reason
he was glad to see us and was comfortable
around us. I always liked Johnny, and was
pleased that he would see us.

He was not going to be in any of the skits,
nor would he be going out of his room for dinner that evening; so we said goodbye and good
luck to him. As we were leaving Taliesin, we
ran into Brandoch Peters, son of Wes, whom
we hadn't seen since he was a boy, but to our
surprise, he remembered our names from the
old days.

After leaving Taliesin, we drove directly to
see the Wyoming Valley Grammar School in
Spring Green that Wright designed in 1956,
and from there we drove into Iowa to see the
Walter residence in Quasqueton, which I had
been fortunate to experience when I first went
to Taliesin.

Barbara at one of our stops while traveling to
Alaska :: 1990

We headed west from the Walter house and drove through Des Moines, completely overlooking the Trier house, which was built in 1956. Somehow neither Barbara nor I noticed it in the Storrer catalog we had with us.

Approaching Salt Lake City, we took the time to locate the Stromquist residence (1958) which had recently been purchased by two gentlemen who had been renovating it for several months to bring it back to its original condition. They seemed to be doing a good job, and they described, in detail, the work they had done. After some cocktails with them in the early evening, the four of us went into town for dinner, and later, Barbara and I took a room for the night.

In the morning we were off for Reno, Nevada, as Barbara felt lucky, but as it turned out, she wasn't. Who would have guessed? After breakfast the next morning we started on our last leg of our trip for home. All in all, we had a great time seeing the Reverend Doty, Johnny Hill and others at Taliesin, the Wright buildings, and driving across America in a new DeLorean.

Sadly, Dolores Dudo, Rocco's private secretary, called me a few months later to tell me Rocco had to undergo brain surgery, and he didn't pull through. I had looked forward to several more meetings with him in the future to exchange more on what he had done since our Army days, but our wonderful meeting in his office was to be our last.

TALIESIN FELLOWS NORTHERN CALIFORNIA

When the Taliesin Fellowship was in Scottsdale, we sometimes traveled there to visit friends who had stayed on, and also to experience the desert again. Barbara enjoyed Arizona so much, I planned to design a house for us near Pinnacle Peak, north of Scottsdale, but in the meantime we purchased a temporary house in Scottsdale, and we made several trips in the next few years to take advantage of it.

On these trips between our California house and the one in Arizona, we would make a layover in the Los Angeles area to see friends from our Taliesin days. On one occasion we found that the *Journal of the Taliesin Fellows* magazine, begun by publisher John Geiger, also a friend of ours from Taliesin, was having a hard time publishing regularly because of a lack of funds. Barbara and I were discussing how we might help John meet the payroll in order for him to continue publishing the *Journal*. We had been aware of some forty former apprentices living between Sacramento, San Francisco, Los Banos, and Monterey, so we thought if we could get them all together we might collectively help the *Journal* flourish. It was in this mode that Barbara suggested we begin a group of former apprentices in the Bay Area. I thought an organization of our own might be a way to show some houses to the public, for a fee, and send the proceeds to Geiger in order to keep his excellent magazine running in the black.

I suggested she call our old friend Bill Patrick whom I had known before going to Taliesin. She asked if he would like to become a part of this new venture, and if so, would he mind holding our meetings at Midglen, (his house and office) as it would be more central for the anticipated apprentices from the Bay Area to attend.

Barbara called Bill, who wanted a day or two to think it over. When he called back in the affirmative, he said he had called Mr. Wright's West Coast representative, Aaron Green, who thought it a good idea and said he would be there for our first meeting at Midglen.

Barbara thought I should become president of this new organization, but I said to her it would be better if Patrick would assume the honor, since his place would be closer for most people to attend. She called Aaron Green, whom she had worked for in the past, and discussed the position of officers in our new "Taliesin Fellows Northern California," which I had named.

Simply a great person.
Barbara on one of our
earlier outings
: : 1963

Barbara waiting for a
taxi whle on vacation
in St. Martin
: : 1990

We sent out about forty notices of our forthcoming meeting, and about thirty-two apprentices showed up, including Aaron, who nominated Bill Patrick for president, Barbara Nisbet for secretary and Earl Nisbet for treasurer. All were elected by a show of hands, disregarding the fact that no one ran against us.

Our new Taliesin Fellows were very enthusiastic about raising money for the Journal; several of the new members knew the present owners of several of Wright's California houses, and we would probably be able to open their houses to the public by selling tickets.

During the coming months we were able to raise money by showing the Bazett (Frank)

house in Hillsborough, the Hanna house at Stanford, the Buehler house in Orinda, the Berger house in San Anselmo, the Morris Gift Shop in San Francisco, the Fawcett house in Los Banos, which was supervised by one of our new members and former apprentice, Bob Beharka; our most remote showing was the Albin house in Bakersfield.

Our members had voted the percentage of the earnings to be sent to the Journal towards its subsistence, and as treasurer, I was very pleased to write those checks.

Barbara enjoyed traveling to places she had not been before; so between working on our house, visiting southern California and Scottsdale, and attending meetings at our newly formed TFNC. organization, we managed to travel to Brazil to see her son Danny married in a Catholic church. A few months later we went on a vacation, with friends, to Hawaii for two weeks, then months later, with the same friends, I drove the four of us to Baja, Mexico in our motor home. That turned out to be such a fun trip; we did it again the following two years. The next year, with the same two friends, we flew to Cozumel, Mexico, in the Caribbean, to spend a week. We had planned to go on to Belize the following week, but the wife of our friend became ill; so we left for home the next day.

OCTOBER 17, 1989

My mate, Barbara, was in the kitchen of our house in Aptos, packing the last segment of food we were storing in our motor home for the trip we had planned during the past week. No, we were not going to attend the World Series that day; we would be late, for at that moment fans were filling the stadium. No, we were about to leave for a week driving down the coast highway to Big Sur, where we would be camping and enjoying our good earth.

Living in California over the years you feel rumbles in the earth from time to time, and usually you stand still and wait it out, and in a few seconds you seem to be on normal footing again.

While Barbara was packing the last box of food to take with us on our trip, I happened to be close to her in the dining room at 5:04 PM. I felt a small, very hard, jolt, so I said to Barbara, "Let's get out of here; this one feels different." What we were feeling was the Loma Prieta earthquake, which measured 7.1.

I ran for the front door of our house, as I wanted it open in case the house would twist and wedge the door inoperable. I was trying to unlock the door but I was thrown to the floor while hanging onto the doorknob. I looked back, and Barbara was already on the floor and a water pitcher flew past her head and a large Chinese wine vase we had on my mother's hope chest was bouncing on the carpet like a basketball.

I turned my attention to getting the door open again, but as I got to my knees, I too was bouncing up and down, so much so that I cut my elbow on a light switch as I tried to get to my feet by leaning against the wall.

It was said to have lasted about 27 seconds, but it seemed more like 27 minutes to us. Neither of us could get up and stand until it was over.

Finally, when I did open the door, there was a metal cabinet lying across the doorway. It had been about to be placed in the garage, but I hadn't gotten to it. Our next door neighbor appeared at the entry in time to help stand it upright again, and away from the doorway. He had been outside watering his garden and he said he thought our houses were going to touch, they were swaying that much. Each of our houses are approximately three stories in height, but his was constructed on poles set into the ground, which is more prone to swaying than our house, which was hand-dug into the earth.

The three of us then ran out to the street to level ground, and I cautioned us to move away from the overhead electric power lines in case they should break because we would most likely be having aftershocks.

After a few minutes, the aftershocks seemed to be diminishing so I grabbed some tools from the garage and shut off our water and natural gas supply lines to our house. There is always a possibility of an explosion with a gas line leak within a dwelling, and I didn't want to take any chances.

I then went around the neighborhood to shut off supplies to a few other houses. In a few hours it would be dark and we would not have any electricity, gas, or water, so I drove our motor home onto our neighbor's lot directly across the street from our house. It was not being used by anyone; the elderly lady who had lived there was in a rest home and Barbara had been visiting her since she moved.

Fortunately we had just loaded the motor home with supplies and water, but we were too low on gasoline to take a chance on leaving the area. We camped on the hill above us for a week until the filling station had electricity again.

The neighbor's house on poles had approximately $20,000 damage done to it when all was said and done. Two large windows broke in our house; there was virtually no structural damage, but some gypsum boards had developed cracks only in the ceiling joints, so the house fared well. Our possessions were another matter. Everything on an open shelf fell off onto the quarry tile floors and broke. The refrigerator ended up three feet from the wall with everything on the floor. Bottles of this, that, and the other thing broke and the contents created a smelly mess, which was an experience in itself. I had my mother's collection of cut glass that was fragmented beyond belief. Art plates, bowls, and several raku pieces of Barbara's would be no more. All in all, we probably lost approximately two thousand dollars on the house and eight thousand dollars in art objects.

It turned out we were living approximately seven miles from the epicenter of the Loma

Prieta earthquake; it caused 63 deaths, 3,757 injuries, and over six billion dollars in damage, and more than 3,000 people were left homeless.

At the time the Loma Prieta hit, it was the most costly natural disaster that had occurred in the United States.

It was felt extensively 10 miles away in Santa Cruz, 21 miles away in San Jose, 57 and 59 miles away in Oakland and San Francisco, respectively.

We hope that was the last quake we will ever experience.

The following year Barbara and I went on a dangerous cruise to Alaska, launching, or should I say lunching, from Seattle, Washington. I am not referring to the dangerous seas your ship sometimes plods through to get you to your destination; I'm referring to the dangerous sea of calories you see everywhere you turn, once aboard. We docked at Prince Rupert, British Columbia as the first port of call, following by Sitka, Valdez, Anchorage, and Kodiak before turning about for the return trip to Seattle.

Barbara and I spent a few days with Milton Stricker, an architect, and his wife, Eunice, who showed us some of the interesting houses Milton had designed in the area. We had been friends of Milton for a long time, going back to our days together at Taliesin.

On our drive back to our house in California, we stopped to see the Marin County Civic Center, which Wright had designed some years earlier. We went into the gift shop, because we heard that an owner of a Wright house, Mrs. Berger, was donating some of her time there, and we wanted to ask her who we might talk to about having an exhibit of TFNC apprentices' work.

We met with the lady in charge of booking exhibits, and after I showed her a couple of examples of our work, she said we could have a week for an exhibition somewhere in the near future. At the next TFNC meeting, Barbara and I asked our members to get some of their best work ready for a presentation that would occur in a few weeks.

Collectively we spent many, many hours getting photos and drawings mounted on boards for the showing, to say nothing about getting models of buildings on stands for viewing. Some of our members prepared three-dimensional sculptures that were over six feet in height. Others would be showing painting, abstractions, or some artistic photography.

Before our exhibition day arrived, the Civic Center had mailed out a few hundred invitations to benevolent citizens in the Marin County area for a special showing the day before our scheduled opening. We had rented trucks in order to transport the material to be shown, and several volunteers hung the show, following directions of the lady in charge. We were finally ready, but we had not anticipated the weather. One of the worst storms California had ever seen hit that day, and in a few hours the streets were flooded, and our gallant *art lovers* stayed home in droves. Very few were in attendance the first night, but one hardy soul arrived in a canoe. The storm continued waxing and waning during our entire engagement, and needless to say it was a minor disaster.

ST. MARTIN

A few months went by and Barbara and I decided we needed a complete change; so we made arrangements to spend two weeks in the Caribbean, on St. Martin, which is owned by two governments, the French and the Dutch. There is much beauty to behold as you travel around the island, and the sailing is a dream come true.

After a few days of exploring the Dutch side of the island we noticed that a main, well-traveled street was called *Nisbet*. We had been on it several times. It was a long street, and seeing the street sign again and again, it aroused my curiosity to the extent I wondered if our family could be related. We finally entered a bank to

ask a clerk if she knew how *Nisbet Street* got its name. She didn't know, but she would go into a back room to ask her boss if he could give us an explanation. In a few moments she came back to tell us they didn't know how important this Mr. Nisbet had been to have a street named after him, but she went on to say, "He was black."

Shortly after arriving back in California, I suggested to Barbara we should think about getting married. We had just gotten together to get a house built, and on various things kept us busy from day to day; so neither of us thought of marriage. We had a marvelous time living the way we had during the past few years, but I thought the time had come to get hitched, and it just so happened Barbara's best friend was a Unitarian minister, and she had recently been sent to Phoenix to take over a congregation.

Barbara called her to say we wanted to be married in Arizona, and would she do the honors; "Of course" was her reply. I was looking a couple of months ahead to Mr. Wright's birthday that would fall on a Saturday, June 8, 1991. I hoped we could get permission from the CEO, Dick Carney, to be married that day in the living room at Taliesin West. Actually, when I was living at Taliesin, at Spring Green, Dick lived in the adjacent room; so we were friends for forty

years at that point, which was why I wanted to be married on that day; Barbara and I also had known each other for forty years.

JUNE 8, 1991

I made an appointment for Barbara and me to see Dick. We didn't let on why we wanted to see him, and when we were shown into his office we noticed he greeted us with a scowl, instead of a smile on his face. We found out later some former apprentices had tried to come back to Taliesin to live, but for one reason or another, they didn't work out, and Dick thought we too would be asking to return to Taliesin. When he heard our real reason for this meeting, he said, "I think that is a wonderful

Announcements mailed thoughout the San Francisco Bay Area for the forthcoming TFNC exhibit of former FLLW apprentices
:: 1995

PHOTO: PATTY BADENHOP

his wife, Patty, helping in the kitchen. She had always wanted to live at Taliesin, but had never had the opportunity.

We were planning to have the reception at Mrs. Wright's garden and pool area, which was just off of her private quarters. Barbara and I, with the Badenhops, cleaned the pool and brought some beach balls to float in the water. We also brought all the potted plants we could find that weren't tied down to the area for color, besides setting up the tables with colorful cloths and cut flowers. By the time we set up the champagne and hors-d'oeuvre table, we were finished, and the garden lighting made it all come alive.

Barbara and I helped apprentices Effie Casey and Arnold Roy move extra chairs and more plants to the garden/living room, where our actual ceremony would take place.

We also helped set up the dining room by covering the tables with turquoise cloths, which was Barbara's favorite color, and placing silverware and glasses at each place. Our friends brought in the flower arrangements we had ordered from a shop in Scottsdale.

Our next mission was to decorate the theatre where all would be gathering after dinner. By the time we had finished placing flowers in strategic locations and added colorful place mats at each seat, the atmosphere was dazzling.

There were quite a few extra people in attendance on June 8, 1991. In celebrating Mr. Wright's birthday each year, Taliesin invites people in the Scottsdale area who had donated some of their time to act as docents, guides, or booksellers for the benefit of the school, for an evening of cocktails, hors-d'oeuvres, dinner, music, and entertainment. Ours was a formal affair, with ladies in beautiful flowing gowns, and male guests looking fit and proper in their tuxedos.

It was enchanting to exchange vows with Barbara before her minister friend, Bette Doty, in one of Mr. Wright's most beautiful living rooms, and it felt good to be at Taliesin again,

idea," and he called Indira Berndtson to get together with us to plan the service, the meal, the champagne gathering, and the musical entertainment, which would take place later in the Cabaret Theater.

Indira was quite helpful along with some of our friends from California who came out early to help with the preparation of food and some general housekeeping chores. I recall our friend Alvin Badenhop, over six feet tall, cleaning windows that had been somewhat neglected, and after forty years. I was again captivated by the serenity of that great spacious enclosure from the harsh external desert just a wall away.

When our ceremony was completed, and our toasts made, I coveted a special momentous photo of our special day; so I asked Barbara to pose with me before the fireplace so we could hold hands. With our free hand, each touched one of the two main stones I had helped find and place nearly forty years earlier.

My old friend, Kamal Amin, whom I first met at Taliesin in 1951, took the photograph that recorded the culmination of our milestone. Many other photos of the evening were taken and Taliesin photographer Greg Williams presented a nice video to Barbara and me the next day.

The Taliesin volunteers and our friends seemed to mingle pleasantly, and fortunately we provided enough good food and champagne along with the evening's presentation of some Vivaldi violin pieces played by a young lady from Scottsdale; our friend from Menlo Park, Fred Clarke, played several classical selections on his guitar. The last person to perform for everyone was Barbara's son, Daniel, who played and sang some country songs on his guitar. All the music was well received for all to retain fond memories of Mr. Wright's birthday celebration on June 8, 1991.

Dick Carney, CEO of Taliesin at that time, offered Yvonna's (Mr. and Mrs. Wright's daughter) quarters, the Sun Trap, to Barbara and me for our first night as husband and wife, or should I say, wife and husband. Mr. Wright designed this small but unique apartment for his daughter, who enjoyed it for years, but she was gone at this time.

We appreciated a place to stay after a late evening saying goodbye to friends who made the trip from California.

In the morning we had a nice breakfast with the fellowship, and we thanked Dick again for letting us use the living room for our ceremony.

My old friend Alvin Badenhop and his wife Patty were also able to take a room for the night at Taliesin, as we were planning to follow them to meet a client of Alvin in Colorado. This, then, would be our honeymoon, following a yellow Pontiac through six states.

We drove from Scottsdale, Arizona, north to Flagstaff, then we headed east to Albuquerque, where we turned north to Denver. At Denver we headed west on Highway 70 passing Vail and on to Eagle, where Alvin's client was expecting us.

From left: Taliesin photographer, Greg Williams, Barbara Morrison Nisbet, Rev. Bette Doty, and the author. The stone above Rev. Doty's head was found by the author, and dropped while bringing it down the mountain, losing 2' of length. The rounded stone above the author's shoulder was found in an indian chief's hideout in Cave Creek, AZ
: : June 8, 1991

PHOTO: ALVIN BADENHOP

PHOTO: KALAL AMIN

From left, Ingrid Morrison, wife of Danny Morrison, Barbara (Morrison) Nisbet's son. Barbara Nisbet, author's wife, standing between two stones he brought for the fireplace hood. Marriage was on the birthdate of Frank Lloyd Wright : : June 8, 1991

Alvin and Patty Badenhop on his client's site. Eagle, CO :: 1991

We spent two days looking at the site for the house Al would be designing, and looking at more beautiful scenery than we had expected. There was grandeur in every direction from wherever you were.

After Al completed his business with his client, we pointed our automobiles west again, and we fell in behind the yellow Pontiac. We went through Grand Junction, Colorado, and somehow wound our way on small back roads, all the way to Salt Lake City. From there we stayed on route 40 through Winnemucca, finally arriving at Reno.

Barbara at a Carmel Guiter Society gathering. Carmel, CA :: 1984

The four of us had a nice breakfast in Reno before we started our engines to head for the San Francisco Bay Area, where all of had been living. Sometimes, even years later, if I close my eyes and concentrate, I can still see the back end of a yellow Pontiac, mind you, I'm speaking of a General Motors issue from Detroit.

SECOND SEVEN AND A HALF MINUTES OF FAME

After a few days rest, Barbara and I drove to Monterey for an evening's dinner. We had already been members of the Classical Guitar Society of Carmel, and after the completion of our dinner, we attended a guitar recital performed by Terrence Farrell, an acquaintance of ours, who invited some of the Society members for a reception at his house following his recital.

Several people were already there as we were welcomed inside. There was wine and cheese and crackers to munch on as we mingled to talk to some of the other guests. We mainly spoke of the wonderful guitar playing we had just heard, but before long we were introducing ourselves to others who usually asked what one does for a living.

Barbara had been talking to one gentleman as I returned with a glass of wine for her, and she proceeded to introduce me, by name of course. When he heard my name he asked if I was the one who designed a cabin in the Santa Cruz Mountains a few years back. He went on to say he had seen the *Better Homes and Gardens* publication of it and saved the article, hoping that I would design a house for him some day. Practically in the same breath he told us his brother is an architect, but he didn't care for his work.

He asked me for my business card, but years have gone by and I have still not heard from him.

This, I feel, is my other seven and a half minutes of fame.

THE INCREDIBLE ROY RANDOLPH

I am certain most people know, or who have heard of the actor and conservationist, Leo Carrillo who was born in Los Angeles on August 6, 1880.

He was part of an old and respected family who's roots go back to the conquistadors, and his own father became the first mayor of Santa Monica, California.

Leo worked for a time as a newspaper cartoonist before he went to New York to become an actor on Broadway. Later he went to Hollywood where he appeared in more than 90 films. Although he was known from coast to coast with cinema exposure, he was best remembered from the television series, the "Cisco Kid," on which he played the sidekick "Pancho."

He served on the California Beach and Parks Commission for eighteen years and played a major part in the State of California acquiring Hearst Castle at San Simeon, the Los Angeles Arboretum, and the Anza-Borrego Desert State Park.

Because of his contribution to the state, the Leo Carrillo State Park, on the Pacific Coast Highway in Southern California was named after him.

Many know of his contribution to the Motion Picture Industry, and have seen his "Star" on the Hollywood Walk of Fame at 1635 Vine Street. What most people do not know is that Leo adopted a young boy and raised him like his own son. This youngster went to the best schools and learned to speak Spanish like a native in the company of the Carrillo's. This would become an advantage to young Roy Randolph later on when he was in the C.I.A. during World War II.

From the moment he was growing up in and around Hollywood, he was meeting and dining with the various stars of the day.

Leo Carrillo was a very popular person in the days of movie making and stars would come to the Carrillo Casa for food and drink

The incredible Roy Randolph. Puerto Vallarta, Mexico :: 1996

and merriment, and just to have an entertaining evening with the affable Leo.

One of the many entertainers that often made his appearance with Leo was Bill 'Bojangles' Robinson, who began teaching Roy Randolph to dance. In the successive months, dance became exhilarating for Roy, and he learned all the steps and dances he could. In the next few years he made his living in designing chorography for the movies, and in teaching actors to dance for their performances.

The studio hired him to teach young Shirley Temple to dance, for her first several movies. By this time Roy was well known around Hollywood, and many stars would look to him as a friend.

Roy had gotten a very good education by the time WWII came along, and he enlisted in the army where he became a C.I.A. agent. After his training, and because of his perfect Spanish, he was sent to South America to mingle with various communities in various cities to ferret out Nazies who had fled Germany to live incognito in a city, such as Rio, Buenos Aires, or Caracas. He traveled to many cities during his time in the service and was able to turn over four Nazies to the military police.

Immediately after the war years, he returned to Hollywood to teach dance and he made a home for himself in the Palm Springs area in California. While there he became a friend of Lily Ponds, the great Opera Singer, and he gathered other friends around him to contribute to local museums and theater. In the succeeding years, he did so much for Palm Springs the city made him an "Honorary Mayor."

Not only did he travel extensively in South America, he also saw a great deal of Mexico because of his ease of getting around by speaking Spanish. He loved most of Mexico, but he decided to live in Puerto Vallarta, and travel to Hollywood for occasional work in the movies.

He thought of a brilliant way to have a place of his own in Puerto Vallarta without it costing him an arm and a leg. At that time P.V. was not the tourist attraction it is today and it might not work now, especially with stricter building codes.

In any event, he sought out the owner of an eight-story hotel and proposed he build a penthouse on the roof of the building. Roy would bear all of the costs, which would become rent free upon completion for 20 years, or upon his death, when it would revert, in fee, back to the hotel owner. A contract was drawn, signed and soon Roy had a place of his own in Puerto Vallarta.

It wasn't long before he noticed the children of P.V. didn't have a regular school. They were being taught in the open air under a thatched roof where it would become rather grim in the rain.

He decided something should be done about it, and he started to promote civic "Brick Parties" whereby one would be admitted to the dance, food, and festivities by bringing building bricks for a proposed new school. He had many of these parties over the years and he was able to build an eight room brick schoolhouse for the children of P.V.

Here again, he did so much good for the community, they made him "Honorary Police Chief" of P.V. This happened just before I met him.

I had a lull in my real estate ventures so I decided to spend a month or so in Puerto Vallarta. A friend of mine's wife had been in P.V. for a few months and I asked if she could find a small house for me to rent. She arranged for a house on a cliff overlooking the entire beach area, and it also took in the westerly sunsets from the living room.

I woke up to a knock at the front door the first morning I was there, and there was Roy Randolph, looking for the previous tenant. I explained this was my first morning in P.V. and I didn't know anything about the party he was inquiring about. I asked him to come in and while we were talking, I felt an immediate kindred sympathetic spirit with him. Apparently he felt something special in me after my telling him of my time spent with Frank Lloyd Wright, and he suggested he drive us to town for breakfast.

There was less than half a dozen times in my life when I have felt so comfortable around a person, within the first fifteen or twenty minutes of conversation, I knew we could become genuine friends, and that happened between Roy and myself.

He took me to his friend's houses in P.V. for parties and musical gatherings, and we also went on short day trips for sight seeing. We drove to an art colony south of P.V. where all of the individuals paint or sculpt nearly all day long.

We went to evening musical performances as well as hanging out on the beach during the day. I met a nice woman by the name of Dorothy, from New York, about this time and she was willing to be included in our alcoholic escapades. Roy thought we might like to see where his friend Richard Burton had made the movie "Night of the Iguana," in 1964. We boarded a boat for the trip to Yelapa, which is about fifteen to twenty miles south of Puerto Vallarta. Roy told us some tourists think they are going to an island to see the "Iguana" site, as they have to go by boat; there are no roads leading to the area. After visiting the movie site, we spent a night at a small hotel on the beach, and in the morning we had a nice breakfast and swim in the lagoon before we boarded the boat bound for P.V.

Roy was about to lose his penthouse a few months before I arrived so he purchased a new house in a new subdivision just a few miles north of town, and it was just a few doors away from the house of Elizabeth Taylor.

He was preparing a surprise party for Richard Burton and Elizabeth Taylor, which would be given, at his house. He asked Dorothy and me to go with him for a couple of days so he could instruct his help in what to purchase and what things needed doing.

Dorothy and I were invited to attend what would be a most interesting evening, but a day or so before Burton and Taylor were to arrive, Roy received a phone call from Burton saying he and "Liz" had broken up again, and they would not be coming to P.V.

I stayed for another week and left for California when Dorothy went back to New York. She and I corresponded for a time but 3,000 miles is arduous to overcome, and soon the both of us discovered it was easier not to write.

I went back to P.V. in 1997 to spend a month in the same house, and of course to see Roy. On this trip I met Zelda, who was vacationing in a nearby townhouse. We spent a great deal of time with Roy doing similar things, with one exception. He had planned another brick party, and I was pleased he asked my help. I designed a poster with a stylized little boy and girl holding hands on their way to school. The posters were about 2' wide and 3' tall, and were printed gratis by a friend of Roy, and dozens of them were placed all over town.

It turned out to be a great party and enough bricks and cash were acquired to build another room on Roy's school.

Just before I was to leave for home, Roy presented me with a gold card he had printed to entitle certain friends of his to belong, and meet in a private club of his in Palm Springs, which he said included TV, stage, and movie celebrities. Sadly, before I was to attend my

Friend Zelda and author in Puerto Vallarta :: 1997

TOP
Roy Randolph, companion Dorothy, and author at Randolph's house for last minute details for surprise party for Richard Burton and Elizabeth Taylor :: 1996

MIDDLE
Author and friend Dorothy in Puerto Vallarta :: 1996

One of Barbara's raku pots and the cover of her proposed Italian recipe book being exhibited at Cal Poly, San Luis Obispo, CA posthumously :: 1996

first meeting, his secretary sent me a letter notifying me of his recent passing.

SEVEN AND A HALF MINUTES FORWARD

Barbara and I had known Keith and Marge Riley several years before they asked me to do a redesign and an addition to their house. Marge is a psychoanalyst; Keith is a brilliant

computer programmer, who wrote a program for the U.S. Navy to have a safer way to load big guns on their ships to counteract the problem which caused an explosion on one of their ships, killing some sailors in their maritime exercises.

We would get together for excursions around the Bay Area to places of interest we would enjoy. It was delightful to spend time with them, when possible, as they lived quite a distance away in the East Bay. We were able to spend weekends with each other from time to

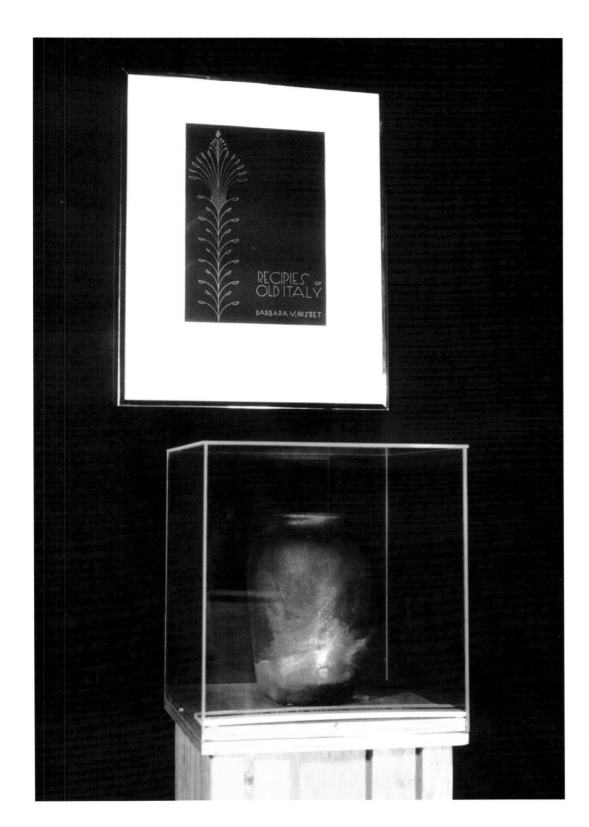

Barbara's Cal Poly exhibit
of her raku vase and her
contemplated book,
Recipes of Old Italy
::1996s

time, and we would usually have dinner at a favorite restaurant, but on occasion we would host each other for dinner at our own abode.

At one opportunity to have a most delightful dinner at the Riley residence, we were chatting over coffee and cheesecake when Keith asked me directly, "Earl, what would you say was the best thing you obtained from being at Taliesin?" Without missing a beat, I said, "Barbara," and Barbara followed with, "That's really nice, Earl." As Cronkite would say, "And that's the way it was."

Barbara was one of the very first persons I met at Taliesin, and from the very first day we worked together I felt she was a very special lady. Over the years many others came to know what a sweet and sensitive nature she possessed. She was always thinking of others, to the point where she would visit infirm friends in hospitals or rest homes on more occasions than some of their relatives. She always brought gifts of flowers or books, or something that might interest the person she was visiting.

She was never looking to get something out of these contacts for herself; she was simply thinking if she were not able to get out, how nice it would be if someone brought her flowers. Barbara was just that kind of a person and all who knew her would acknowledge the integrity within her.

One day Barbara and I were having lunch with our friend and TFNC member Duke Johnson, and he mentioned his son was studying architecture at Cal Poly, at San Luis Obispo. Immediately Barbara asked Duke to have his son supply us with a telephone number of someone with whom we could discuss having an architectural exhibit at the college. In a few days, Duke called us with the name and number of the person.

I called the woman in charge of exhibits and after talking, and sending some photos of our Marin County exhibit to her, we arrived at a date for showing about six or seven weeks later.

In the meantime, Barbara's mother, who was living in San Francisco, was not feeling well;

Barbara would visit her every few days, and stay over to cook and clean.

One time her son was also visiting, and he noticed Barbara did not look too well; so he took her to a hospital in San Francisco to have her checked. The doctors examined her, but they found nothing wrong.

Several days later she was visiting her son in Marin County when she had the same symptoms again, so he took her to a hospital in Marin County. The doctors there also found nothing wrong, but Barbara was not herself. Her mother had gotten better, and we drove to Scottsdale for an appointed dinner at a friend's house.

As soon as our hostess saw Barbara she went next door and returned with a doctor friend to speak to Barbara, After five minutes of discussion, he said she should have a head scan upon our return to California.

We checked into a hospital where Barbara had a scan, which showed a large brain tumor that had developed over the past several months.

She had an operation to remove the tumor; she also had several bouts of radiation. Unfortunately, it was only a stopgap measure, and she simply grew weaker each day until she needed professional help. I arranged for her to have a nice room, which pleased her, looking out upon a beautiful garden under some massive pine trees in Monterey, California, where she slipped away about ten days later.

Again, I experienced another great loss; my sweet, gentle, and kind wife was gone. She had been so healthy-looking and vibrant in spirit before she became ill; her friends were astounded when they were notified of her demise.

Of the many letters of condolence written to me, the following letter from Bruce Brooks Pfeiffer, from Taliesin West, expressed the loss of Barbara most admirably.

Another very sad thing about losing Barbara was that she enjoyed traveling. We had discussed some of the places she wanted to see, and I had intended to journey with her to Japan, Egypt, China, Spain, and Italy, in that order.

We had known of a seemingly wonderful way to see Japan through an organization begun by Mr. and Mrs. Sam Cohen, who lived in the East Bay. We attended a get-together meeting at their house to learn what the Japanese American Culture Exchange Program was about.

Sam started this organization some twenty-plus years prior to our attending the meeting. You pay a flat fee for round trip airfare. All lodgings and meals are included. Each day you stay with a different Japanese family in a different city. The host family takes you to historic or interesting places near their home during the day, and you sleep at their home. Arising in the morning, you have breakfast with the family, and upon completion, they take you to the next train depot or bus station, where you meet others from the trip. After your arrival at the next city, you're introduced to your new host, and the process begins again. In my estimation, this is a marvelous way to experience a country when you do not know the language.

We signed up that evening, as it seemed a perfect way to see Japan.

We talked so much about this particular trip, I felt certain she would enjoy it immensely, but she passed away two weeks before the flight. Somehow she must have had a premonition about her health, because during our discussion about traveling to Japan, we each promised to make the trip even if one of us could not.

I was saddened by Barbara's absence, but I did make the trip. I know I was morose most of the time. Often I did not have lunch with the others. I instead would purchase an apple to eat in a park, or wherever there was solitude. I would meet up with the group later in time to take the bus to the next destination.

It was a fascinating way to get around in a country full of beauty and mystery. I saw the wisdom of Barbara's promise, and mine to her.

THE FRANK LLOYD WRIGHT FOUNDATION
FRANK LLOYD WRIGHT SCHOOL OF ARCHITECTURE
THE FRANK LLOYD WRIGHT ARCHIVES

September 30, 1995

Dear Earl -

For quite some time I have been out of the office, and also out of touch with things, only to return and discover that Barbara had died. I can not tell you what a shock that is, when you both were here last year she seemed so energetic and vital, as I always remember her.

I fully realize that nothing anyone can say or do can lessen the pain and anguish - but you know how much we loved Barbara - and perhaps that - along with wonderful memories - can be of some help?

My love and deepest sympathy -

TALIESIN WEST □ SCOTTSDALE, ARIZONA 85261-4430 □ 602 860 2700   FAX 602 391 4009
FRANK LLOYD WRIGHT ARCHIVES   FAX 602 451 0234
TALIESIN □ SPRING GREEN, WISCONSIN 53588-9304 □ 608 588 2511   FAX 608 588 2090

I would probably not have gone without that. At the next meeting of the Taliesin Fellows Northern California the members decided to dedicate the upcoming shows at Cal Poly, San Luis Obispo, and at Cal Poly, Pomona to Barbara.

We assembled the items used for the Marin County exhibit, and trucked them to San Luis Obispo where Duke and I helped set up the show. Barbara had done raku pottery for years, and just before she became ill, she was putting together a cookbook based on authentic old recipes from Italy. I prepared a stand for one of her raku pieces, and I also took a photo of the cover layout of her cookbook so they could both be displayed.

The show turned out to be a great success, with students asking the architects questions after the showing.

Letter of condolence from Bruce Brooks Pfeiffer, Director of Archives, Taliesin West

Duke set up the show in Pomona, with the help of some students, as I had scheduled a Celebration of Life memorial for Barbara at a church in San Francisco. I needed to be on hand to make the arrangements, but I underestimated the number of people who would be attending her memorial. Many had to stand the entire hour, while others related her good deeds. Her friends traveled from Seattle, Portland, Scottsdale, Long Beach, Florida, and many Bay Area locations.

Her good friend Bette Doty gave a beautiful eulogy; they had known each other for years.

I had some displays with photographs of Barbara on trips and other letters of interest. One of the pieces for all to see was this portion of a letter sent to me by Keith and Marge Riley:

"Barbara was a sweet person and we know how close you were. I remember one time when you were visiting us Keith asked you what was the greatest benefit you had gotten from Taliesin. You looked across the table and said "Barbara." She, obviously touched, said "That's really nice, Earl." We were all touched. We don't get to see other couples express genuine affection for each other very often. Thank you for letting us share that moment with you."

VARIATIONS ON A THEME

Variation is obtained by arranging the basic triangle in congruent combinations of two, three, four, and six elements. Various colors and perforations in the elements will give countless effects.

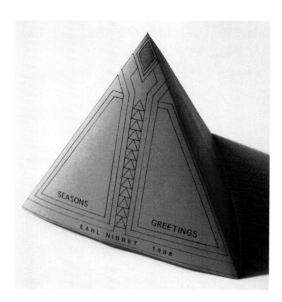

ABOVE
Three-dimensional Christmas card based on the triangle :: 1998

RIGHT
Variations on a theme depict triangles working together in diverse fashion :: 1998

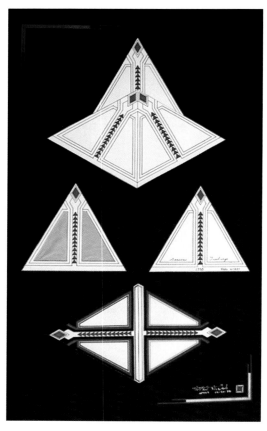

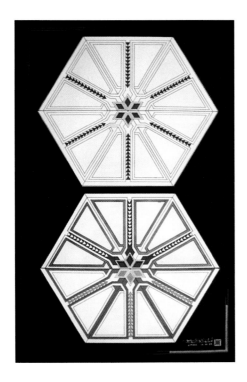

LEFT
Theme 1

RIGHT
Theme 2

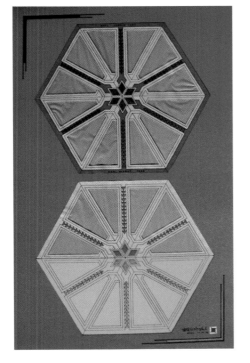

LEFT
Theme 3

RIGHT
Theme 4

CHAPTER SEVEN : :

WORLD TRAVEL

TO TRAVEL OR NOT TO TRAVEL

Several times, Barbara and I discussed world travel. She enjoyed the excitement of experiencing new places and meeting new people, and I wanted to take her to places that most interested her. We had decided, following our proposed trip to Japan, that we would travel next to Egypt, as she was enamored with the early history of that country. We would then take a trip to China to see that special scenery which would be flooded when the world's largest dam was completed.

Although Barbara's heritage was Italian, she preferred to see Spain next; like me, she was captivated by their gypsy music.

But she was gone now, and I had taken the trip to Japan alone, with, I hope, Barbara looking over my shoulder.

In 1998 I took a tour to Egypt to behold some of their ancient culture in evidence after nearly 3,000 years of continuous rule, in the pyramids and temples along the Nile.

Most modern cultures count their histories in hundreds of years. China is the only country that can come anywhere close to the longevity of ancient Egypt.

From a distance, the pyramids of Giza are a marvel to behold. However, as you enter the passages to the Great Pyramid, then to the inner recesses to view the burial chamber, you

get an eerie feeling. The hairs on the nape of your neck activate in a strange way. History was once alive here; you can almost feel what the workers experienced as they were creating one of the Seven Wonders of the Ancient World.

Walking through the towering pillars in the Hypostyle Hall at the Karnak Temple of Amun, you again feel something special when you realize you are probably walking in the footsteps of kings, and Cleopatra herself. The same can be said of wandering through the Luxor temple.

Thebes on the east bank of the Nile was the land of the living. The west bank contained the Valley of the Kings, where more recent mummies of pharaohs were placed in tombs cut deeply into solid rock rather than using pyramids, because of looting. These new tombs had walls and ceilings that were beautifully decorated so that the journey to the Kingdom of the Gods would be easier for the deceased pharaoh.

When seeing the Great Temple of Ramesses II at Abu Simbel, one marvels at it in two ways. First, for the powerful image before you, and secondly for the international engineering which went into saving this temple from being inundated in the 1960s when the High Dam at Aswan was being constructed, raising the waters of Lake Nasser. UNESCO sent hundreds of workmen and engineers to cut apart the

Author photographing Abu Simbel which was relocated to higher ground in the 1960s by UNESCO to avoid being inundated after the High Dam at Aswan was complete
:: 1998

temple and reassemble it on high ground where the rising waters could not touch it. When viewing it in its new location, you are not aware of the saw cuts that had to be performed for the repositioning.

MY TRIP TO CHINA (1999)

October 1, 1999 was the 50th anniversary of communism in the People's Republic of China, and the tour I traveled with landed in Beijing on October 7. After our first breakfast at the four-star Beijing Capital Hotel, we were bussed to Tiananmen Square, the world's largest, to see it decked out in its entire splendor.

Besides the permanent buildings surrounding the mammoth square, one could see a great number of floats that had been brought in from various provinces throughout China, each depicting something of relevance from that particular area. Huge banners hung from many of the main buildings, and for added color, thousands of potted flowers were lined up against buildings, or placed in massive clusters where they would be most effective. Even without the buildings, and the twenty-foot high portraits of Mao Zedong, the flowers in this vast area were overwhelming.

FORBIDDEN CITY

Just off Tiananmen Square is the Forbidden City, once the home of the powerful Ming and Qing dynasties, who restricted access to members of the royal family and their households, hence the name Forbidden. The buildings contained vast works of art and other treasures of antiquity.

The Summer Palace is the magnificent residence of China's last empress Dowager Cixi, and has the largest imperial garden in the world. The layout of different buildings falls on quite a systematic arrangement, and the designer's use of rocks, plants, pavilions, ponds, cobble paths, and other garden styles creates a poetic effect as you stroll among them.

A unique marble barge was constructed on the edge of her private lake, Lake Kunming, which is large enough to cruise. A 700-meter-long covered corridor with exquisite color paintings, on the ceilings, links the buildings and gardens together, and enables tourists to more easily appreciate the whole scenic area. It is a veritable museum of classical Chinese garden architecture, and was begun back in 1750 as a gift to Emperor Qinglong's mother. In 1860 most of the buildings were destroyed when the British-French Allied Army burned them but were renovated in 1888 by Holy Mother Empress Dowager Cixi.

Within the next few days we viewed the Great Wall of China, which was begun 2,000 years ago at Shanghaiguan Pass on the east coast and stretched 4,000 miles to Jiayuguan Pass in the Gobi Desert. It has been estimated the quantity of brick and stone used for the great Wall could create an 8' high wall that could surround the globe.

We next visited a cloisonne factory, an art form unique to China, where various stages of the process was being performed while we watched and asked questions, and spent a most interesting day.

In Shanghai, we visited the new Provincial Museum, established in 1952, boasting a collection of 120,000 pieces of Chinese cultural relics in twenty-one categories, including bronze, ceramics, calligraphy, painting, sculpture, furniture, jade, and ivory carvings, coins, and wood and lacquer wares, which would make any city in the world proud.

They have their own laboratory for scientific conservation of cultural relics, which has won several prizes for restoring and mounting ancient Chinese painting and calligraphy, as well as repairing and restoring ancient bronze and ceramics.

Their exhibits spanning from the Neolithic Age to the Qing Dynasty and contemporary time contain beautiful representative works of art from each time period.

Soon we were where I'd wanted to be, cruising on the Yangtze River viewing some of the most fascinating scenery along the Xiling and Wu Gorges. The way Mother Nature pushes these hills straight up out of the bowels of the earth for hundreds of feet is most extraordinary. By the time we reached the city of Guilin we were awe-struck as it is one of China's most beautiful cities. As you cruise the meandering Li River you are captivated by the lovely views of the limestone hills, which have inspired poets and artists since the founding of the City of Legends 2,000 years ago. At nearly every turn you will find cormorants trained by fishermen to dive into the river, catch the fish in their beaks and return them to the boats.

We next experienced a major engineering feat, seeing the massive Yangtze Three Gorges Dam project, which was over 50% complete at the time of our visit. In fact, the dam was my reason for being in China. When their work is completed, thousands of homes, businesses, and artifacts will be flooded and the Yangtze's course will be altered forever, rendering the Yangtze Valley unrecognizable.

THE TERRA COTTA ARMY

The tomb of China's first emperor, Qin Shihuang, is still to be unearthed and is reputed to contain extravagant palaces and pavilions

Hong Kong, where the old and the new are compatible
:: 1999

filled with rare gems, but the terra cotta warriors and horses of the Qin Dynasty was discovered recently in March, 1974. Two peasants were digging a well and came upon them by accident. When unearthed, the three discovered pits contained approximately 8,000 terracotta warriors and horses, and about 10,000 pieces of weaponry. They were so splendid and magnificent in detail they are now regarded by some as the Eighth Wonder of the World. Permanent structures now cover these important artifacts.

THE CHILDREN'S PALACE

There are several schools for gifted children throughout China referred to as Children's Palaces, however, the one in Beijing is the only one we observed on our trip.

Since the one-child policy in the People's Republic of China is altering family roles and child rearing practices, there are concerns about the possible harmful effects of too much attention and pampering. It was found in a Chinese study these little emperors and princesses were more egocentric, less persistent and less cooperative than children with siblings.

Some of the country's most gifted children are housed and schooled in the arts, and they seem to be quite happy in their surroundings. Most of them are serious in their endeavors, but at the same time, have smiles on their faces.

It is possible to see three- to five-year-olds perform colorful and highly choreographed dances, and five- to seventeen-year-old children practice calligraphy and art. You might see children of any age practicing or performing on traditional musical instruments, and when they notice a visitor admiring their talent, smiles beam across their faces. If these youngsters were having problems, you wouldn't know it by observation.

Their music, whether a solo performance or with a group, was a delight to hear, and seeing examples of their artwork showed development beyond their years.

Next we flew to Hong Kong to experience one of the most modern cities in the Far East. Hong Kong was a British Crown Colony until 1997, when it was returned to Chinese rule. Under the policy of "One country, two systems," Hong Kong enjoys autonomy from the mainland, and continues to have its own legal system, currency, customs, immigration authorities, and police department.

I could have spent more time in Hong Kong, but we were scheduled to fly to Bankok, known by the Thai people as the City of Angels. The ornate buildings along the rivers and canals were fascinating to see; ancient traditions still prevail here.

We had a smooth flight back to Vancouver where I caught another flight for home.

ON TO SPAIN (2000)

Paco, a flamenco guitar player friend, and his wife called one day to ask if I would care to join them in Madrid, to attend a month-long Bienal de Flamenco in Seville.

We planned to meet in Madrid and spend a few days at clubs where flamenco music was played by artists Paco knew. When it was time to leave, they would rent a car and we would motor to Seville to attend approximately thirty flamenco performances in thirty days.

It was springtime when we drove south through provinces of colorful vegetation in full bloom. The beauty of the countryside remains in my mind.

Paco had arranged for our hotel rooms near the center of activities, as we would be walking to most of the flamenco performances. We drove only to distant venues because the festival only occurs every other year, and parking is a major problem.

Flamenco is a southern Spanish art form existing in three forms: cante, the song, baile, the dance, and guitarra, guitar playing. Gypsies were often referred to as the originators of its creation throughout Andalusia. Early Arabs, Moors, and some Muslims also had influences on this art form.

Early flamenco was mainly vocal, accompanied by rhythmical clapping of hands, (toque de palmas). Soon dance was added for vigor, and it was left to composers such as Julian Arcas to introduce more formal guitar playing.

Around 1869, flamenco was developing in music cafes (cafes cantantes) to its definitive form. The more serious form expressing deep feelings (cante jondo) is also from that time period.

Flamenco dance was the major attraction for the public in those cafes cantantes. Guitarists featuring flamenco dancers soon gained a reputation, and from 1915 on, these shows were organized and performed all over the world.

Lately flamenco dance has changed. Female dancers now seem to showcase their temperament, rather than artistry. The flamenco guitar that formerly accompanied the dancers now became a soloist art form, with the great modern virtuoso Paco de Lucia being the pioneer of that development.

Mass media has brought flamenco to the world stage, but it has always been and will remain an intimate, personal kind of music. You have not listened to authentic flamenco if not experiencing a juerga with a small group of friends at midnight somewhere in the south of Spain, when there is nothing around but the voice, the guitar, and the body undulating in the moonlight.

I do hope Barbara was available to look over my shoulder for each of the performances, as they were as good as they get.

COSTA RICA (2001)

My cousin Hal Durian had been going to Costa Rica for the past six summers on vacation from teaching history at a southern California high school, and this year he asked if I would like to accompany him. I had often thought about going to Costa Rica, and since he knew the country so well, I thought this would be a great opportunity, so I readily accepted.

I had already read about Costa Rica, the spider monkeys that would race through the forest canopy, the crocodiles that swim their many rivers, the numerous species of birds that are so abundant. Many of their animals are not known in the states, such as their armadillos and capybara, which is the world's largest living rodent, and beautiful, lush vegetation everywhere you go. Some of the birds that can be seen in Costa Rica are bobolink, bobwhite, cuckoo, heron, egret, falcon, owl, pelican, vacamar, vacana, macaw, toucan, and many more that you might already be familiar with.

Although Costa Rica is less than half the size of Ohio, it is the home to more than 800 species of birds, more than can be found in all of North America. About 25% of its land area is protected, with about 10% of its area designated as national parks. It is a land of natural splendor and spectacular diversity. You may visit rain forests, then dry tropical forests, then white-sand beaches with craggy coastlines, to soaring mountains and active volcanoes.

With this in mind, I arranged a flight to the Ontario, California airport to meet my cousin where we would begin our trip. We flew to Panama City, where we waited about an hour to catch another plane bound for San Jose, Costa Rica, which was founded in 1737. From the airport outside of San Jose, we took a taxi to the same hotel Hal had been staying in for the past six years.

We went to the desk to register, and the clerk remembered my cousin at once from previous visits. Hal then asked for his old room or the least expensive room in the hotel. I immediately asked for the second least expensive room they had left. His room was on the third floor and mine turned out to be on the fourth floor. Hal said he would come to my room after he put his things away. The porter opened the door to my room and I went into a bright glare coming from two sources on the opposite wall. When I put on my sunglasses I could see narrow streets in the foreground and larger buildings in the background with most of the exterior walls and roofs covered in corrugated iron sheets, which were mostly rusty. I gave the porter a few dollars for taking care of my bags, and he left.

Soon my cousin came to my room and went to the window wall and said, "You have a very nice view here." I then asked "From which window?" It was the next day before I saw the room he had rented. It was in the central portion of the third floor, and it had no windows at all. No wonder he liked my room.

The next few days were spent going to places in San Jose Hal thought I would enjoy. Several breakfast, lunch, and dinner places plus watching kids play soccer a time or two. We also went to an evening concert at the Teatro Nacional, one of the oldest buildings in Costa Rica, to hear a choral group presenting Verdi's Requiem. The theater's interior is considered the country's most impressive architectural accomplishment, built in neoclassical German style.

I asked Hal if there was a zoo near our hotel. He said there was, and we proceeded to take a taxi there. I suppose it was a zoo because it had gates in front, you needed tickets to get in, had an armed guard, and it had a typical souvenir shop where you could purchase post cards or stuffed or carved animals. We bypassed the souvenir shop and walked to an area that had crocodiles and turtles living together in the same open concrete tank. The water was so brown you couldn't see all the inhabitants at once. The longer you stood to look at them, the more you realized they were actually in there.

Next stop was to see some native animals in a deep enclosure, which used to be a blue concrete stream around the perimeter of the tank, but that was also brown with feed, brackish water, manure and leaves, and it was a wonder all those animals were not sick.

We saw a huge cage filled with monkeys climbing tall barren trees that had been placed in the center. They looked relatively happy for their lot in life, but its certain they would all leave if the doors had been left open.

We then saw a cage with the world's largest living rodents, called capybara, living in it. The water again was brown and brackish. I had seen just about enough of the zoo by then,

but we also saw a cage set into the jungle planting that was about sixteen feet long on each of its four sides and had a chain link roof about eight feet from the ground. We discovered two jaguars in the cage. What I observed was a larger and older one would just lie there and look out of the cage, while a smaller and obviously a younger one that must have been placed in the cage recently, continually paced around the four sides of the cage. That did it for me and I asked Hal if he was ready to go back to the hotel. The answer was "Yes," and we left.

On the thirteenth of June Hal and I decided to take the Costa Rica Highlights Tour, which would take us through four of their seven provinces.

A small bus called for us at our hotel and we were driven through the city to pick up others who were going on the same tour.

Our first stop was at one of the largest coffee plantations in the country where our guide explained the growing of the coffee beans and how they process the beans for shipping throughout the world in bags of about fifty pounds each. We then went to breakfast at the plantation before setting out for the next stop, which was the Poas Volcano (2704 feet). By the way, Costa Rica produces very good coffee throughout the country but the coffee we had at this plantation was the worst coffee I experienced all the time we were in Costa Rica.

Nearing the volcano, we experienced what the locals call the poor man's umbrella, a giant leaf that sometimes reaches four feet in diameter and has a sturdy center stalk by which to carry this lofty object of vegetation. As we rose in elevation it became a bit cooler and there was evidence of a great deal of mist forming. In fact the locals call it the cloud forest. It looked as though we were in an airplane amongst the clouds. For that reason I decided not to climb higher to the observation point to look down into the volcano. Hal and most of the others did go, and when I saw Hal again, I asked him

Author's cousin, history teacher, Hal Durian, about to slice a "durian fruit" for guests. The spiny, football-size fruit with an obnoxious odor is a true love-hate situation. Millions regard them as "hell on the outside, and heaven on the inside." They are mainly grown on tall trees throughout Southeast Asia. A limited season and a short shelf life makes durians quite expensive. The exotic flavor of the custard, yet odoriferous flesh, is for some a treasured food :: 2001

PHOTO: BARBARA DURIAN

to describe the view from the top. He said that the moisture was so thick that you could only see about six feet in front of you. No one could look into the volcano on that visit, and soon we were on our way again.

We then went on past high volcanic edifices, through deep canyons, jungles and streams, then stopping at La Paz Waterfall, which, they told us, never stops flowing. Then on to a coffee break at a hummingbird gallery. The owners of this rest stop have several hanging feeders for hummingbirds along a long veranda, where dozens of birds feed at a time. There are several varieties that have been attracted there which dart straight up from below your site level and suspend themselves and look over the feeders before they decide where to feed. You can almost reach out and touch the birds, as the feeders are only about two feet from the walkway. The owners told us they must wash and clean the feeders each evening before adding fresh liquid, since the birds could possibly become sick and die from infections. From their terrace we could look down and see the impressive 250-foot-high San Fernando Waterfall across the canyon.

Soon our group was again on the bus and our guide was explaining the sites along the way. We were now on what they call the Caribbean Plain, with its warm tropical weather and vegetation, driving past colorful small towns, cacao and banana plantations, pineapple fields and even Brahmas bull ranches.

Our next stop for a buffet lunch was at Selva Verde Lodge, which translates into *Green Jungle Lodge*, and is built alongside a rushing river surrounded by colorful gardens and a natural jungle. After a nice lunch we were able to cross the river by walking on a suspended bridge, which swayed with each step you took. On the other side we found marked trails through the jungle that gave you a chance to look for green and red frogs, three-toed sloths, monkeys, birds, capybaras (world's largest living rodent), and possibly a jaguar or two. My thought was it also gave them a chance to look

for you. We happened only to see frogs, monkeys, many birds, and the three-toed sloth.

Our next bus ride was very short and brought us to the banks of the beautiful Sarapiquì River, where we boarded a very long and narrow boat with another group of visitors, all on the lookout for iguanas, monkeys, crocodiles, sloths, turtles, and colorful birds. The boat held rows of two passengers on either side of a center aisle. I didn't make an actual count that the boat could take but it seemed that there were about forty-eight of us that day. We started down the river and the captain would slow the boat at trees that contained families of monkeys or where he could point out iguanas to the tourists. The passengers soon got into it and would shout out to the captain they were seeing something and would point it out. Our guide had binoculars and was soon telling the captain and the tourists what he was seeing. The sun was high, and looking up to see some of the wildlife was difficult. When the captain was notified of something to see, he would turn the boat around so the passengers on the other side could also have a chance to see what was happening. It was not an easy task as the boat was quite long for its width and the river was rushing. This happened several times when our guide excitedly shouted to the captain "I see a very rare two-toed sloth up there," pointing straight up into the sun and the treetop.

I immediately asked, "Which foot are the toes on?" I got a few smiles from the passengers, but a frown from our guide. I was thinking to myself that a two-toed sloth might be very rare, but couldn't one of its toes have been bitten off in a fight?

The sloth, although very slow, was apparently climbing to the very top of the tree it was on and people were told to look for a bundle of fur near such and such branch, all the while looking into the sun. As the captain was turning the boat around again so the other side could get a look, I asked, "Why don't you shoot it and pass it around?" Some outright laughter came from some, and I received another frown from our guide. Soon we were cruising again and we saw a small crocodile, on a bank, which did not move or blink its eyes even after four or five minutes. My mind drifted off to Disneyland for some reason.

Beyond the edge of the river we could see we were passing working banana plantations with their tractors, homes, vehicles and sheds that were necessary for the harvest of their crops. We were nearing the end of our hour-and-a-half river cruise when I shouted to my cousin, who was on the other side of the boat and several rows back, "Hal, I think I see a jaguar." Hal, and several passengers started looking in the direction that I was looking, then a few seconds later I said, "Oh, no! it's only a Chevrolet." I received more frowns than laughter this time.

We returned to our hotel via Brauilio Carillo National Park, a protected area of almost 500 square kilometers of towering mountains and virgin forests containing rare woods, giant ferns, and colorful flowers. Because we were in the cloud forest, it rained nearly one, and-a-half-hours, out of the two hours it took us to get back to the blue skies of San Jose. Of course we returned to the narrow streets along with a multitude of busses, trucks and automobiles.

My cousin had told me, at one time he read in the *National Geographic* magazine that Costa Rica has one of the world's best and healthiest climates. I suppose that might be true if you don't inhale. In the city of San Jose I found the dust and diesel fumes almost too much to bear at times. Sometime while walking the narrow streets you had to hold your breath till the trucks and busses cleared the area, but soon there would be another two or three coming along. That was my particular problem in this otherwise beautiful land.

After Hal and I got back to his house in southern California, I thought I would look up an Army buddy whom I hadn't seen for a few years. I called Loran Estes and he invited me to a brunch the next day, where he met with

friends each Sunday morning in Long Beach. After picking me up he drove us to the appointed place, and I saw his old friend Marilyn Hastings, mayor of Seal Beach, CA, whom I had already known, and met a couple of his new friends, and we talked about old times and Army days. We were having our brunch outside in the back of this popular restaurant, in their patio area, when everyone there began to look at the next couple coming in for breakfast. The man was about seven feet tall and the woman was almost five feet tall. Several of the diners had stopped eating while this Mutt and Jeff couple were being seated, and one of Loran's new friends asked, "I wonder what she sees in him?"

"His knees," I replied.

After our nice brunch, Loran drove us to his sister's house where she showed us some of her work as an artist, and various artifacts collected while she and her husband were in New Guinea. She also showed us some things her husband had drawn for the Walt Disney Studio, where he had worked from its inception. It was truly interesting for both of us to see, since Loran had also studied art in his younger days.

Soon we were on our way, and I would be flying home in the morning.

MY ENGLAND AND HOLLAND VACATION

Let me tell you about my recent trip to England and Holland. The main purpose of my trip was to see where my father was born, where he grew up and worked in England before coming to America. The Holland part of the trip was to see where my grandparents on my mother's side were born and raised.

I decided to go in May, before school was out and where I had the possibility for clear weather. I flew from San Francisco to New York and on to London, where I landed at Heathrow Airport. I then endeavored to take the Underground train with my luggage, which had been broken on the trip from New York to

London. Somehow the pullout handle that you use to pull your bag was broken off and gone. I had to pull it hunched over; it was much too short without the extension handle. I stayed in a hotel that I had booked from the states, which turned out to be my first mistake. The room contained its own bathroom, but it was so small, I thought I was wearing the bathroom when I entered. It was a far cry from being spacious or commodious. The hotel claimed to be a four-star hotel, but I did notice three of the stars were missing from their sign. It was quite late the night I arrived at my hotel, so I watched television for a while. While I was lying in bed a cramp started to affect my left leg. In trying to get out of bed, by placing my elbow on a telephone shelf, which was attached to the headboard, the entire shelf sheared off, and it, the telephone, and I went crashing to the floor. I had to place my large bag and prop some telephone books under the shelf so it would look proper when the maid came in to make up the room. The first thing I did next morning was to seek out a hardware store in order to buy some wood glue. After the maid had finished with my room, I glued the shelf back onto the headboard, since I didn't want to have to explain to the hotel what had happened. All in all I did get a pretty good night's rest that first night. Later, after having a continental breakfast, I grabbed my umbrella and went outside to notice the skies were gray and cloudy, but I proceeded to purchase a day pass to ride the buses around the city of London. This is a good way to acquaint yourself with where you are in relation to your hotel. My hotel, by the way, was near Victoria Station.

After a soggy lunch of fish and chips, I headed for the Victoria and Albert Museum. I wanted to see the Frank Lloyd Wright exhibit of the Kaufmann office that had been designed by Wright in the thirties and was built by Manuel Sandoval, a good friend of mine, who is no longer with us. It was a thrill to see, but there was not much illumination on this exhibit and people were using flash to take pictures of it. I

tried with my camera, but the flash didn't seem to want to work. I asked if they sold pictures of the exhibits in the museum, but they said no! I visited for a few hours then made my way back to the hotel for the night.

The next day the skies were blue and bright, so I left my umbrella in the hotel, and purchased another day pass for a bus ride and took a different trip. I got off the bus to walk around the Piccadilly Circus area. About an hour and a half later a deluge of water descended, and soon the streets were flooded. All you could do was to stand in doorways, go shopping, or have something to eat and wait it out. I wanted to look around the area some more and not go back to my hotel defeated, so I popped into a shop and bought another umbrella. I spent the day walking in the rain and riding steamy busses from which it became difficult to see the sights.

The next day I purchased my usual day pass and started off in another direction. This time I had boarded a two-tier bus, and I went aloft to see the sights from a different perspective. This turned out to be an interesting trip as I was seeing important buildings and small shopping areas from time to time. People got on the bus, off the bus, and soon I was the only one upstairs. A couple of stops later, the driver shut off the engine. I waited for it to start up again, and when it didn't, I went down to see what was going on. Nothing was going on! The driver was gone and I was the only person on the bus. I tried to get off through the emergency exit, but it wouldn't open. All I could do at this point was to wait for the driver to return. In about thirty minutes he came back and was furious to see me on the bus. He said, "How did you get on the bus?" I said, "I couldn't get off the bus." When he found out I had only been in London for three days he forgave me. Soon we became friends, of sorts when I told him that he had to have great skills to drive a large bus on such narrow streets. By the way, it rained all this day too. I was going to stay in London a few days longer to see more sights, but I thought it might be better to rent a car for a week and drive to Wales and Scotland. I wanted to take in as much of Great Britain as I could, and try to get out of the rain.

I had already made reservations from the states to hire a car for a week from a well-known company for $176, all-inclusive, no extra mileage charge. When I looked at the London map to see where I had to pick up the car, it seemed so far away, it was as if it was in another country. I called them to see if I could get the pickup point changed to a location that was about six blocks from my hotel. They told me that particular location had been closed, and the only other close location was a couple of miles away, and I agreed to go there; so I checked out of my hotel and went by cab.

The car they provided was a brand new Peugeot with only 75 miles on it. I asked them to draw me a sketch to get from their shop to the main highway out of London heading for Stonehenge, but they gave me a copy of a city map they had highlighted. That was just what I didn't want. It didn't clearly give me the number of blocks to turn right or turn left as the case may be. With this highlighted map, I was looking for the correct way, but all the signs are so small it was difficult to read, especially in the rain. I had only gone about ten blocks or so, desperately trying to stay to the left side of the road while looking for my way out of London, when I heard a loud wham! At first I thought I had hit a pedestrian, but looking into the rear view mirror, I saw that it was a tall center-divider post that I had struck. I then looked at the left door mirror and saw the mirror had been knocked out of its housing and was dangling by the electrical wires. It was completely useless to me till I could pull over and try to do something about it. I could not seem to judge where the left front wheel and fender was on this car. Every so often I would clip a curb going around the corner to the left. There were some people on an island in the middle of a wide road the first time this happened, and needless to say, they jumped back a bit when the wheel hit.

I finally found the correct road out of London, but it had taken me about two hours to do so, and it was while I was in Hyde Park I found room enough for me to stop and put the mirror back into its housing. I don't know if it ever worked electrically or not again. The glass was not broken and I never did find the switch that adjusts the mirror, but by ducking my head it was close enough for me to use.

As I said, I was on the right road to Stonehenge, but they don't have road signs saying "Stonehenge" so many kilometers. They have signs to the next hamlet, town or burg, and you have to know all the burgs along the way to your destination, else you are lost. I was lost all the time, as the signs are not only small, it was always raining. Because of the rain, it would pay you to have a navigator; that I did not have, and also I didn't know what direction I should go. I only knew my destination. Then you have to be conscious of, and consider the roundabouts.

If you haven't driven using English roundabouts, you haven't lived. A roundabout is a place where you approach a paved circle in the middle of the road, and drivers are coming from sometimes five orientations to change directions for their final destination. You have to move over, from lane to lane, within this circle and be lucky enough to exit the correct turnoff to take you on your proper course. This, of course, is also known as mechanized Russian roulette. Often the names on the little signs look like the hamlet you are now seeking, but no! It was Hampshire instead of *Spamshire*, and you now head down the road for twelve to twenty miles before you are lucky enough to spot another roundabout and try to get back on the correct road again.

Every so often I would have to pull over to check the map to see when I would have to change roads in order to figure out where I wanted to go. Sounds great, except there is nowhere that you can pull off the road except for designated rest stops. They have no shoulders on the roads I drove so you have to depend on the paved stops, and they can be, and usually are, miles apart.

I finally arrived at Stonehenge and it was quite impressive and a joy to see. After taking enough pictures, I proceeded to enter the rental car and the alarm went off, beep-beep-beep. I frantically kept pressing the gadget on the key-chain and it finally went silent. Each time I locked the car after that, it always went beep-beep-beep till I finally hit the right combination to silence it. I never did figure out how to set the alarm or how to unset it when you wanted to get back into your car. I just left the automobile unlocked after that. I had all my things locked in the trunk, and the trunk didn't go beep-beep-beep when you opened it.

My next destination was Bath. I had planned to see the buildings and baths there, but by the time I finally arrived, it was getting a bit late and I never did find a good place to park and the first thing I realized was that I was heading out of town. Traffic was beginning to build up, and at the exact same time I hit another curb, I heard a strange woman's voice saying, "You are coming to M-4 and there will be a twenty-minute delay, use alternate route A-38 to avoid delay." At first, the hair on the back of my neck stood up because I thought I had hit a woman or an object. Then it sounded like an automated voice, and it kept repeating the same message every few minutes. I couldn't find a way to shut it off till I saw a red light to the far right of the dashboard. I pushed the button in desperation and it stopped the message, but it would still come on from time to time. I could finally stop it but I never did find out how to keep it from coming on in the first place. I didn't need it at all, as not only did I not know I was coming to M-4, I had no idea where an alternate route would be. I thought I was on the way to Cardiff at that point, but when I looked at the next road sign about twenty miles down the road, I found I was heading for Warminster, which happens to be on the way to Stonehenge.

I finally came to another roundabout and headed for Oxford. I wanted to see and walk around Oxford, because my wife Barbara had taken some enjoyable and knowledgeable classes there one summer. After a couple of missed turns, I finally came to Oxford, which is a charming area, but it was getting late and I began looking for a place to eat. That didn't turn out to be the easiest thing to do either. I finally found a place to park within walking distance of a restaurant I had spotted. By the time I parked, walked there, and went to the rest room, they had stopped serving dinner. I didn't feel like having a pint and hard-boiled eggs, which was all one could order; so I got in the car and headed out of town. In about a half-hour I spotted a nice pub in a small hamlet, and I was fortunate to have quite a nice dinner there.

After dinner I asked the waiter and the bar-maid how to get to Stratford-on-Avon. It was probably no more that thirty miles from there, but neither of them could tell me how to get there. I finally asked the owner who was able to tell me the way, he probably went there, once! The reason for my wanting to go to Stratford-upon-Avon was that although my father was born in Southshields, which is in the north, near Scotland, he had lived in Stratford as a small boy for a short time. The directions were actually great. I only got lost twice and there were convenient places to turn around. I was getting very low on fuel by the time I arrived and the only gas station I saw was closed. It was quite late and I didn't see a motel or hotel to look for a room so I pulled into a one-way street and parked for the night. I liked one-way streets in Great Britain, as you couldn't get into too much trouble on one. The only trouble I thought I might get into was sleeping in the car on the street. I had been sitting up for about an hour when a van parked on the other side of the street from me. No one got out of the van; so I thought, another lost American. I didn't look at the van at all, and I hoped they were not looking at me.

The driver's seat on my rental car would not lie back, or I could not find out how to lay it back, as they do in America, so I just kept sitting up listening to the rain on the roof for hours. Finally I got so stiff I decided to get into the back seat as it was then about three o'clock in the morning and so far no police came to chase me away. I unlocked all the doors from the inside before I got out of the driver's seat then beep-beep-beep. I jumped into the back seat and locked all the doors and pressed the gadget on the key-chain like crazy. The beep-beep-beep finally went silent. My heart was pounding and it reminded me I had to go to the rest room. There would be no rest room for a few hours yet, until the gas station reopens. By then I was so tired I thought if they threw me in jail, at least I would have a bed to sleep on; so I relaxed and slept for a few hours.

The morning brought new showers from time to time; I filled up at the service station I had seen the night before and looked at the map to see what my choices were. I had thought I would enjoy driving on small country roads looking at the countryside and taking pictures from time to time, but the roads are too small with no shoulders to allow you to pull over to let cars pass. You spend more time looking in the rear-view mirror to see the cars pulling up on you than you can spend looking at the scenery. Even on small roads, the cars go fast and they continually beep for you to go faster or to pull over, but there is no place to pull over. At this point I had had it. I finally asked a gas station attendant how to get to a main highway so I could head directly for London.

A half-hour or so later, I finally found the main highway to London. It was a six-lane road-way with a center divider, called M1. As soon as I got on it the rain came down in buckets. There was a slow lane to drive on, and the middle lane was basically for trucks, and the outside lane was for fast traffic. They usually drove about seventy miles an hour in that lane, but when I was in it, I drove about eighty-five

miles an hour, so very few drivers would catch up to me. The main trouble that day was the rain came down faster than the wipers could take it off the windscreen. Even so, I felt safer driving in the fast lane than being beeped off the road in the slow lane.

At this point all I wanted to do was to get the car back early enough so I could receive a refund for the rest of the week. All went well till I got about twenty miles from London. It was mid-morning by this time, and I thought all the commute traffic would mostly be over. But no! We were stopped on the highway and crept the entire twenty miles a car-length at a time. It took me about two hours to get to the city limits. If I could then get the car back to the dealer within two hours, I would probably not be charged for an additional day. I actually drove around in circles looking for and asking directions to the dealership where I had rented the car. It was about the fourteenth person, I asked, who told me it was just around the corner from where we were.

I drove to the check-in area, and turned the car in. It was twenty-three and-a-half hours later, and I had put on seven hundred miles on the odometer. I mentally computed the miss-directions that occurred. I had roughly seen about three hundred and fifty miles of scenery. They finally charged me about the same price for the day, as they had quoted me for a week. That certainly was enough driving for me in England.

I decided since I was packed I would go to the airport and see about getting my flight changed so I could leave this day for Amsterdam. I was still dragging my baggage with the broken handle when a cabby asked me where I was going. We haggled about price, as I only had so much left in English money, but he agreed to take me all the way to the airport for the money I had. I was going to take the Underground, but this turned out to be much better.

The flight to Amsterdam was nice, but I was routed through Paris and I had to wait in the de Gaulle Airport for about four hours in order to catch my flight to Holland. Upon arriving at the Amsterdam airport, I changed some money and tried to figure a way to get to the hotel I had also booked from the states. I was looking at a map to see where I had to go, when a cabby helped me. He showed me the hotel where I was supposed to stay was not convenient for evening activities. He actually took me to a hotel just three blocks from the center and main restaurants. The room I booked was so small that there was only about one foot of space between the edge of the bed and the walls, and there was about three feet of space at the foot of the bed.

Before going out for dinner I took a shower, but I failed to notice the shower curtain did not fit the enclosure. It missed by about an inch or so on either side and when I had finished there was a flooded bathroom floor to mop. I used the bath mat and wrung it out a couple of times, which seemed to take care of it.

I went out for my first meal in Holland. I saw Mexican, Italian, Greek, Chinese, Japanese, Vietnamese, and some fast food places like McDonald's, and there were fish and chips places, but no Dutch restaurants. I actually saw some Dutch restaurants the next day, but the first night, I settled for a barbecue place, since many people were already eating there, and it was OK, but not great.

I had been advised by friends to see and do certain things while I was in England and Holland, but the rains kept me from doing some of them in England and I was determined to do more in Holland. The next day I rode some trams and buses to get the lay of the land. I found a large supermarket and bought some nice fruit and tomatoes, then I walked to the canal to watch boats go by as I had lunch. It was not raining at this time but it was overcast; so I had one of my two umbrellas with me as I walked about till evening, when I went back to the hotel to sleep.

The hotel I was staying in was on a corner and there was major roadwork going on with workmen laying a large new pipeline in the street and around the corner. In fact, when you went out the front door you had to walk about two hundred feet in either direction to get around a chain-link fence. Since the desk girl said she put me in the back of the hotel because of the street noise, and because of the construction, I had the feeling that the hotel was almost empty. But no! The next morning they gave me a call and told me I had to check out in fifteen minutes so they could make up the room for the next people. I asked if I could get another room in order to stay there, but they said they were full and I hadn't told them I wanted to stay longer. I packed and checked out.

Since I was now without a place to stay in Amsterdam, I decided to get on a train for the city of Groningen where my mother's parents came from, but it is located almost as far north as you can travel in Holland. I exited the tram and dragged my bags to the train depot where I purchased a one-way ticket to Groningen as I planned to stay some time there to look up my roots. It was still raining some, but it was nice to see the countryside pass by without getting wet and without having to drive in it. After about three hours of travel the train stopped at Groningen, the last stop north. We departed the train and I had to walk to the bus depot Quasimodo-like pulling my bags, as I still didn't have an extension handle on my large bag. The center of town was quite a long way away, so a bus ride was necessary. I struggled to a bus stand where there were a number of red busses. After my questions, I was told that I would have to go to the yellow bus station, about a block away. I was pretty tired by the time I arrived at the yellow bus station, and I sat down on a bench next to an elderly lady. We started up a conversation and I told her I wanted to see where my grandfather and grandmother lived; so I showed her an official paper that was a birth certificate. She translated it for me, since it was printed in Dutch, and then said, "They didn't come from Groningen, they came from Kloosterburen." My heart sunk through the bench I was sitting on, and I asked her how I could get to Kloosterburen. She said I had to take the green bus; so I went to the green bus station and waited about an hour before a bus pulled up.

I asked the driver if his was the right bus to get to Kloosterburen. He said, "You can't get there from here." Apparently his bus goes farther north but stops some kilometers from Kloosterburen. He said if I really wanted to go, I could ride with him to the end of the line, and he would call for a taxi to meet the bus, and the taxi would take me the rest of the way. I hoped my grandparents were looking down and seeing my efforts about this time, as that was it for me. Having no idea of what I would find there, and if I would be able to get back to the train station should there be no hotel in Kloosterburen, I just started dragging my bags back to the train station, where I purchased a one-way ticket to Amsterdam.

Later I uncovered a few facts about the Province of Kloosterburen. An air photo shows the little village, near the sea, which has a *Dutch Reformed Convent* dating back to the 1100s. There are only 4 or 5 streets within the populated area, and there certainly is no hotel.

The countryside is flat and the wind whips through the area most of the year. I now understand why my grandparents yearned to depart their homestead.

After the three-hour train ride, I was again in Amsterdam, but now I had no hotel room for the night and it was starting to get dark. Fortunately the rain had stopped and I no longer had to use my umbrella while dragging the bags all over the city. I got on a tram and headed back towards the area where I had formerly had a room. I got off nearby my former hotel and asked a young man about a hotel. He advised me where I could get a nice hotel within three or four blocks. Off I went and secured a place to stay for a couple of days. It was near

all the activities I had already seen and was only a couple of blocks away from the Van Gogh Museum, which was one thing I came to Amsterdam to see.

The next day was sunny and bright. I took a canal boat ride and saw some pleasant sights along the way. In the afternoon I walked to the Van Gogh Museum and found out it would be closed for the next few weeks for renovation. I had a bite to eat and talked to the owner about the Van Gogh Museum being closed. He then told me about another museum where they had many of Van Gogh's paintings. I thanked him and walked to the ticket office at that museum only to find they were closing for the day. Later I saw a painting by Van Gogh on a postcard rack, but refused to buy one. The next morning, I cut my Nederland excursion short and headed for the airport, and home.

DUKE AND EARL VISIT THE PRINCE

My old Taliesin friend of the fifties, Duke Johnson, had never been outside the U.S., so I suggested we might sometime go on a trip to Europe together in order that he might see some of the world beyond our borders. A few weeks later he had given it some thought, and he let me know that he had made arrangements to purchase a Volvo station wagon, by flying to Sweden to pick it up and drive it around Europe before the factory shipped it to the USA. He was going to stay a month to see some of his relatives in Goteborg, then drive on to Rome to visit Giovanni del Drago, an Italian prince, whom we both knew while living at Taliesin. I decided to accept his offer to share the trip, and I booked a seat on the same KLM plane he was taking to Sweden by way of Amsterdam.

We left San Francisco on October 6, and had a two-hour layover in Amsterdam before heading to Goteborg, the home of the Volvo factory, where Duke's cousin Guert Niellson lived. Guert is an architect, and it was he who made arrangements for our hotel stay, just a block away from his residence.

We saw the local sites of Goteborg, with Guert leading the way to some of the city's most interesting places. My back was giving me trouble at that time; so Guert made arrangements with a physical trainer to have me take two massages. I stayed in Goteborg while Duke and Guert took a trip north to Stockholm, the original home of Duke's grandparents. They looked into some old records and found out where Duke's relatives had lived, as well as tracking down a number of other current relatives.

The Johnsons' were planning to have a reunion in two days in the south of Sweden, where some of the family had lived in the past. At the reunion in a meetinghouse next to the family church, I counted about seventy relatives there for the gathering, and afterward we saw the grandparents' homestead.

We left soon after for Italy by following a relative, as a guide, to a hotel in Malm, and the next morning we drove the car to a ferryboat bound for Kiel.

The first day in Germany we drove leisurely through the rolling countryside and past the cities of Hamburg, Hannover, Kassel, and Frankfurt at eighty-five miles an hour; and then spent the night in a quiet hotel in the small town of Guxhagen. After breakfast it was back to eighty-five miles an hour again until we arrived at Zurich, where we intended to spend a night, or at least several hours, to attempt to locate a brother of another friend from Taliesin days. We hadn't established a meeting time for visiting, and after many phone calls to him, without success, we had dinner and drove on to Lugano. While driving through the many tunnels of the Swiss Alps, we marveled at the engineering accomplishment of boring through super massive stone and the size and length of some of them. I noticed telephones in them placed for emergencies, which had been spaced at regular intervals; so I started counting them to myself and then would tell Duke we just went through a fifteen-telephone tunnel, or six-telephone tunnel, or however many telephones were attached to the walls. One was about a hundred and twenty-telephone tunnel, which surprised us both. The next day we arrived in Milan, and we were now on course to visit Prince Giovanni, who was actually living in his castle overlooking Lake Bolsena in Tuscany, about forty-five miles north of Rome. He also owns an island in the lake, which has two historic buildings where Pope Leo X lived for some time to escape persecution. After leaving Milan we passed through Parma, Modena, Bologna and Florence before arriving at Lake Bolsena. As we got close to Giovanni's house, which was built around the 16th to 17th century, we went down a narrow driveway and through an archway so narrow we had to pull in both side mirrors to get through. We found we were next to Giovanni's house but on the wrong side.

Giovanni has been living both in Rome and at the lake since his return from Taliesin and the states. The castle is built adjacent to the church and has forty-six rooms; it quite fills the landscape when seen from a distance. He was telling us that he has been restoring the castle since his return, since the place was bombed during World War II. The bombed-out roof was the first thing to be replaced, and he was careful to restore the architecture of the period. All of the rebuilding had been done with this thought in mind. He said the place had been looted and all of the paintings, silver, sculptures and art objects were missing when he started the reconstruction.

All the rooms have paintings of museum quality, and some of the replaced paintings are actual portraits of his grandparents and great-grandparents. In the major rooms some of the paintings are ten to twelve feet high and eighteen to twenty feet long. Most of the eighteen-foot-tall windows' drapes were destroyed, but his restoration matches the scenes in the paintings, gold crests and all.

Because of his failing eyesight, Giovanni has a friend living with him to drive him from place to place, and he also has a couple who cook and serve, and another woman who cleans, does laundry and other odd jobs. A policeman lives there and dines with Giovanni on occasion; in the five days of dining in the main dining room with the policeman, we saw him about three times, but we never found out where he worked.

Giovanni took us on a tour around the surrounding area showing us castles, churches, and other historic buildings that were built hundreds of years ago. Near his own castle is the basilica of San Pietro, which is believed to date to the tenth century. After visiting the basilica, we went to Rome with Giovanni, who had business to take care of there. We stayed overnight in his restored town house, built about 1890, and is located just a stone's throw from the American Embassy. He also has people living in his house in Rome who take care of the place while he is away and who cook for him while he is in Rome. Giovanni is a great cook in his own right, and cooks when he feels like it; he made some wonderful meals for us in the five days we were with him.

While Giovanni was taking care of his dealings, Duke and I visited the Pantheon, on our own, an incredible building with its fabulous interior and famous dome. We learned that Victor Emanuel, from Turin, who unified the Italian language throughout the country, was buried in the Pantheon. After lunch we went to the Coliseum, which of course is another impressive masterpiece. We visited the Arch of Constantine and spent some time at the Roman Forum, which is in very sad condition, with most of it on the ground or missing altogether. We had wanted to stay another day or two in Rome to see the Castle Sant'Angelo, Vatican City, St. Peter's Square and Basilica, the Sistine Chapel with Michelangelo's paintings, and to walk along the Via del Corso, but Giovanni had to get back to his house at the lake. We

were running out of time to do many other things we had planned; so we decided not to return to Rome again on this trip.

On our last night with Giovanni, Duke and I invited him to dinner and he suggested we go to a nearby hill town for which Tuscany is noted. It was rather close to his house, so we drove a few miles and came to a restaurant where Giovanni knew the owner, who was also the cook. After meeting the owner/cook, he excused himself to prepare something for us, which had the approval of Giovanni. After we had been seated in one of the two dining rooms, the only other couple in the room heard us speaking English and started a conversation with us. They were from Portland, Oregon and had been in Italy for a couple of weeks. Soon, people started to come in for dinner and each couple or foursome had to say hello to Giovanni who then introduced Duke and me. This happened about six times, and the couple was so amazed, they asked if he knew all the people in town. He said these people were from Rome and he happened to know them all; they come to places like this for weekends. Giovanni also told us he had been mayor of the town and had persuaded all the towns around Lake Bolsena to connect to a sewer treatment plant for the lake's protection.

The next morning, after our good-byes to Giovanni, we invited him to come to the states and stay with us when he could do so. We left with wonderful memories and headed for Orvieto, another great historic hill town. After our visit there we went on to Siena where we had lunch at the Piazza del Campo, one of the most beautiful squares in Italy. Siena flourished, after the middle-ages, as a trading center that was on the route from northern Italy to Rome. The primary focal point has to be the thirteenth-century slender tower on the square. In modern times, they have two horse races around the square in July and August where they move the people to the center of the square so horses can race around the perimeter. There is much betting on the outcome of the race and the citizens run out and even beat the riders if they feel they should ride faster. The riders also beat each other to further their advantage, and after the race they have a celebratory dinner party, with the winning horse sitting at the head of the table.

From Siena we again returned to Florence, which was on our way to Venice, where Duke wanted to see the art of Venetian glassblowing. Duke had taken a class in glassblowing recently, and had been quite interested in art glass ever since. While in Florence we had gone astray quite a bit of the time and didn't see as much as we would have liked, and after lunch we headed for Venice.

After arriving, we arranged for a hotel stay on the island in Venice, then drove around to do some sightseeing. After a lavish meal in a nice restaurant we went to bed in order to get an early start to see glassblowing. One blower made a beautiful vase, and then made a glass horse by manipulating molten glass with a piece of metal held in his other hand. There was no blowing required at all to make the horse, and it was completed in about four minutes. It was a fine piece, and one of the spectators in the room purchased it for his young son who was with him. We were told a novice glassblower is apprenticed to the master glassblower for fifteen years before he is considered capable to work on his own; after the glassblowing, we visited some shops selling fine art glass to compare with what we had just seen.

We took a water taxi to the Piazza San Marco and took pictures of pigeons landing on people, dozens at a time. We walked about for some time and saw St. Mark's Basilica with its Byzantine facade. Although it was nice to be in Venice, it was difficult to take good pictures; the fog was quite heavy and it was misting from time to time.

Duke got his fill of glassblowing and now it was my turn. For years I have been interested in the making of guitars and violins. We were so close to the center of violin making in Italy that I suggested to Duke we spend some time

in Cremona, where the legendary Antonio Stradivari was born and lived from 1644 to 1737, producing the best violins the world has ever seen and heard. Duke wasn't interested in violin making per se, but after visiting the Stradivari museum in Cremona where hundreds of items are on display that Stradivari used in making his violins, Duke came out with a great appreciation of the art. I had been used to seeing many forms, tools, and jigs that some of my guitar-building friends used, and even I was impressed with the hundreds of drawings Stradivari used in the construction of his violins.

Our next destination was Genoa, because we wanted to drive along the Italian and French Riviera before heading north to Sweden to drop off the Volvo for shipment to the states. When we were near Genoa, we both wanted to see the Carrera marble quarry, so we headed into the mountains following the signs. We heard blasting on occasion, but a lot of the marble seemed to be cut in place with immense power saws. There were many trucks continually coming down the hill with large pieces of marble on their beds. Several had minimal tie-downs, and you could see the high pieces sway a bit on their way down to the dock where many ships were waiting to fill their loads. We had lunch next to the quarry in a workman's type of small restaurant, where none of the waiters spoke English. Another diner helped us order, and we had one of the best meals in all of Italy, with the exception of Giovanni's, and the price was about half of what we had paid elsewhere. From the coast road, about fifteen miles away, we were able to look up and see the quarry where we had been; we noticed it took up a great deal of the side of the mountain. Only when we were actually there could one grasp the enormous size of the operation; it has been active for centuries generating some of the best marble the world has ever produced. They seemed to be working three different colors, gray and white, green and white, and all white, which was predominant. Duke purchased several pieces of marble, including a chess set that was so heavy he decided to ship it home rather than try to get it aboard an aircraft.

We returned to the coast highway; I wanted to drive to Portofino and on to Monaco before heading north through France.

Driving along the coast was extremely slow compared to the eighty-five-miles an hour we had been used to driving on the main highways. Even when we were cruising at eighty-five, we would be passed by German cars doing about one hundred and ten. They seemed to be in convoys of two or three cars at a time. As soon as they went by, in another few seconds another group would pass.

Portofino is a charming place, but the roads are so narrow you have to sometimes wait for the oncoming cars to clear before you can proceed. Parking is also a nightmare, even with the police in control, but after waiting about three-quarters of an hour, we were able to get into a garage to park. We walked down to the harbor and took some pictures before having lunch overlooking the sailboats and watching sight-seers milling about.

We got back to the coast road where the going was still slow, but we were heading for Monaco and the French Riviera, where I had wanted to go ever since I had been in France during the war. I could tell that Duke was getting weary of the slow pace that we were covering, or should I say, not covering. In any event, we were finally about two miles from Monaco and Duke spied a sign to the right that would take us up to the main highway. Without a word, he took it, and we soon were going eight five miles an hour again, but we were never to see Monaco.

Since we were now in France, Duke thought it would be a good idea to visit the city of Dijon. In one of the restaurants where we had dined, he used a package of Dijon mustard that had a date stamped on it. He wanted to find out from the factory if that meant that it shouldn't be used past that date, or was it dated more or less like wine to show when it

was packaged. We did go through Dijon but somehow or another we didn't get around to looking up the mustard factory.

We next went through Metz on our way to Luxembourg. It was raining quite heavily when we arrived in Luxembourg and as usual, it was extremely difficult to find parking. After circling a couple of blocks for a time a parking garage was taking customers, and after parking the car we walked in the rain to find a place for lunch. We were in the heart of the city and we found a business-type luncheonette that turned out to be quite good; however it was disappointing to be in such inclement weather and we didn't take many pictures, although the city was quite impressive.

Again we were on the road, now driving through Belgium, part of Germany and into Holland. The countryside was quite beautiful in all three countries; it was difficult to tell the difference between them except when you arrived at a toll station for paying fares. They each took their own money, of course, and if you were not careful in the lane you chose, credit cards might not be accepted. Without having the right coins, soon the cars behind you would start beeping till things got sorted out by an attendant carrying various countries' coins for change.

We were again heading for Sweden to drop the car off for shipment to the states, and we were now very close to Groningen, the county seat, where my grandparents were from. I had told Duke of my recent unfortunate trip to Holland to seek the place where my grandparents were raised, but I had no success. He said that we should try again, and when we arrived in Groningen we asked where the archives are located for the city. When we were in the office of archives, we told them what we wanted, and a very nice man, who spoke English pretty well, helped us for a couple of hours. We got some copies of old documents showing the names of my grandfather and grandmother, but since it is in Dutch, it will have to be translated at a later time.

We then drove through Germany by way of Bremen and Hamburg on our way to Denmark. We both wanted to see the new bridge that had been constructed between Copenhagen and Sweden. Actually, we saw two bridges that were quite similar in construction with center towers, and cables attached, suspending the roadway. Both were simple and beautiful though each a bit different. We continued on to Malm where we had a great lunch in an old building in a park that reminded me of a private hunting lodge. In fact, we had to ask if it was all right for visitors to dine there, and they said of course, and we were seated. The entire building was constructed of heavy timber, both outside and in, and it was obvious it had been there for many years. The ceiling was of high sloping beams carved and painted with subtle ornamentation, and many of the windows overlooked the beautiful park. We had a meal of reindeer meat, which we also had tried in Switzerland, and by now we were calling it Bambi, but it turned out to be very good. Duke and I will probably never have it again, as it was just something to have while you were there.

Duke tried to call a cousin of his that was living in Malmo without success, so we decided to go on to Goteborg where Duke wanted to see a demonstration of Swedish glass blowing. His cousin Guert had again arranged for rooms for us and we settled into the hotel. An hour later, Guert called to inform Duke the glass blowing factory was closed for the weekend so we were not able to compare the glass blowing of Venice. We stayed on for a pleasant weekend and dropped the car off for shipment, after Guert and his wife took Duke and me to the airport where we headed home to California.

Bill Patrick, also formerly at Taliesin, met us at the airport in San Francisco, and after an afternoon tea that his wife Kinuko prepared, we chatted for some time about our trip, and soon we were heading home to deal with jet lag.

PALMS I HAVE KNOWN

Having traveled in quite a few countries and islands on our speeding spheroid, it became clear to me how mighty and diversified is the palm tree.

For instance, they can be short and rugged in one country, and tall and graceful on an island in the Pacific. What is obvious is they are most favorable on their home ground.

For centuries the coconut palm in the Pacific is the most useful of native growth. The islanders use the coconut milk as a drink, and they also cook rice and fish with the liquid. The coconut meat is used directly as food and an oil for lighting. The shell is used for cups and bowels, while the husks are fired for cooking.

Growing close together, the palms form an overhead canopy for shade during hot weather. The fronds are woven tightly together and

Egyptian date palm trees in downtown Cairo :: 1998

Good friend and business
partner Jim Moore in his
most recent auto
:: 2004

used for roofing their houses while straight
trunks are used in construction. Also hollowed
out trunks are used for outrigger-sail-boats.

Finally, even the trunk lobe at the base is
sometimes used for a large fire when many
people are to attend. Nothing in the coconut
palm goes to waste.

In general, the palm tree has evolved differ-
ently in various climates and conditions. Some
are short, stocky, and quite bushy, while others
have rather thick and stiff leaves.

The *Zamia Maritima* or Cardboard Palm
in Thailand is one of those with stiff, thick,
and broad leaves, and grow to a miniscule
height.

The *Licuala Spinosa* or Spiny Licuaia Palm is
found in Southern Thailand and can be identified by its rather open fan shaped leaves, which
are almost rectangular in form with squared off
ends. Another palm in Thailand, with a fan leaf,
is the *Licuala Eleganas* or unknown. This fan
shaped is large, and closely knit, with a long
thick stem, and could be used for an umbrella
in an emergency.

The *Cycas Revoluta* or Sage Palm in Japan
grows to approximately 15' and looks like a
feather duster with a thick handle.

The *Rhapis Excelsa* or Lady Palm in China
has very open, narrow, glossy, green-leaves,
and resembles a bush rather than a tree.

On Fiji you might see the *Pritcharbia
Thurstonii* or Thurston Palm. Its trunk is modest
in height, but the fronds stretch vertically from
the trunk and fan out in all directions. Another
unique palm found in Fiji (in the Garden of
the Sleeping Giant) is the *Johannesteijsmannia
Altifrons,* which has a solid broad leaf, 18–20"
in diameter, and could be used as an umbrella.
It is normally about 6–8' in height.

Egypt has several varities, but the *Phoenix
Dactylifera* or Date Palm is short, and quite
bushy, with wild looking fronds, but it is a top
producer of dates.

The *Elaeis Guineensis,* or African Oil Palm,
has a very short bushy trunk, compared with
its overall height. The fronds grow skyward to
about 7 times the height of the base.

In Mexico you might see, but not recognize
this vegetation as a palm tree because it most
resembles bamboo. It is the *Chamaedorea
Seifrizii* or Mexican Bamboo Palm. It is known
for its smooth bamboo-like trunk. It has graceful
open leaves, similar to a house plant, and it also
produces fruit.

On St. Martin you might run across the
Acoelorrhaphe Wrightii or Silver Saw Palmetto
Palm, which can be identified by the fullness
of the tree leaves that begin by growing very
wide at the ground level.

The *Syagrus Romanzoffiana* or Queen Palm
is a native of Brazil capable of heights to 60'.
They are extremely graceful with their lightweight fronds swaying in a breeze. They are
quite common along the sandy beaches. Their
trunks are solitary gray and are ringed with
old leaf bases.

You will notice a profusion of *Dypsis
Leptocheilos* or Teddy Bear Palm in West Palm
Beach, Florida, identifiable by a 6–8" diameter
smooth trunk. The fronds produce an abundance of shade with their graceful and lacy
form.

Should you someday travel to California
you must be sure to see the *Slimierectus Tallus*
or Tall Tree. This species of palm is most stately
and grows upwards to 60–70'. An unusual

feature of this palm is that they seem prone to grow in rows, and another characteristic is they are usually found next to tall buildings or malls.

CLOSING THOUGHTS

People, places, and circumstances in our lives influence us all, and I am certainly not an exception.

For example, what is paradise to many can be total boredom to some. In my case, after nine months of absorbing the carefree lifestyle for which Tahiti was noted, I realized that at any time I'd be asked to leave the island by a representative of the French government. I had already overstayed my allotted time by three months, this only by the fact that my friend, the Chief of Police, had greased some wheels on my behalf. What I needed was a creative outlet based on my architectural background, which would not be possible in Papeete, given that my time was literally running out. So, I traded

Tahiti's paradise for another form of island paradise: Hawaii. I chose Hawaii as a result of my meager funds, rather than returning to California, because I had met some very nice people from Hawaii in Tahiti, who said they would be glad to help me begin an architectural practice in Oahu.

In retrospect, the three people who have made the greatest influence on my life were my parents and Frank Lloyd Wright.

Even before I began helping my father in his hardwood flooring business, I'd ride along in his Ford truck to wherever he would be submitting a bid for the client's work. Once the terms were agreed upon, my dad would extend his hand, and with his handshake explain to the client that regardless of any extenuating circumstances, he or she would receive excellent workmanship for the agreed-upon price. The handshake was my father's bond.

He also impressed upon me the importance of being considerate of others, by making the

Sunset from author's balcony, Aptos, CA : : present

effort to see their point of view before making a snap judgment. In addition to being an impeccable and trustworthy craftsman, Charles Nisbet was "exactly what he preached."

My mother made life's shortcomings easier for me to grasp and, therefore, to accept. Regardless of what might occur, nothing would exasperate her. She felt there was always another way to handle unforeseen negative events, and with that in mind she would tackle the problem and make things right. During the depression, she explained that although we had little money at the time, whatever losses we might suffer, her flexibility would see us through. Years later, this philosophy kept me on track.

While building my home overlooking the Pacific, with dreams of building yet a larger house with better materials, circumstances in a business venture made that impossible. At the time, I was involved in an apartment house investment in another state, put together by an unscrupulous realtor/attorney. For months, we investors were repeatedly asked for additional funds to keep the project alive. Eventually, I lost a great deal of money on that project. When the six investors learned the realtor/attorney could not be sued for recovery of funds, my wife, Barbara, was amazed that I could manage to sleep at night. I based my acceptance on my mother's way of handling life's trials.

Many of us have regrets when reflecting back on our lives. Again, I am no exception:

I regret that my father, who made his own hand-cranked ice cream each summer, while experimenting with natural fruit flavors from my parent's orchard, was not able to experience today's extensive list of flavors.

I regret that my mother did not have a voice coach to help her develop her lovely singing voice.

I regret that my brother, Harry, did not live long enough to experience the completed renovation of the Statue of Liberty, which he'd contributed to.

I regret that my wife, Barbara, did not live to see the development of the *Taliesin Fellows Newsletter*, which she originated.

I regret that I didn't do more paintings for friends over the years. Also, that I didn't have the opportunity to design more buildings: e.g., a church, hotel, restaurant, resort, and/or municipal buildings.

I regret not having been to Monaco, but perhaps that will be forthcoming.

I have absolutely no regrets for my years spent with Frank Lloyd Wright, a most amiable and gracious person, with whom I had a phenomenal working relationship. He certainly changed my life in a positive way by developing me into a whole man, as he used to explain to us in the fellowship.

Now, as I watch beautiful sunsets from my balcony overlooking the Pacific, and listening to waves breaking on the shore, I reflect back to Frank Lloyd Wright's wisdom. I realize would not be enjoying this environment if not for his brilliant way of teaching one to do everything.

I APPLAUD THE MASTER!

FIN